WHEN THE WORLD STOOD ON THE BRINK OF NUCLEAR WAR

WHEN THE WORLD STOOD ON THE BRINK OF NUCLEAR WAR

SUPERPOWER FACE-OFF: THE SUEZ CRISIS AND THE HUNGARIAN UPRISING

FRONTLINE BOOKS

First published in Great Britain in 2025 by
Frontline Books
An imprint of
Pen & Sword Books Ltd
Yorkshire – Philadelphia
Copyright © Norman Ridley
ISBN 978 1 03613 023 7

The right of Norman Ridley to be identified as Author of this work has been asserted by him in accordance with the Copyright, Designs and Patents Act 1988.
A CIP catalogue record for this book is available from the British Library.

All rights reserved. No part of this book may be reproduced, transmitted, downloaded, decompiled or reverse engineered in any form or by any means, electronic or mechanical including photocopying, recording or by any information storage and retrieval system, without permission from the Publisher in writing. NO AI TRAINING: Without in any way limiting the Author's and Publisher's exclusive rights under copyright, any use of this publication to "train" generative artificial intelligence (AI) technologies to generate text is expressly prohibited. The Author and Publisher reserve all rights to license uses of this work for generative AI training and development of machine learning language models.

Typeset by Lapiz Digital
Printed and bound in the UK by CPI Group (UK) Ltd, Croydon, CR0 4YY.

The Publisher's authorised representative in the EU for product safety is Authorised Rep Compliance Ltd., Ground Floor, 71 Lower Baggot Street, Dublin D02 P593, Ireland.
www.arccompliance.com

For a complete list of Pen & Sword titles please contact
PEN & SWORD BOOKS LIMITED
47 Church Street, Barnsley, South Yorkshire, S70 2AS, England
E-mail: enquiries@pen-and-sword.co.uk
Website: www.pen-and-sword.co.uk
or
PEN AND SWORD BOOKS
1950 Lawrence Road, Havertown, PA 19083, U.S.A.
E-mail: uspen-and-sword@casematepublishers.com
Website: www.penandswordbooks.com

'It was simply unimaginable to me that the United States would oppose its own allies in Egypt but fail to oppose the Soviet Union in Hungary.'
János Kádár

CONTENTS

Chapter One: The Soviet Occupation of Hungary 1
Chapter Two: Colonel Nasser and the Suez Canal 14
Chapter Three: The Sevres Protocol 48
Chapter Four: 22-24 October 60
Chapter Five: 25-28 October 91
Chapter Six: 29 October 115
Chapter Seven: 30 October 127
Chapter Eight: 31 October 144
Chapter Nine: 1 November 151
Chapter Ten: 2 November 160
Chapter Eleven: 3 November 165
Chapter Twelve: 4 November 171
Chapter Thirteen: 5 November 180
Chapter Fourteen: 6 November 186
Aftermath 190

Appendix 1: The Sevres Protocol 195
Appendix 2: 16-point resolution of Budapest students 197
Notes 199
Sources 212
Index 217

Chapter One

THE SOVIET OCCUPATION OF HUNGARY

'It's all a load of shit, that's what it is!'[1]

As the tide of the Second World War had inexorably turned in Europe in September 1943, with U.S. and British forces advancing through Italy, a secret agreement was made between the Hungarian and British governments to the effect that Hungarian forces would surrender to either British or American forces when the latter reached the Hungarian frontier. At the same time U.S. airborne troops were preparing to land on Hungarian soil as a precursor to a U.S.–Hungarian alliance. Unfortunately, Allied plans faltered as German forces pre-empted them and put into operation *Unternehmen Margarithe* occupying the country on 19 March 1944 in their last desperate efforts to halt the Soviet advance. On 15 October 1944, in *Unternehmen Panzerfaust,* they removed the wartime Hungarian government of Admiral Miklos Horthy and replaced him with Ferenc Szálasi. Horthy had tried and failed to conclude a last-minute truce with the members of the Hungarian anti-Hitler coalition and agree surrender terms with the advancing Soviet army, some of whose forces were already occupying the extreme eastern regions of Hungary. Despite Horthy's departure, it was clear now that if Hungary was to be liberated from the Nazi yoke it would be by Soviet forces.

The German occupation of 1944 had started a Hungarian economic crisis with the ruthless exploitation of Hungarian resources and that had been followed by the privations and devastation, both to infrastructure and population, resulting from great battles fought out between German and Soviet forces on Hungarian soil. The battle for Budapest saw more than three quarters of its buildings destroyed or damaged. By preventing Horthy from seeking an armistice with the Soviets the Germans had not only extended Hungarian involvement but ensured that Hungary ended the war as a belligerent on the losing side with terms forced upon it by the victors which in their case was the Soviet Union. The Soviet Marshal Rodion Malinovsky allowed his soldiers three days of celebratory looting, while special units of the Red Army grabbed all the valuables they could lay their hands on.

A provisional Hungarian government, formed in Moscow and headed by Mátyás Rákosi was installed in the country and negotiated the terms of an armistice with the Soviets. This entailed simply agreeing to whatever conditions were demanded. Rákosi was a life-long Stalinist and favoured the creation of a one-party totalitarian police state. He had been trained in Moscow to organise a Hungarian communist party but served thirteen years in a Hungarian prison for his revolutionary activities. Released in 1940, he returned to the Soviet Union where he became leader of the Comintern, the Soviet controlled international communist organisation. Upon his return to Hungary, Rákosi and his team were well-placed to fill the administrative vacuum, with or without the backing of the electorate, and had the relatively easy task of gaining control of the provincial, county and municipal administrations, which had been destroyed by the military catastrophe. His understanding of practical problems of government gave him a significant advantage over the Hungarian non-Communist political opposition.

Soviet control of the country gave them total administrative oversight of municipal elections in October 1945. To the bewilderment of Hungarian anti-communists, the Western Allies made no protest and remained aloof from Hungarian politics insisting that diplomatic practice excluded the possibility of them interfering in the internal political affairs of foreign countries. Nevertheless, when the elections took place in October 1945, it was the anti-communist Smallholders Party who won a majority. Rákosi was hauled up before his Kremlin backers and roundly castigated for his complacency and inefficiency. Things got even worse for him when the general election on 4 November 1945 gave the Smallholders a decisive majority of the total popular vote. The Hungarian Communist Party quickly saw the error of its ways in allowing free elections and was careful never to repeat that mistake. Thereafter, the Soviets consolidated their victory by establishing military occupation of Hungary through political and economic infiltration and dominated all aspects of Hungarian public life essentially subjecting Hungary to the status of a colony of the Soviet Union. Unsurprisingly, it did not gain the confidence of the majority of the Hungarian people.

The Allied Control Commission (ACC) was a military-led administrative means of ruling former enemy states occupied by the Allies. Under precedent established by the Allies in Italy, Soviet-dominated regimes were allowed to take control of those lands liberated from the Germans by the Red Army. The role of the ACC was to 'regulate and supervise the execution of the armistice terms under the chairmanship of the representative of the Allied (Soviet) High Command and with the participation of representatives of the United Kingdom and the United States' but this applied only to the period between the signing of an armistice and a full-blown peace treaty.[2] The Soviets took full advantage of the credulity and naivety of Western officials which might be generously labeled passive negligence but, in some cases, was best described as active collaboration in the Soviet repression of Hungarian society. Such was the grip of Soviets in Hungary that U.S. diplomats came to bemoan the fact that their ACC presence in the country had no appreciable influence on the course of events there and they were embarrassed by appearing to share responsibility for policies which '[had] nothing to do with American ideals or American interests.'[3]

The Allied concept of Soviet ambitions seemed to have been based on the belief 'for which no credible evidence existed' that Stalin had undergone some sort of transformative experience during the war and renounced his former methods. The U.S. and Britain appeared to share a delusional idea of Soviet aims and methods based on a wilful and perplexing refusal to acknowledge the precedents. Truman went so far as to say that the end of the war had brought 'a victory of an ideal founded on the rights of the common man, on the dignity of the human being, on the conception of the State as the servant – and not the master – of its people' which seemed to project a genuine conviction within U.S. policy-making, that the Soviet Union and the Western Allies had a common goal in Europe and that the Soviet Union could, somehow, be brought into a democratic world community if treated with patience and magnanimity.[4]

There seemed to be little appreciation of how Stalin had been affected by his sense of betrayal and humiliation when Hitler broke the Nazi-Soviet Pact and launched an all-out war against the Soviet Union in 1941. Kramer suggests that his experience had further convinced Stalin that he had to prevent the re-emergence of hostile regimes along the Soviet Union's western flank by installing regimes with a strong pro-Soviet agenda. He was clearly motivated by the dictum that 'whoever occupies a territory [after the war] also imposes on it his own social system. Everyone imposes his own system as far as his army has power to do so.' It was clear that the Soviet Union was in such a position in

1945 and possessed sufficient military and political power to impose its will over Eastern Europe and turn Hungary into what Nikita Khruschev called one of the Soviet Union's 'involuntary allies'.[5] At a time when he was beginning to restore a brutal dictatorship at home, undoing the relative liberalisation of the wartime years, Stalin increasingly came to realise that establishing a protective buffer zone would only be possible by imposing direct communist rule across Eastern Europe but for most countries that would be affected, communist ideology was directly at odds with traditional values and beliefs.

It was not long before the Soviets presented Hungary with a bill for its liberation from the Nazis. Only four days after the end of the war in Europe, secret negotiations were being held to force the Hungarian Provisional Government to agree paying the Soviet Union 200 million dollars in war reparations in goods 'valued at 1938 prices with an increase of 15 per cent for industrial equipment and 10 per cent for other goods.'[6] Reparations also included war booty defined as 'German war material located on Hungarian territory'. Trainloads of dismantled machinery left daily for Russia without being controlled or accounted for and there were endless columns of cattle, horses and pigs being driven toward the Soviet Union. Like the Germans, the Soviets disembowelled whole factories such as the huge Tungsram lighting factory in Újpest which was stripped over a period of two months with its machinery loaded onto more than 600 railway wagons, many of which were shunted into railway sidings, forgotten about with their contents left to rust away.[7]

When the Hungarian Prime Minister, Zoltan Tildy, took the oath as President of the Republic on 1 February 1946 it seemed as if the country was embracing law, civil rights and representative government and that a peace treaty, ending the alien occupation of their country, could be concluded before Communist infiltration had become fatal to their national independence. Communist influence in the government was energetically suppressed, however, so that by the end of 1946 all Hungarian ministries and government agency were at least partially and sometimes wholly responsive to communist directive flowing from Rákosi who, in turn, got his orders from Moscow.

The Soviets plundered and requisitioned food to feed their huge occupation force which created an ongoing national food crisis throughout 1945 and 1946. In January 1946, the average daily ration in Budapest plunged to 480 calories, and even with a slight increase in the coming months, a heavy manual labourer could only expect 1,000 to 1,200 calories per day and an office worker, 600 to 650 which was no better than starvation rations. Conditions were much worse even than in occupied Germany. The $30 million of debt that Hungary had owed Germany was now demanded by the Soviets and, incredibly, the Soviet Union also claimed from Hungary the nearly 300 million dollars which Germany owed to Hungary.

Reparations also included war booty defined as 'German war material located on Hungarian territory which allowed for the removal from Hungary of factory equipment, personal possessions, money and securities and other supplies including American-owned property. In the middle of 1946, half of Hungary's industrial production, and about 90 per cent of its heavy industry, was producing only reparation goods for which there would be no payment. The Soviets actually consistently undervalued these goods which stretched the repayment period endlessly on top of which the Hungarians also had to pay the cost of transportation to the Soviet Union, adding a further burden while the Soviets levied a five per cent surcharge for late delivery.

The level of allied connivance in this crime was made manifest when Major General William Key, the U.S. representative on the ACC and the British representative Major General Oliver Edgcumbe suggested that 'rumours' of the Red Army taking booty from Hungary should be publicly refuted for the sake of retaining close ties with the Soviets and did not question the Soviet General Kliment Voroshilov when he blatantly lied by saying that there had been no requisitioning of food at all during the first six months of 1946. The reality was quite different. In March 1946, the owlish, academic Hungarian Minister of Agriculture, Imre Nagy, expressed 'grave apprehension' over the total lack of western interest in Hungary.[8]

Soviet strategy was clearly to destroy the Hungarian economy by looting, requisitioning, economic penetration, interference with internal economic affairs and restricting economic relations with countries outside the Soviet sphere. Runaway inflation ensued, the limits of which far surpassed even those of the German inflation in 1923. All this was a precursor to the reinvention of Hungary as a communist state. More than half a million Hungarian men, women and children were forcibly taken to the Soviet Union to work as slave labour in camps, mines and farms. Somewhere between a third and a half of them died in captivity. The Western members of the ACC showed no interest in this criminal outrage. When Archbishop of Esztergom and Prince Primate of the Catholic Church in Hungary, József Mindszenty brought up the issue at a full ACC meeting, Key and Edgcumbe agreed with Voroshilov that 'members of the Church ought not to interfere in political matters.'[9]

The damage caused first by war, then by the large-scale removal of Hungarian property by the retreating Germans, and the systematic dismantling and removal of industrial facilities together with all kinds of public and private property by the Red Army, was the fundamental cause of the complete economic collapse of the country. Communications was one of the greatest challenges with every railway line having been heavily damaged and all major bridges destroyed during the war. Most locomotives had been taken away and all the steamers and barges of the river fleet either sunk or removed to Germany. The first stages of rebuilding had to be done with the existing resources and with no assistance from abroad. The result was to extend Soviet control to every sector of Hungarian industry and finance, beyond the hope of redemption by any reasonable effort or sacrifice on the part of the Hungarians. The method of systematic economic disruption together with deep infiltration into the Hungarian economy, was accompanied by a positive programme of political indoctrination.

At the very start of 1947 rumours circulated in Budapest suggesting that members of the National Assembly and even Cabinet Ministers had been arrested by the Political Police on the grounds that they had conspired against the Hungarian Republic. The U.S. Department of State issued a statement declaring 'its feeling of concern at the political crisis . . . precipitated in Hungary [which] appears to threaten the right of the people to live under a Government of their own free choosing.' The arrest and detention incommunicado by the Soviet occupation forces of Béla Kovács at the end of February 1947, and fabricated materials on the alleged participation in the plot of several party leaders, including the Prime Minister, Ferenc Nagy was seen as 'a most flagrant interference in Hungarian affairs' and part of a realignment of political authority in Hungary so that a minority which obtained 17 per cent of the popular vote in the last free election had nullified the expressed will of the majority of the Hungarian people.[10] The communists then used the time-honoured Soviet police methods of accusing opposition parties of engaging in anti-state activities to eradicate political dissidence completely. Political parties in the legal opposition would be entirely eliminated by 1949.

The Hungarian Government declined an invitation to take part in the Paris Conference in early 1947 at which the victorious allies negotiated the details of peace treaties and wartime reparations with nations of the defeated alliance. Nevertheless, as part of the ensuing Treaty, Soviet forces were authorised to remain on Hungarian territory to guard the Soviet line of communications for as long as Austria remained under military occupation. When another election was held in Hungary, the non-communist party support completely disintegration as a result of communist plots to undermine the leadership and fragment the democratic political structures within the country calculated to prevent cooperation between all sections of the Hungarian nation.

Arthur Schoenfeld, the U.S. Envoy Extraordinary and Minister Plenipotentiary to Hungary in 1947 recorded his thoughts in 1948 and concluded that;

> 'more and more repression will be required to sweep the national consciousness clear of the hope of future freedom. As the suppression is intensified, the resistance, open or covert, is likely to grow stronger. If, as some say, the Kremlin's real purpose is merely to make sure of having "friendly" governments on the borders of the Soviet Union, then the practice of Soviet imperialism as exemplified in Hungary is not simply brutal but stupid as well. The record here presented does not suggest that Soviet-Communist methods will call forth the popular support on which governments must depend if they are to endure.'[11]

Political purges duly swept through Eastern Europe in the late 1940s aimed predominantly at non-Communists to consolidate rule from Moscow but after 1949 and the breakaway of Yugoslav communists under Josip Tito, they became focussed more on communists themselves especially high officials who had been instrumental in carrying out the earlier repressions. This resulted in show trials of communist leaders intended to suppress any thought of autonomy from Moscow but primarily to infuse into society a general sense of fear and submission. Mass arrests, deportations and internments in forced labour camps followed. Stalin believed that another war in Europe was imminent, and the purges became part of a mobilization of the East-bloc countries for war. As the 1940s ended, all states in the Soviet bloc embarked on crash industrialization and forced collectivization programs, causing vast social upheaval yet also leading to rapid short-term economic growth. There was a significant expansion of the East European armed forces which absorbed an ever-greater share of resources with very little left over for consumer output. As well as employing terror, Stalin consolidated his power by the presence of Soviet troops, a network of state security forces and the wholesale penetration of East European armies and governments by Soviet agents.

After such a long time under Stalin's control, the Soviet Union suffered a severe shock when he died on 5 March 1953 and the world waited anxiously to see how Soviet policy might change as a result. Nowhere more so than in Hungary where there was a spectacular

Moscow-inspired leadership reshuffle with Imre Nagy being appointed to lead the country alongside Rákosi, despite the fact that the latter had been accused by one of Stalin's potential successors, Nikita Khruschev, as having brought the country to the verge of catastrophe and of being someone who risked being 'chased away with pitchforks from Hungary' as the country faced a peasant uprising against the ruling communist regime.[12] For appearances sake, Nagy was made an equal partner to Rákosi, but, in reality, he was given total control and expected to implement a programme of reform.

Nagy had a long association with Moscow having spent time in the Soviet Union during the 1930s when he acted as a paid informer for the NKVD (Soviet secret police) where he was known as Vladimir Iosifovich Nagy. Under the codename 'Volodya', Nagy denounced over 200 Hungarian émigrés many of whom were executed for 'anti-Soviet activities'. It has been suggested that Nagy initiated the NKVD relationship as early as 1933 to gain leverage against his political enemies within the Hungarian Communist Party, especially Rákosi.[13]

The character of Hungary as a police state was defined by a commonly, if discreetly, uttered dictum that the country was a three-class society comprising those who had been to prison, those who were there, and those who were heading there. By far the largest segment of society represented in the prison system at any one time was the industrial working class who were there for political offences or theft. Pilfering and spontaneous sabotage were common with high labour turnover, waste in factories, futile planning and falsified output figures to meet unattainably high production targets.

Hungary had witnessed its first serious strikes since the war when, in 1953, 20,000 workers of the Mátyás Rákosi iron and steel works, aware of strikes and protests in Poland, had downed tools in protest at low wages and food shortages. To avoid country-wide escalation, the authorities quickly agreed to a significant wage rise but further disturbances broke out in other industrial centres threatening a widespread popular revolt. Khruschev hoped that Nagy would take Hungary on a new path of collective leadership, but he got rather more than he had bargained for when Nagy wasted no time in challenging the status quo by making an unprecedented speech to the June 1953 session of the Hungarian Central Committee condemning the overall strategy of the whole Stalin period. In it he called for an easing of the load on the workers and peasants, a drive for higher living standards, putting an end to the internment camps and turning the economy away from heavy industry to the manufacture of more consumer goods.

Nagy followed up with a speech to the Hungarian Parliament on 4 July 1953, which made public the policies of the 'New Course' he had outlined days before in private session, engendering in the Hungarian population a sense of the possibility of opposition to communist control. In his speech, he referred to 'young Hungarians' which in the normal run of things was not exceptional but in the context of Hungary in 1953 was almost revolutionary. Not since 1945 had the nation been allowed to think of itself as an ethnic entity separate from its role as part of the greater Soviet Union. 'We have made serious errors', he said under the baleful glare of Soviet diplomats.[14] Rákosi, still the most powerful politician in Hungary owing to his position as First Secretary of the Communist Party, made his feelings known. 'Nagy is playing with fire', he said and called for a meeting in Moscow to give him extra authority to clamp down on Nagy's reforms but Khruschev, who was trying to guide the Soviet Union away from the Stalinist line, subjected him to a violent dressing-down. Rákosi was to blame, he said, for the draconian regime in Hungary and it was now up to Nagy to 'rehabilitate' the people.

Far from revitalising the workforce, however, Nagy's strategy failed to elicit a response with workers hating the regime to such an extent that 'they were ready to destroy it and everything that went with it'.[15] Nagy attempted to cement his position within the Hungarian Communist Party against Rákosi, by employing the power of the press, in particular the daily paper of the People's Patriotic Front, *Magyar Nemzet* (The Hungarian Nation) and set up a special Government Information Office. In 1954 he proclaimed that 'We have created a new country, and a happy and free life for the people'[16] Meanwhile Rákosi and Ernő Gerő argued that workers' living standards were too high. It was students and the younger generation of peasants and factory workers sons who became most vocal in their opposition to the government and showed more courage to speak their minds. They showed no interest in abstract ideological discussions preferring to tackle concrete issues such as food shortages. 'We were the first generation that was not scared...we had nothing to lose' said one.[17]

When his policies failed to have the desired effect of improving living conditions, Nagy faced unrest in the population and opposition within the government resulting in an attempt by Rákosi to unseat him. Nagy was becoming increasingly isolated but, as his position weakened, he gained the support of journalists at the Communist Party daily newspaper *Szabad Nep* (Free People) who rallied his remaining supporters and formed an embryonic reformist movement to liberalise the communist regime. Nagy was energised by this support and openly and vigorously accused Rákosi in the Central Committee of causing the economic difficulties by blatant and deliberate actions. This stance was timely and effective in persuading the Committee to support Nagy but Rákosi remained as a threat and managed to win a vote suppressing publication of Nagy's speech. This was ignored by *Szabad Nep*, however, who went ahead and printed it.

The result was dramatic as support grew across the country for Nagy's 'New Course' and for the introduction of genuine democratic reforms within the regime. The movement gained traction in other newspaper offices and universities where Stalinist policies came under repeated attack. Alarm bells rang in Moscow with blame for the debacle falling on Georgy Malenkov who had briefly succeeded Stalin as leader of the Soviet Union for nine days before being appointed as Premier under Khruschev. He was removed from that post in February 1955 ostensibly for 'endangering [by his economic failures] the orderly development of the People's Democracies' but remained a thorn in Khruschev's side eventually fomenting an abortive coup against him in 1957.[18] The accusations levelled at Malenkov were very much aimed at his economic policies which favoured light industry to increase the production of consumer goods and which were similar to those of Nagy and the demise of Malenkov was closely followed by that of Nagy.

The connection between the two events is clear. The situation in Hungary was endangering Soviet foreign policy and had a decisive influence on power struggles in Moscow. First Malenkov was dealt with and then, with him out of the way, Nagy would be next.[19] This was a clear threat to Nagy despite his having appealed to the Kremlin trouble-shooter Mikhail Suslov by saying that his reforms had been approved by the Central Committee and endorsed by Suslov himself. When Nagy suffered a mild heart attack brought on by stress and was forced to retire temporarily from public life in March, Rákosi grabbed the opportunity to reclaim his former position of power. In his absence, Nagy was roundly condemned by Rákosi in the Central Committee for the economic failures of the 'New Course' and, with Malenkov's recent removal clearly in mind, the Committee showed scant support for the absent Premier and voted for his expulsion from both the Politburo and the Central Committee itself in December. Nagy was removed as head of the government on 18 April 1955, kicked off all committees, lost his seat in Parliament and chair at the university and replaced by András Hegedüs. Journalists at *Szabad Nep* were duly purged, and a Stalinist editor brought in.

Moscow, still in turmoil over the succession to Stalin and revision of his policies, was now faced with a number of options for dealing with the situation in Hungary but first had to contend with Khruschev's 'secret speech' to the Twentieth Congress of the Communis Party of the Soviet Union on 25 February 1956 in which he roundly condemned Stalin and signalled a move to revert Soviet policy back to a more Leninist model. Populations in the Soviet Bloc reacted to this speech by anticipating a certain willingness by Moscow to allow a measure of reform and a relaxation of its iron rule.

As a consequence of this speech, Khruschev flew to Belgrade to seek rapprochement with Tito by declaring that Stalin's accusations against Tito were false. Khruschev's whole strategy now undermined Rákosi and his Stalinist supporters in Budapest since they had been at the forefront of criticism and denunciation of Tito manifest in the persecution of Tito's ally, the Hungarian Minister of Interior and Minister of Foreign Affairs, László Rajk, in 1949. As Rákosi had consolidated his rule in a one-party state, he had accused Rajk of being a spy for Tito, an agent for western imperialism and one who planned on restoring capitalism to Hungary. Rajk was arrested on trumped up charges, tortured, subjected to a show trial and then murdered along with his family. As a consequence of Khruschev's support for Tito, Rajk's reputation was now rehabilitated despite his earlier role in secret police terror campaigns and Rákosi found himself reeling from the repercussions and scrambling to retain his hold on power. He was forced into making a humiliating declaration of Rajk's innocence but blamed the ÁVO, (*Magyar Államrendőrség Államvédelmi Osztálya*) State Security, for his death.

The ÁVH (*Államvédelmi Hatóság*), referred to as 'the iron fist of the working class', had replaced the much reviled ÁVO in 1950.[20] The Hungarian police chief Sándor Kopácsi said that this new secret police authority treated the ordinary police with contempt. The ÁVH had taken over the wartime Gestapo building at 60 Andrassy Place and faithfully perpetuated their methods to terrorise opposition to the communist state. Rajk had been only one of many high-profile victims of ÁVO brutality.

Rákosi responded by further trying to purge the Hungarian Communist Party of dissent to his rule. He planned mass arrests of writers, intellectuals of the Pétőfi Circle and senior civil servants but at the top of his list was Nagy. Nagy was an easy target because his stubborn loyalty to party procedures and rejection of all forms of factionalism made it difficult for him to defend himself. Nagy had even reprimanded the *Szabad Nep* journalists for their publication of speeches in support of him at confidential Central Committee meetings. Even now, he would not endorse students who sought his approval for subversive writings in the *Szabad ifjúság* (Free Youth) journal, but his support grew not only amongst the intellectuals but also within the wider community. It was also clear that support for him had not altogether vanished in Moscow when he got a visit from a powerful ally of Khruschev, the small Armenian dark-skinned Anastas Mikoyan who forced Rákosi's resignation in favour of another, but significantly less effective Stalinist leader, Ernő Gerő. The imposition of the hardliner Gerő was, in fact, a setback for Khruschev who was fighting for his political survival predicated on an easing of Stalinist dogma and rigidity and showed that there was significant resistance in the Politburo, especially from Molotov to that development.

Public pressure now built for official recognition of government culpability in Rajk's murder and when, on 6 October 1956, his body was disinterred for reburial in the Farkasrét Cemetery where Party officials would deliver eulogies, a huge crowd lined the streets of Budapest to see his coffin pass by. It was an event described by historian Johanna C. Granville as the 'dress rehearsal of the revolution.'[21]

For many, Rajk's funeral marked the end of Stalinism in Hungary. It was not lost on them that 6 October was the anniversary of the Austrian execution of Hungarian freedom fighters in 1849. Workers and students across the nation met and discussed the political situation. It was a potent manifestation of the strong public opposition to the regime. Afterwards hundreds of students marched under Hungarian flags towards the city centre singing revolutionary songs and shouting anti-Stalinist slogans unhindered by the police who believed it to be an official rally. The students, surprised and encouraged by the lack of police action to break up the march, now thought that opposition to government was being tacitly tolerated and increasingly spearheaded the movement for reform.[22]

Within days, student meetings in universities throughout the country were debating reform of the government and urging demonstrations in support of Władysław Gomułka in Poland. This demonstration of student anger caught opposition politicians a little by surprise. Most had not envisaged more than a slow, orderly reform of the system and it took them some time to agree to supporting such a radical movement that was out of their control especially when a demonstration planned for 23 October was officially banned with warnings that demonstrators would be shot. That did not deter some students who now led a revolution that 'had developed a life of its own.'[23]

This movement in Hungary was heavily influenced by events taking place in Poland. After Khruschev's 'secret speech', a factional struggle had broken out within the Polish Communist Party in a country which was the only East European state to be made aware of the contents of the speech at the time. To head off a political crisis, the Polish government proclaimed an amnesty for some 36,000 individuals who had been unlawfully arrested and imprisoned. This did little to dampen popular resentment of the regime and on 28 June 1956, a massive and well-organized workers' demonstrations for 'bread and freedom' broke out in the city of Poznań. The sheer scale of the demonstration and the attention given it by the world's press did not deter the authorities from acting to suppress it with brute force killing some seventy protestors. The Polish government suffered massive criticism for the actions of the security forces and was forced to debate the return to positions of power of activists led by Gomułka, who had been the party's leader until 1948. At that time he had been removed from office and imprisoned for expressing policy views regarded by Stalin to be intolerable but he escaped execution and had been released from prison in December 1954. Now, on 21 October 1956 he was fully rehabilitated and was elected Party First Secretary, very much against the wishes of the present incumbents of the Kremlin, it must be said. He had defied Soviet threats and been able to defend himself against a delegation of Soviet state and military leaders headed by Khrushchev by promising that he could be trusted to responsibly manage Poland's relations with the Soviet Union and calm the internal situation down. When the final results of the elections for new Central Committee were known, the deputy chairman of the Council of Ministers of the People's Republic of Poland, Konstantin Rokossowski, who had led the suppression of strikers on 28 June failed to make the cut. He returned to Moscow and urged Khruschev to intervene militarily in Poland. He was rebuffed and did not return to Poland in any official capacity. Life for Gomułka was made marginally easier when the Kremlin's attention was diverted by unrest that had broken out in Hungary.

Chapter Two

COLONEL NASSER AND THE SUEZ CANAL

'The lawyers are always against our doing anything. For God's sake keep them out of it. This is a political affair.'[1]

British Prime Minister Sir Anthony Eden

The Suez Canal was opened for the general use of the world's shipping on 17 November 1869, by the *Compagnie Universelle du Canal Maritime de Suez*, which operated by virtue of a concession from the Egyptian Government. The British Government had originally opposed construction of the Canal but soon came to recognize its commercial value and strategic importance so when the ruler of Egypt found himself in urgent need of funds, the British Government purchased shares in the Canal amounting to more than 40 per cent of the company's total holdings giving Britain an important voice in its administration. After British forces intervened to suppress an Egyptian Army revolt in 1888, they remained in the country as a virtual force of occupation and Egypt, to all intents and purposes, became a British protectorate. In that respect there were some similarities with the Soviet occupation of Hungary after 1945 although that point should not be argued too strongly.

On 29 October 1888 the Constantinople Convention was signed by the United Kingdom, Germany, Austria-Hungary, France, Italy, The Netherlands, Russia, Spain, and Turkey establishing an international regime to govern the status and use of the Suez Canal. The convention provided that the Canal should always remain open, both in time of peace and of war, to all commercial and war vessels, without distinction of flag, and including the ships of belligerents. No hostile act or act of interference with its free use could be committed in the Canal itself, its ports of access, or within a three-mile radius of such ports, by any state.

During the First World War shipping continued to use the Canal with only minor interruptions. At the end of the war Britain took steps to strengthen its legal position to protect the Canal but during the Second World War it was assumed that both sides of the conflict were quite prepared to put it out of action if it suited their purpose. Britain had declared an official protectorate over Egypt on 18 December 1914 which lasted until 28 February 1922 when it was ended in response to growing nationalist pressures in Egypt and the country was declared to be an independent sovereign state. However, the British reserved certain matters to the discretion of the British Government until such time as the two countries could conclude agreements respecting them. This included security of the Suez Canal and the defence of Egypt against all foreign aggression or interference.

British occupation of Egypt was terminated by the Treaty of Alliance between the United Kingdom and Egypt on 26 August 1936 but Britain still retained the right to establish military garrisons in the Suez Canal area and in fact had its largest military base in the Middle East on the western bank of the Canal. Article VII of the Treaty provided that Egypt was obligated in the event of war to furnish Britain with facilities and assistance, including the use of ports, airfields, and means of communications until such time as the parties could agree that the Egyptian Army was capable of taking over responsibility.

After the Second World War, however, an upsurge of Egyptian nationalism saw the Egyptian Government try unsuccessfully to terminate the 1936 Treaty. With their country now a member of the United Nations, they had become frustrated by the presence of British troops which they considered to be excessive and beyond levels envisaged in the Treaty but the emergence of a Cold War between East and West drove British policy towards retaining a strong presence in Egypt which they considered to be vital to the defence of the Middle East.

Egyptian forces had been humiliated in the 1948 war with Israel and that sparked a movement, led by Gamal Abdel Nasser (*Gamel 'Abd al-Nasir*), to drag the country out of its feudalism, embodied in the monarchy, and imperialist subservience. The Egyptian army had been modelled on the British and, despite its defeat in 1948, had evolved into an efficient and cohesive force. Nasser's political philosophy was encapsulated in his work *Philosophy of the Revolution* in which he saw the elimination of the "white man" from the Middle East and Africa, and a universal Islamic Empire with limitless power, a Pan-Arab state from the Strait of Gibraltar to the Indian Ocean.[2]

Anglo-Egyptian relations continued to deteriorate as British troops in the Canal Zone were harassed to the point where, on 26 January

1952, well-organized extremist elements in Cairo staged anti-Western demonstrations, which resulted in some loss of life and considerable property damage. Egyptian police were killed in a skirmish with British troops as martial law was introduced. The Egyptian Wafdist government was dismissed by King Farouk (*Fārūq al-Awwal*), who assumed personal rule. Then on 23 July 1952, a successful coup by the Egyptian military forces led by Lieutenant-Colonel Nasser established a military junta calling itself the Revolutionary Command Council (RCC). King Farouk was ousted, and Egypt ultimately was declared a republic on 18 June 1953. Land reform and the abolition of political parties were the hallmark policies of the new administration which quickly broke the power of the upper classes. Talks were started on the removal of the 70,000 British forces encamped in the Canal Zone. Britain was not averse to seeing its commitment reduced given the sporadic guerrilla operations mounted against British troops, a growing volume of anti-British propaganda flooding the bazaars and marketplaces of Cairo and, not least, the excessive cost of maintaining its bases there.

In his Paper of 2001, 'Suez-Sinai, 1956: The International, Strategic and Military Aspect', Michael J. Cohen considered the context in which the Suez crisis of 1956 developed believing it to have been a consequence of the Atlantic Alliance preparations for a third world war between the N.AT.O. allies and the Warsaw Pact countries. In the event of such a conflict breaking out, the Soviets were expected to achieve their primary goal, the conquest of Western Europe, within one month, and their secondary goal, the conquest of the Middle East and the British Base at Suez, within three months. Given Soviet supremacy in conventional weapons, the only realistic chance of opposing Soviet action lay in the allied strategic air offensive, which essentially meant the U.S. Strategic Air Command and its increasing reliance on its nuclear capability. Up until the mid-1950s this meant B-29 and B-50 aircraft but these did not have the range to reach the Soviet Union from U.S. air bases so there was an urgent requirement for overseas air bases from which to attack strategic targets inside the Soviet Union. Two countries that the U.S. used in this way were Britain and Egypt. Indeed, Cohen argues that the main American raison d'être for keeping up their ties with Britain was to secure forward air bases for its strategic bomber force. In Egypt, the Abu Sueir air base in Egypt extended its runways to accommodate the B-29 heavy bombers.

It was intended that in the event of global war, American warplanes would launch the strategic offensive from Egyptian airbases against Soviet targets which would have the consequence of making Egypt a target for Soviet retaliation. A Western-led Middle East Command was set up under a British plan codenamed SANDOWN. Its purpose was to defend Suez against a Soviet offensive long enough for a strategic air offensive to be launched from Abu Sueir. For logistical reasons the optimum defence lines along the Taurus mountains in Turkey and the Zagros mountains in Iran were considered impractical without U.S. ground forces and so the plan adopted the Ramallah Line which, in effect would have immediately surrendered the northern half of Israel to the Soviets.

In the Spring of 1953, however, the U.S. decided that this was not acceptable and chose instead to set up a new defensive line further north in Turkey, Iraq, Iran and Pakistan. British planners went along with this idea and on 19 October 1954 signed the Anglo-Egyptian Agreement. This replaced the Anglo-Egyptian Treaty of 26 August 1936 which had provided for the establishment of military installations and supporting facilities along the Suez Canal garrisoned by British troops. The aim of the Agreement had been to win Egyptian goodwill, but it singularly failed to do so. There was continual Egyptian propaganda against Britain and the Egyptians tried to undermine the pro-British regimes in the area. The new agreement provided for the gradual evacuation of the British garrison from the Suez Canal base by 18 June 1956 after which the Egyptian military forces would assume gradual control of the base, and custody of designated base installations. The agreement was to terminate seven years from its signing during which time Britain had the right to re-enter the base with its military forces in order to put the base on a war footing if it was attacked by an 'outside Power'. It was this significant aspect that became the fundamental justification for British intervention in 1956.[3] This was a 'hollow pretence' put out to appease critics, says constitutional law Professor Vernon Bogdanor, and one that was not taken seriously by most people.

Britain had arranged to supply arms to Egypt in March 1950 but cancelled the deal six months later when Egypt had demanded that all British troops leave the country. Egypt had been receiving significant funds from the U.S. for economic development since 1952 and U.S. diplomats had worked hard to persuade the country to buy U.S. arms at low cost but all to no avail. The non-economic terms of the deal required Egypt to join an anti-Soviet defence pact, but Egyptian public opinion would not allow it then just as it had thwarted the British deal of 1950. Egypt tried to overcome public opposition by attempting to make secret and informal commitments to the defence of the Middle East in exchange for arms but both the British and the U.S. insisted that the alliance had to be formal and public.

Egypt meanwhile had been purchasing Czech small arms since as early as 1946 but the supply had run dry because of Soviet support for Israel in the 1948 war which was thought to have been crucial to Israel's victory. At that time, Israel was the only country in the Middle East to offer any hope of the Soviet Union gaining influence in the region but Soviet support for that country seriously weakened its chances of ingratiating itself with the Arab nations. While the U.S. had accepted the state of Israel in practice (de facto) the Soviet Union had recognised it in law (de jure). Stalin had a binary view of the world in which a country was either communist or non-communist which left little room for developing relationships with non-aligned countries who wanted to remain neutral. He had been very cautious in his dealings with Arab nations seeing them as firmly entrenched in the Western camp, but when Khrushchev had succeeded him, Soviet policy changed by recognising that non-aligned countries might build closer ties with the Soviet Union without adopting its draconian politics. By opening negotiations to sell arms to Egypt, the Soviet Union was trying to win influence there but it would have little say in how, and against whom, those weapons might be used. Such moves were threatening to end a lull in the arms race between Israel and the Arab states that had been designed to maintain a balance of power in the region. Egypt indicated straight away that it would be very interested in buying tanks, aircraft and ships from the Soviet Union and Czechoslovakia, but the Soviets were taken aback by the immediacy of the response and had to step back and consider how to reply. They could not be seen to be pouring arms into the region but on the other hand they were worried that the Egyptians were just using them to exert pressure on Britain to restart its arms deliveries. The Egyptians persisted in looking for a deal and went directly to the Czechs in October 1951 to agree the purchase of tanks, armoured vehicles, jet fighter aircraft and sundry transport vehicles. All this would be paid for through the export of Egyptian cotton.

As a result of this impasse, the U.S. and Britain looked elsewhere to build their anti-communist alliance and turned to Iraq, Turkey and Pakistan with whom they created the Baghdad Pact in February 1955 but although it was created to further U.S. interests, that country was not in fact a signatory. In April, the U.S. Secretary of State, John Foster Dulles said, 'It might be necessary for the United States at some future time to join the Pact in order to prevent its collapse, but at the moment we do not wish to do so because of the many extraneous elements involved in it.'[4] This ensured that Britain continued to hold two strategic air bases in Iraq, at Habaniyya, and Shaiba. Iran and Turkey, in particular, had known long and troubled relationships with the Soviet Union and Russia before that and the hereditary mistrust between the countries had prevented the Soviets from expanding their political philosophy in that direction. The Pact, whilst building a defence against Soviet expansionism was also designed to marginalise Egypt and force it to think again about its relations with the Western Powers but that country chose instead to seek an alternative alliance with Saudi Arabia and Syria which threatened to ignite a rivalry between Iraq and Egypt for leadership of the Arab world. There were, however, deep-rooted political and ideological differences between Egypt and Syria which prevented the rival alliance from achieving a stable framework. This was deeply troubling for Nasser who saw the Western Powers surrounding Egypt with a pro-Western alliance in a conspiracy to remove him from power.

Very soon Egypt became frustrated by delays in the supply of the Czech arms. Time and again supplies were withheld without good reason. After Nasser's coup, the new Egyptian President, General Mohamed Naguib, turned again to the U.S. for an arms deal to cement the loyalty of the Egyptian armed forces to the new regime but again the U.S. placed such terms on the deal that it was politically unacceptable to Naguib. Attempts were made to reignite the Czech deal and get it moving this time. The real change in negotiations came with the death of Stalin, who had been amused by Middle Eastern politics but had never shown any interest in getting involved, and the rise of Khruschev whose world view now encompassed a different East-West dynamic. For him the Middle East was becoming a vital pivot in cold-war relations with the rapidly increasing reliance of Western economies on oil. There was also the sense that the next stage in the struggle for the growth of Soviet influence would focus on the liberation of colonial and semi-colonial peoples.[5]

The Soviet Union now took a keen interest in expediting the Czech arms deal but Nasser was anxious to keep it secret so that the British did not get wind of it and stop their arms shipments which had started up again. Intense negotiations began with numerous delegations shuttling between Cairo, Prague and Moscow. When the Czech arms deal finally started to bear fruit, it brought the prospect of either Egypt, employing its new weaponry to take revenge on Israel for its defeat in 1948, or Israel launching a pre-emptive strike before the Egyptian army could make use of its new weapons. Both Britain and the U.S. made strenuous effort to persuade Nasser to renounce the arms deal fearing that it would 'complicate if not block the achievement of two major U.S. objectives in the Middle East: an Arab-Israeli settlement and the creation of effective regional defence arrangements against

Communism [and reduce] the potential of local communists for political subversion.'[6] In Israel, however, Prime Minister David Ben-Gurion was more pragmatic and instructed his Chief of Staff to prepare for war. His country's wider strategic aim was to ensure that no single Arab state on its border gained sufficient military strength to launch a unilateral attack. To this end, destruction of the Egyptian Army and Air Force before they could fully assimilate the influx of Soviet arms became a priority. Preparations had begun by concluding a major armament deal with France in anticipation of launching an attack against Egypt in late 1956.

The state of Israel had been in existence for less than ten years. The Israeli people enjoyed immense good will in Western liberal circles but the country was small, fragile and surrounded by enemy states. Britain, in particular, clung to its entrenched pro-Arab sympathies and recalled that the Israelis had hanged captured British soldiers Sergeants Clifford Martin and Mervyn Paice in 1947, albeit in retaliation for the British hanging of Jewish prisoners. They could not, however, ignore the new democracy making the desert bloom with its horticulture and asserting itself as a nation determined to defend itself against all-comers. Its leader Ben-Gurion had gone to Palestine from Poland in 1906 and fought with Britain's Jewish Legion in the First World War. After the Israeli state was established in 1947, he saw himself as the personification of its historical destiny and led it confident in its strength and purpose.

In Britain there was a powerful political lobby rueing the passing of the Empire and the Daily Express succinctly encapsulated this in the Egyptian context by saying on 17 June 1954, 'Britain has made too many surrenders since the war...Now Britain must stand firm. To make any further surrenders, to yield any further resources, would endanger not only the wellbeing of the Empire but its security too.' However, a government report in the same year concluded that it 'could not discover anyone who thought that the Egyptians were in the least likely to attempt to close or sabotage the [Suez] Canal.'[7]

The situation reached a crisis point on 19 July 1956, when the U.S., Britain and the World Bank cancelled the promised guarantee for a loan to Egypt to build the high dam at Aswan. On reflection, Western financing of this ambitious project had been problematic right from the start. In 1955 Dulles had outlined U.S. aspirations as wanting to 'reach a point at which Egypt would be willing in effect to turn away from Russia as a source of arms...and to agree to open negotiations for a settlement with Israel' so that the U.S. and Britain might 'offer to supply Egypt with her reasonable arms requirements, assist in the financing of the [Aswan] High Dam, bring influence on Israel to agree to a just settlement, and help Egypt to play a role of leadership in the Arab world.' Essentially it would bind Egypt to the West and reduce the risk of increased Soviet influence in the region. Dissenting voices in the U.S., however, saw them facilitating 'a socialised economy in Egypt' and even Nasser was reluctant to commit to an early accommodation with Israel which he believed would not enhance his prospects of becoming the leader of the Arab world. There was a general consensus that Nasser could 'not cooperate as he is doing with the Soviet Union and at the same time enjoy most-favoured nation treatment from the United States.'[8] The response of the Soviet Union was to call for calm and for the West to 'soberly' take into account 'the new circumstances and spirit of the times'.

Britain was equally convinced that the Aswan Dam project had been flawed from the start as shown by a memo sent by the British Prime Minister, Sir Anthony Eden to the British Foreign Secretary Selwyn Lloyd on 18 March saying, 'We have no present interest in…pressing on with the [Aswan] dam.'[9] By July, Nasser was getting sufficiently concerned to send his ambassador back to Washington in order to try and convince Dulles to go ahead with the scheme saying that 'the differences between the two sides were not really important but Washington had made its mind up that Nasser was pursuing policies in the Near East opposed to reasonable U.S. objectives and supporting Soviet objectives. On 19 July, a National Security Council (NSC) meeting concluded that if the dam project went ahead the austerity imposed upon the Egyptian economy to pay for it would make Nasser very unpopular and there was little confidence that the relationship between Nasser and the U.S. would survive long enough to have any reasonable guarantee that Egypt would ever repay the loan. When Dulles met the ambassador later that day, he didn't even wait for him to introduce the subject before cutting him off abruptly, giving him a lecture on why the offer of a loan to finance the Aswan Dam had been withdrawn.

The manner in which Dulles did this was an affront to Nasser, whom he called 'nothing but a tin-horn Hitler'. Churchill once said of Dulles that he was 'the only bull who carried his own china shop around with him.'[10] Nasser, who had just returned from a conference on Brioni with Marshal Tito, was 'staggered and embarrassed' by the news that threatened to unseat him.[11] He was, however, in a strong position at home. He had survived an assassination attempt by muslim extremists and enhanced Egypt's reputation and status internationally with a series of agreements with major powers. After a number of long consultations with his Cabinet, he retaliated against the sleight, in a three-hour speech on 26 July by announcing the nationalizing of the Suez Canal and ordering Major Mahmoud Younes' Army Corps of Engineers to take control of the Canal Company offices in Cairo, Port Said and Ismailia. Part of his justification was that revenues from the Canal would be required to pay for the Aswan Dam now that Western finance had been withdrawn but there is some evidence to suggest that Nasser had planned to take over the Canal anyway and saw the loan termination as a convenient excuse. It was a shock for the U.S. and, at a stroke, deprived Dulles, who had hoped to restore the loans in return for closer cooperation, of one of his most effective negotiating tools. Britain anticipated some reaction from Nasser and, realising that because he could do little to hurt the U.S. it would be Britain who would suffer the consequences of his ire.

In Britain and France there was a 'bewildered rage' at Nasser's nationalisation and [12] the crisis had the effect of bringing about a 'spectacular revival of the Anglo-French 'entente cordiale'.[13] Eden's invective knew no bounds as he likened Nasser's move to Hitler's occupation of the Rhineland. The British Prime Minister had made no secret of his disdain for Nasser and had even, as British Minister of State for Foreign Affairs, Anthony Nutting reported, called for his assassination.[14] Nasser's opinion of Eden was little better. He found him condescending and patronising all of which led to a lack of willingness of either one to see the others' point of view.

Eden had succeeded Winston Churchill as Prime Minister in April 1955 after a distinguished career as Foreign Secretary which had given him unrivalled knowledge of world affairs but left him sadly lacking in the understanding of Britain's social and economic problems and he failed to grasp the way in which these and Britain's rapidly diminishing role as an imperial power constrained the country's freedom of action in foreign affairs. His health, however, was being brought into question. During a visit to the U.S. in early 1956, his private secretary Sir Evelyn Shuckburgh recorded that he found Eden 'thin and nervy...not at all well or happy.'[15]

The British Labour Party opposition in government had initially supported Eden. Its leader Hugh Gaitskill had deeply deplored 'this high-handed and totally unjustifiable step by the Egyptian Government'.[16] This, however, was a statement from which the Parliamentary Opposition progressively distanced themselves over the coming weeks. The French note of protest was so violently worded that the Egyptian Ambassador refused to accept it. Andrew Foster, the United States Chargé d'Affaires in Britain, reported to Washington that the British Cabinet were considering economic, political and military measures against the Egyptians, regardless of the illegality of such a move. British commanders in the Middle East had been asked to formulate plans to seize the Suez Canal and Foster was requested to find out what Washington's reaction would be if the plans were actioned. U.S. President Dwight D. Eisenhower responded with a strongly worded letter advising Eden of 'the unwisdom even of contemplating the use of military force at this moment' and suggesting that Eden 'rethink his position', a statement that Eden conveniently took to mean that 'the President did not rule out the use of force'.[17]

Eisenhower had been the Supreme Allied Commander during the latter stages of the Second World War and then was Supreme Commander of all N.AT.O. forces before retiring from military service in 1952 when he ran for and was elected to the office of President of the United States. By the end of 1955 he was recovering from a heart attack but was well enough to campaign for a second term of office. He relied heavily on John Foster Dulles, his Secretary of State, to advise him on dealing with the world beyond the U.S. Shuckburgh bemoaned the fact that whilst Eisenhower and Dulles appeared to have 'continuity of policy, serious ideas and courage' Eden seemed 'frivolous by comparison.'[18]

Support for Eden came from Lloyd who backed him up by saying that the Americans always followed where others had led but Eden was acutely aware of how much Britain needed U.S. support to retain its place at the top table of world powers. The British Chancellor of the Exchequer, Harold Macmillan, was all for keeping up pressure on the U.S. by maintaining a belligerent pro-war stance towards Egypt. His comment to Dulles about Nasser having gripped the throat of British imperial power did not quite have the effect intended since one of the pillars of post-war U.S. foreign policy was the replacement of Britain as the world's foremost imperial power by the U.S., which Dulles described as 'a tightrope between the effort to maintain our old and valued relations with our British and French allies on the one hand, and on the other trying to assure ourselves of the friendship and understanding of the newly independent countries who have escaped from colonialism.'[19]

Already by the Spring of 1956 intelligence assessments from his Joint Intelligence Committee concerning Egypt were being routinely ignored by Eden. He had by now come to see Nasser as beyond redemption and someone about whom he regarded himself as the ultimate authority. It was a dangerous practice to select the pieces of intelligence that fitted a particular preconceptions and denied Eden of developing a more balanced overall view. The argument he most employed to bolster his position was to compare Nasser to the fascist dictators that had brought the world to the cataclysmic fate of all-out war in 1939.

It should be remembered that, at this point, Nasser had placed no restrictions on shipping passing through the Canal although the ban on Israeli ships that had been in place since 1948 remained. Even the British Cabinet agreed that he had done nothing illegal. All that changed was the administration of the waterway and the channelling of revenues which would now go to Egypt. In Britain, however, this was seen as a direct challenge to its prestige and authority in world affairs and soon became a test of its resolve to halt its decline as an imperial power. Eden was already highly exercised by Soviet efforts to increase its influence in the Arab world which he saw as a threat to Britain's oil supplies. The abrupt dismissal on 24-hours' notice by King Hussein of Jordan of Lieutenant-General John Glubb as commander of the Arab Legion (essentially the Jordanian army) was an acute embarrassment for the British Government and was seen by Eden as Nasser's handiwork. This may have been an overestimation of Nasser's influence in the Arab world but he was not slow to embarrass Lloyd by congratulating him, tongue-in-cheek, on the following day for 'having arranged for Glubb's dismissal in order to improve relations between Egypt and Britain.'[20] This taunt irrevocably hardened Eden's attitude of hostile disdain for the Egyptian leader which had begun to take on the characteristics of a personal vendetta. Shuckburgh recorded in his diary, '[Eden] seems to be completely disintegrated...petulant, irrelevant, provocative...Poor England, we are in total disarray.'[21] British Intelligence claimed to have information from an agent inside Nasser's inner circle who told them that Nasser was 'an out and out Soviet instrument'. Eden took this at face value and added it to his litany of charges laid at Nasser's door despite the British Ambassador in Cairo disputing the accuracy of the claim.[22]

Eden as Foreign Secretary to Winston Churchill, had signed the Anglo-Egyptian Agreement with a clear understanding that the era of imperialism was over and that it was no longer possible in the modern world to rule over others without their consent but he still believed that Britain had a major role to play in world affairs by holding onto a ring of strategic positions, such as the Suez Canal; and by trying to ensure that there were friendly governments in areas of strategic importance, such as the Middle East. The signing, however, had not pleased Churchill or many in the Conservative Party which burdened Eden with the reputation of being weak, especially after he succeeded Churchill as Prime Minister.

Glubb's sacking prompted a vitriolic riposte from Eden when he told Nutting that he wanted Nasser 'destroyed' regardless of any consequences that might result in 'anarchy and chaos in Egypt.' It was the case, however, that Eden's violent temper was known to get the better of him, especially when he was under stress or over-tired. Throughout his tenure of office, Eden had been plagued by gallstones, diverticulitis, and Cholangitis. In 1953 he had undergone an operation for the removal of his gall bladder, an operation that had gone badly wrong when his biliary duct was accidentally cut. This left him with lingering medical issues and an ongoing question of a second operation at some point. One of the side-effects of his recurring illness was sleep deprivation. After his sudden angry outbursts he would apologise and people close to him took his tantrums lightly knowing that they did not reflect his true feelings but others outside this circle 'took these outbursts to be more serious than they were.'[23]

Eden's response to Nasser's declaration to nationalise the Canal, contrary to the general perception that he oozed bellicosity, was calm and considered. His first thought was to take the issue to the U.N. but he realised that the Soviet Union would block any progress there. He wrote to Eisenhower saying, 'we cannot afford to allow Nasser to seize control of the Canal in this way [if we do] our influence and yours throughout the Middle East will, we are convinced, be irretrievably undermined.' Eisenhower had made his position clear on 31 July when he said that 'every peaceful means [must be] thoroughly explored and exhausted.'[24] While Eden and Macmillan saw Nasser as posing a serious threat to British interests, Eisenhower was determined to see him as only one of the many irritations he had to deal across the globe. He seemed, however, to offer some support for 'reasonable counter measures' according to his diary of 8 August but military action seemed far from his mind. There were influential voices in Washington such as Herbert Hoover Jnr., however, who warned that the British could not be trusted, and it was here that the suspicion of a British military response took root but it was an opinion that had arisen without foundation.

The only evidence suggesting that Eden's immediate reaction was to urge military action comes from a book written years later by Willian Clark, Eden's Press Secretary, but Eden's diary entry for the time makes no mention of it.[25] Already at this stage, Eden had been approached by Mollet to collaborate with France and Israel against Egypt but the Prime Minister had vehemently turned down the proposition and stressed the importance of keeping the Israelis out of it. Furthermore, the British Chiefs of Staff made it abundantly clear that they had received no directive from the government for military action and certainly had no inkling that the removal of Nasser was the ultimate political objective. They made it clear to Eden that, in any case, they were in no position to mount any sort of quick military operation.

The French Prime Minister Guy Mollet had been focussed on European affairs and had been in office for only six months when the Suez crisis exploded. Nevertheless, he shared Eden's personal loathing of Nasser and called the nationalisation of the Canal 'an outrage' but in Paris the idea of military action against Egypt was one that had been building for some time primarily because of Nasser's support for the Algerian nationalist movement and the nationalisation of the Suez Canal was simply fuel added to a fire that was already smouldering.[26]

Their eagerness to secure an ally in this venture without indepth discussions to harmonise objectives, however, was a serious mistake. Like the British, they too had significant overseas military commitments and they too lacked the resources to undertake a military adventure such as the one to which they seemed to be blindly committing themselves. The evidence seems to suggest that, at the outset, the whole venture was intended as a bluff to bring Nasser down by the mere threat of force and little time was spent actually contemplating the consequences if that bluff was called.

The British Cabinet discussed 'the fundamental question [of] whether they were prepared, in the last resort, to pursue their objective by the threat, or even the use, of force, and whether they were ready, in default of assistance from the United States or France, to take military action alone.' They agreed that 'essential interest in this area must, if necessary, be safeguarded by military action, and that the necessary preparations to this end must be made...even if we have to act alone, we could not stop short of using force to protect our position if all other means of protecting it proved unavailing.'[27] However, the Cabinet agreed that the Egyptians must be subjected to the maximum political pressure backed by the threat and, if necessary, the use of force. The Chiefs were then officially instructed by Cabinet to prepare a contingency plan and timetable for military operations against Egypt but one that would only be employed with reluctance. This was a long way from starting a war. With that in mind, the Cabinet then formed the Egypt Committee, chaired by the hawkish Macmillan, tasked with keeping it informed about the 'situation arising from the recent action of the Egyptian government in respect of the Suez Canal.'[28] One of the first decisions of this committee was to make every effort to 'place the Canal under international control [but] our immediate objective was to bring about the downfall of the present Egyptian Government.'[29] By contrast, to emphasise his own non-military approach, on 28 July Eden froze all Egyptian assets and banned the export of all war material to that country. His own view was still that the situation should be resolved through negotiation. There is nothing to suggest that he was actually ready to commit himself to military intervention at this stage but his hubris, embarrassment, anger and wilful blindness to Britain's woefully inadequate military resources was leading him blindfold into a catastrophe.

The Suez Crisis caught Britain in the middle of a painful military transition phase. It found itself with too many commitments to deal with simultaneously and lacked a strategy view as to how best to allocate resources. It had chosen to retain its status as a global power by developing a large enough independent nuclear deterrent to ensure creditability but, for political and economic reasons, still felt compelled to maintain a conventional military presence around the world not least in the Middle East which was considered the most important of these commitments because of its economic importance. Faced with the Suez crisis, it was clear that political considerations would prevent the use of nuclear weapons leaving only the option based on an airborne and amphibious assault by numerically superior forces. The problem was that Britain could not deploy such forces quickly. They were unbalanced for conventional warfare with most of their forces deployed in global counter-insurgency operations. Britain simply did not have the wherewithal to fight even a medium-sized conventional conflict in the Middle East.[30]

Dulles had visited the Middle East and had gained a desire to strengthen it against communist influence but made the mistake of confusing nationalism with communism. Eisenhower not only identified the region as a front in the global struggle against communism but also saw the logic of greater U.S. involvement in the region and his performance during the Suez crisis would create a template within which future U.S. administrations would frame their policies. He was aware of the importance of Middle East oil to the U.S. economy not so much from a supply perspective but rather in terms of U.S. investment in an industry which, according to a U.N. economic review, had grown in revenues from $500 million in 1953 to $940 million in 1956.[31] His administration was not ready to give Nasser up as a lost cause just yet and saw its priority as keeping Egypt, one of the less troublesome Arab countries, in the Western camp and as an important bulwark to Soviet penetration in the region. In this context the U.S. looked on the Canal crisis merely as a question of re-asserting international control and saw diplomacy as the correct way to resolve the impasse rather than resorting to what they called eighteenth century imperialist and colonialist methods. Eisenhower's approach is best summed up by his remark that 'Western powers must not appear before the world as a combination of forces to compel adherence to the status quo.'[32]

Another one of the U.S. priorities was the security of its naval bases in North Africa and the southern flank of N.AT.O. The U.S. Sixth Fleet had been temporarily put on alert as early as 7 July and ordered to move to within 48-hours sailing of Egyptian waters but returned to normal duties on 11 July, and again put on alert after Nasser's nationalisation speech. The U.S. Chief of Naval Operations, Admiral Arleigh Burke, ordered the fleet, which comprised 50 ships and 200 aircraft led by the aircraft carriers, USS *Randolph* and USS *Coral Sea*, to make 'unscheduled moves…so that people will get used to it' and not draw any conclusions.[33] It might be noted here that both carriers routinely carried small detachments of F2H Banshee aircraft capable of delivering nuclear weapons. Burke was actually one of the few in the U.S. who advocated further punitive action against Nasser saying that 'Nasser must be broken [preferably] by economic and political means but if these proved insufficient and the British resorted to force, we should declare ourselves in support of their action' but Eisenhower took issue with Burke and said that Nasser was merely the embodiment of 'the emotional demands of the people of the area for independence.'[34] If the British were set on going to war without the backing of the U.S. calculating that they would come in later on their side, Eisenhower was adamant that 'they could not work that particular trick again.'[35]

Openly stating that the British Government was taking an aggressive stance and threatening military action would, at this stage, have been foolhardy in the extreme since it would give ample time for international opposition to build as well as giving Egypt and its allies the opportunity to make defensive preparations. That would only be the case if it had serious plans, however. If a bluff was intended to pile pressure on the Egyptians to negotiate then it would be quite a normal and effective tool. The problem was that the bluff worked against the U.S. more than against the Egyptians and acted very much against British interests. Macmillan, who to a great extent was acting independently of Eden who still looked for a diplomatic solution, had done his utmost to 'frighten' Eisenhower's Deputy Under-Secretary of State, Robert Murphy, by convincing him that Britain had already taken the decision to use force and this gave rise to alarm in the White House. The effect there was to make it impossible for the U.S. to give any possible support to Britain's threat of force as a diplomatic tool because it believed that Britain had already chosen the path of war and Eisenhower could not allow himself to be drawn deeper into that scenario and appear to be a belligerent. The U.S. position at this stage seems to have been that Britain could not consider any sort of military intervention without their support and they were clear in their own minds that this would not be forthcoming. By making Britain aware of this, Eisenhower believed, he could allow the Suez crisis to slip down his agenda and let the war of words go on without his involvement while he got on with the business of campaigning for re-election.

Dulles, however, was sufficiently unnerved to go straight to London which Macmillan saw as a 'very good development'.[36] The problem now was that the U.S. State Department had taken Macmillan's view that military action was all but agreed upon to be British Government policy but in reality Eden still considered it to be essentially a bluff to destabilise Nasser's position and force him into accepting a diplomatic solution. Dulles may well have been slipshod with his remarks to Eden when he said that if Egypt refused to consider 'reasonable proposals' then the situation would be created which might 'call for a different approach' which might include 'force if necessary.'[37] Eden certainly thought he could take U.S. support for granted, regardless of what Eisenhower and Dulles said on the record but there is a dearth of evidence in the archives to suggest that the U.S. ever adopted such a position.

Macmillan, and probably Eden as well, made the mistake of thinking that Dulles had a great deal of autonomy in directing U.S. foreign policy in the way that the British Foreign Secretary had for Britain. In fact, Dulles was unable to act independently of Eisenhower, who ultimately made all the decisions and Eisenhower made his position clear; he wanted a peaceful solution. Dulles was certainly more sympathetic to the British view than his President and this is what came over during his 'long-winded' speeches (Eden likened him to a preacher)[38] but his objectives were firstly to draw Britain into a framework of negotiation by giving them the impression that the U.S. would not rule out a military solution if all else failed, and secondly to obfuscate and delay the process to give time for anger to dissipate and for the risk of war to fade.[39]

On the U.S. side their most egregious error was in not recognising the level of influence that Macmillan had over British policy and Macmillan, chairman of the Egypt Committee, was much more hawkish than Eden. They mistook British Prime Ministerial power to be equivalent to that of the President in the U.S. This, no doubt, had grown out of Eisenhower's experience of dealing with Churchill during the Second World War when his powers as Prime Minister had been greatly enhanced. Macmillan, however, was the second most powerful politician in the British Government and Eden's main rival for the premiership, and he spoke for many in the Conservative Party who demanded firm action against Nasser. The U.S. did not fully grasp the extent to which Eden, whom they perceived to be more conciliatory, would have to make concessions to that viewpoint and his word could not be taken as definitive of British policy. It was Macmillan, not Eden who was key to British foreign policy over Suez.[40]

For his part, Macmillan would misread Eisenhower's position. While he continued to believe that the U.S. would 'lie doggo' and not interfere with Britain's plans for military intervention, he, as Chancellor of the Exchequer was painfully aware that the U.S. was putting pressure on sterling by refusing to support it against speculation. It was a clear message that the U.S. would employ other means to thwart British moves while publicly taking a neutral stance. Macmillan, however, continued to give his Cabinet colleagues the impression that the U.S. would tacitly support British action against Nasser and his opinion carried a great deal of weight when it came to Cabinet votes.

The British Chiefs of Staff had been asked to attend the British Cabinet on 27 July and invited to present military options available to Britain to occupy the Canal Zone. They went away to discuss it and arrived at their first conclusion that was to put an imprint on the whole venture and subsequently remove the option of surprise as a component of any military action. Their thinking was predicated on Second World War experience, and by serious concern about the new weapons with which the Soviets had equipped the Egyptian forces resulted in an insistence on detailed planning and the formation of a massive and well-prepared force. The entire concept for any invasion of Egyptian soil involved the application of overwhelming force especially in the context of amphibious landings. The military revolution caused by advanced technology, atomic weapons, supersonic aircraft, guided weapons and a new generation of submarines was acknowledged but not yet evaluated due to lack of experience in deployment. The first memo sent to Cabinet by the Joint Chiefs suggested that any unilateral action against Egypt might require up to six months' preparation.[41]

On 31 July, the planners came up with their first detailed plan, Operation Musketeer, which was accepted by the Egypt Committee three days later. The French had offered immediate cooperation and had sent Admiral Nomy to London on 30 July to take part in the planning process. They, themselves, had already been working on a variety of options for the removal of Nasser, most of which had involved joint action with Israel, and were able to bring some of their ideas to the table. Their contribution to any task force would be a sizeable naval force including two aircraft carriers and a battleship along with a large number of fighter-bomber aircraft. They also had a much more sophisticated airborne capacity with a well-trained and experienced paratroop division. The involvement of Israel may well have been sought by the French to offset their innate distrust of the British whom, they suspected, might, at some point, take unilateral action that might leave the French embarrassed and dangerously out on a limb.

The first Musketeer plan drawn up on 9 August envisaged an attack through Alexandria, on the west side of the Nile delta, after a two-day aerial bombardment of Egyptian Air Force bases. British and French commandos would then launch a pincer attack on Alexandria supported by a naval bombardment. The Royal Marines were to secure the port while the French were to attack over the beaches to commandeer the west and south-west exits from the city. At the same time, French and British parachutists were to secure the road leading to Cairo. It was anticipated that the Egyptians would engage them around Giza. The projected date for the attack was 15 September. All this was planned seemingly without regard for the fact that British forces in the Mediterranean area had been configured only for show-of-force and internal security missions. The Royal Navy had only one carrier task force in the Mediterranean and the army had all of its twelve infantry battalions tied up with counter-insurgency operations on Cyprus. The Royal Air Force had no first line units in the area. But worst of all, there was a lack of suitably developed British controlled ports or airbases from which to stage a major operation into Egypt. Any runic divination based upon these readings would hardly encourage an optimistic forecast.

Alexandria was favoured as an entry point from a practical perspective if a large-scale battle with Egyptian forces was envisaged. It had an excellent airfield and first-class port installations and a more secure route into Cairo. However, it was a major urban area, requiring significant forces just to secure the city, and it was 150 miles from the Suez Canal. Port Said would work better if a surgical strike to take control of the Canal Zone was preferred but it was something of a nightmare from an operational perspective. Its beaches were too shallow for landing craft and its harbour was cramped. Communications to the Egyptian mainland would be along a twenty-five-mile causeway including a single bridge capable of taking the weight of a tank and the nearest airport was fifty miles away.

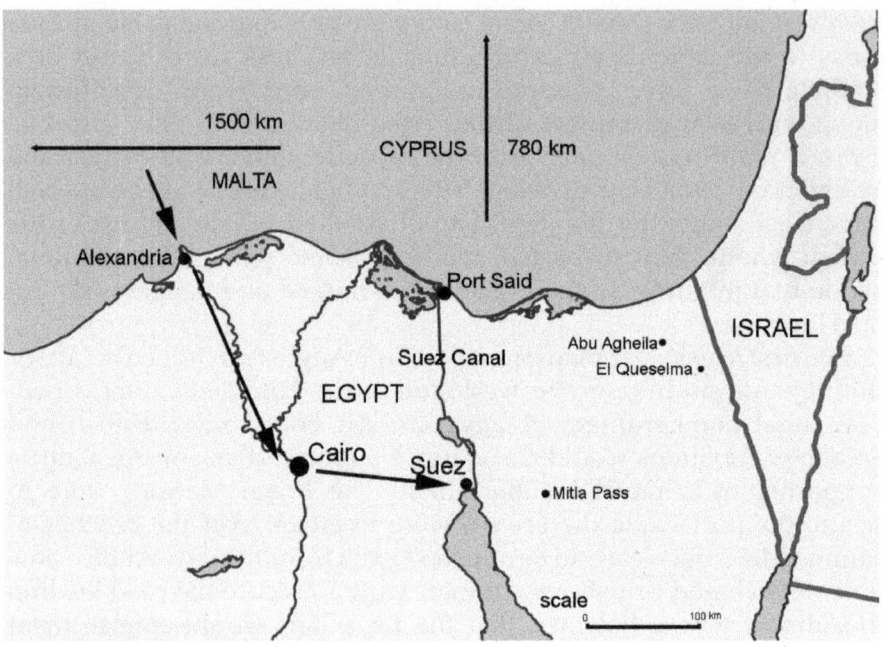

The Musketeer Plan

The French government committed itself to supporting any military operations and had been involved in preliminary talks but, to maintain secrecy, were not given details of the 9 August plan. The British military planners had not particularly welcomed French involvement which they saw as a political expedient and did their best to ignore them. They believed that they already had sufficient forces to go it alone. The last thing they wanted was to have to accommodate an ally with whom they had no formal military relationship outside of N.AT.O. At least they would be able to maintain control by virtue of the French commanders being subservient to British at all levels. The ruddy-faced and bristly-moustachioed General Charles Keightley, Commander-in-Chief of the British Middle East Land Forces, whose headquarters were in Episkopi, Cyprus, was appointed Allied Commander-in-Chief for Operation Musketeer. Vice Admiral P.E.M.J. Barjot was designated Allied Deputy Commander-in-Chief, but at the same time, he was Commander-in-Chief of all French forces participating in the operation. Major-General André Beaufre was, reluctantly, dragged from his command in Algeria and brought in to command the French army contingent of an Anglo-French Task Force.

Many difficulties lay in the path of military intervention, however. The British troops nearest to Egypt were two armoured regiments in Libya, but it was inconceivable in terms of the Middle East political situation for an attack to be launched on an Arab state from another Arab state. British forces in Cyprus were heavily involved with trying to suppress the EOKA nationalist guerrillas and in any case had no air or naval facilities capable of supporting an invasion force. Malta was the only British base able to accommodate an armada and that was at the very least four days' sailing time from Egypt. The French had similar issues with no troops available at short notice close enough to be deployed. To address these issues the British and French set up a planning section in Churchill's wartime bunker complex under the River Thames that Beaufre called an 'uninviting cellar...where much time was wasted.'[42]

The defenders ranged against any invasion force would be something of an unknown quantity. Egyptian armouries had been recently replenished with modern weapons and Soviet instructors had been brought in to train the armed forces, indeed some units might even be manned by Soviet 'volunteers'. To avoid underestimating the opposition, the British and French Task Force was set at 50,000 British troops, half of whom were reservists, 30,000 French, 70 British and 30 French warships, 3 British and 2 French aircraft carriers. Such a force could only be effective with clear planning and specific objectives but Keightley was unable to accomplish either due to Eden's obsessive secrecy. Because of this lack of clarity from the start, the military commanders had to plan for a range of contingencies which, obviously, took much longer and led to confusion. Furthermore, the fear of failure led them to overcompensate by massing a force rather larger than should have been required. Nasser, meanwhile, calculated that the risk of invasion diminished with each passing week.

British intelligence failures compounded their misfortune. The Egyptian security services had dismantled the British SIS network in the country leaving an intelligence blind spot depriving the British government of any strategic insight into Egypt's internal activity. It was known that the Egyptian Air Force was now equipped with 110 Soviet-built supersonic MiG-15 fighters and 48 Ilyushin Il-28 bombers but they posed a much lesser threat that was feared. The MiGs in particular were a problem since they outperformed anything in the attacking air forces but few Egyptian pilots were trained to fly them in combat and the 'volunteer' pilots from the Soviet Union had not yet arrived. In any event it was doubtful if the Soviets would have allowed their own pilots to become involved.

Similarly, the 300 Soviet tanks that now filled the proud ranks of Egyptian military hardware lacked trained crews. The half a million men boasted by the Egyptian army was made up, in large part, by hastily amassed and poorly trained conscripts. All this, said the planners, demanded an air and naval bombardment of Port Said followed by a naval invasion supported by paratroops. The 'tall, elegant, lively and intelligent but volatile' Lieutenant General Sir Hugh Stockwell, commander of all land forces for the invasion was a stubborn man who instinctively refused to take Beaufre seriously and barely listened to any comment or suggestion he had to make.[43] He was forthright in his distaste for the Port Said plan which he called risky in the extreme and would put the landing forces through a bottleneck where they would be at the mercy of saboteurs who could blow the bridges and leave them stranded.

The British White Paper on Defence published at the beginning of 1956, had placed emphasis on the need to be prepared for limited wars, which clearly encompassed their intended action in Egypt, but eight months later the British Army was in a poor state for action. A third of its manpower was teenage conscripts who generally lacked enthusiasm for military life and who tied up many of the experienced personnel in training. The force needed to secure Alexandria was calculated to be three divisions two of which would need to be brought in from strategic reserves in Britain. Time would be needed to call up reserves for the divisions deploying from Britain and to assemble the necessary shipping. It was thought that the strength of the Egyptian Army was in its armoured brigades but even there its leadership was considered weak and incapable of conducting mobile operations. Therefore, it was planned to destroy the Egyptian Air Force quickly then draw the Egyptians into a mobile battle where superior Western tactics and leadership would prevail. The Suez Canal could then be seized but Macmillan told the Chiefs of Staff on 10 August that occupation of the Canal Zone would not, by itself, solve the problem of Suez. That could only come about if occupation was simultaneously combined with the removal of Nasser from power. The unanimous opinion by the Chiefs of the Staff was that it would take a minimum of eight weeks to prepare which was a setback for Eden who pressed for a quicker response. Maintaining secrecy would become ever more problematic the longer the delay.

Eden now hit another obstacle. The senior legal adviser to the Foreign Office, Sir Gerald Fitzmaurice, was supported by the Attorney General, Sir Reginald Manningham-Buller, when he told the Prime Minister that there was no legal basis for armed intervention of a neutral state to protect property or to guarantee freedom of passage through the Canal or to prevent further violence. 'The Suez Canal is not British property, nor is the Suez Canal Company', he said.[44] No international court would uphold Anglo-French claims since the Suez Canal Company was registered in Egypt and was subject to Egyptian law. The British Cabinet was told on 27 July that 'All [Egypt] had done, in essence was to buy out the shareholders [and offer full compensation] but the Cabinet members nevertheless agreed to exert 'maximum political pressure [backed by] the threat, and if need be the use, of force.'[45] Eden chose to ignore what he called legal quibbles and turned instead to Lord Kilmuir, the Lord Chancellor, whose legal qualifications in no way made him an expert on international law. Kilmuir told Eden that Egypt had broken the 1888 Convention by its 'invasion', despite there being no actual evidence of an invasion, and had nationalised an 'international asset'. It was, in his view, guilty of aggression against the signatory powers.[46]

It was very much a case of Eden hearing what he wanted to hear and that did not include advice from his Foreign Office. He was not interested in any advice that was contrary to his own view and he was clearly not going to accept that a country that still had imperial status and had stood up to the might of Nazi Germany was going to be dictated to by a Middle Eastern 'upstart', even one with powerful friends. It was from this point that he started to dictate foreign policy without the benefit of advice from his Foreign Office. British Intelligence operated through the Foreign Office Permanent Undersecretaries Sir Ivone Kirkpatrick and Patrick Dean, who had been expropriated by Eden to set up an alternative communication corridor which was protected from outside influence or scrutiny and effectively excluded the broader machinery of government from policy decisions.[47] He could not so easily ignore the opinion of the First Sea Lord, Earl Mountbatten, uncle of the Duke of Edinburgh, however, who told him that war with Egypt would do nothing to solve the problems of the Middle East, but Mountbatten was persuaded to tone down his criticism and not get too involved in politics.

It was at this moment that wiser heads should have prevailed and urged a more cautious approach. No Western country apart from France supported military intervention. The prospects of a diplomatic resolution with full U.S. support were strong and, what seemed to have been left out of the reckoning for the British was the cost of failure of any military adventure. For the Israelis, it was just another episode in what they saw as their existential struggle for survival and the French would have ridden that storm of failure without prejudicing their main objective of crushing the Algerian independence movement. It was the British who, most of all, failed to anticipate the effects of their action on their relationship with the U.S. who had most to lose by their precipitate action.

If Eden had hoped that his plan would remain secret he was soon disabused of that notion. It was reported in the newspapers that the two aircraft carriers, HMS *Theseus* and HMS *Bulwark*, were taking on ammunition and supplies at Plymouth and loading with troops bound for the Mediterranean. The French Mediterranean fleet was put on a war footing as all roads in the south of France became clogged with military transports heading for Toulon. There had been some hope that all this preparation would somehow go unnoticed especially by the U.S. in whom Eden had little confidence of support for his escapade but that was becoming more unlikely by the day. Reservists were called up without Parliamentary approval which was technically illegal. The condition of some of the equipment was awful. Trucks and armoured vehicles kept in storage since 1945 were barely roadworthy. Parts were missing or had been cannibalised to keep others on the road and it all had to be painted yellow for use in the desert. The litany of equipment failure was almost risible.

The command structure that was set up proved to be no better. A combined headquarters with forward command post was not created until after the initial plan was completed and many of the major commanders could not give it their full attention because they were tied up with supervising preparations for the actual invasion. The main commanders did not assemble in Cyprus until just before the invasion. At the first joint meeting, Stockwell presented Operation Musketeer to the combined staff which annoyed Beaufre who wasn't happy that British plans had got so far advanced without French input. The plan, which was not received with great enthusiasm, gave the impression that planners were hoping that the preparation time would allow for a diplomatic solution to emerge. Beaufre was the exception. He was looking for a quick response before diplomatic pressure could build to oppose military intervention and even render it impossible. Operation Musketeer had four phases

Phase I: Air Battle to destroy Egyptian Air Force (3 days)
Phase II: Amphibious/Airborne Assault (1 day)
Phase III: Main Landing & Build-up (6-7 days)
Phase IV: Advance on Cairo

and included the following principles,

1. Low risk.
2. Destruction of the Egyptian Air Force as a prerequisite before any landings.
3. Rapid link-up between the seaborne and airborne forces.
4. Rapid disembarkation of forces.
5. Avoid entering Cairo.
6. Avoid attack on the actual Canal which would provoke Egyptians to block it with sunken ships.

It was obvious that most of the invasion force would arrive by sea but both British and French amphibious capability was severely depleted and the nearest friendly ports to the proposed invasion site, 250 miles away in Cyprus, were underdeveloped and totally inadequate. Malta had excellent harbour facilities but it was 950 miles away. In the end, a combination of sites in Cyprus, Malta, Algeria. and Britain was used. The air component was limited by the fact that jet fighters on Cyprus lacked the range to operate over Egypt and although French fighters would be secretly deployed to Israel, the main fighter force of 140 ground-attack aircraft would have to be from the three British and one French aircraft carriers. Jet bombers could be flown from both Malta and Cyprus. Paratroops, which would be mostly French, would have to be dropped in waves due to the shortage of appropriate transport aircraft.

British and French armed forces had been weakened by lack of funding and over-commitment to colonial duties. Both used conscripts to make up large parts of their forces. Equipment was generally out-of-date and poorly maintained. The 10th French Parachute Division, based in Algeria made up the bulk of the airborne contingent while the British contributed the 16th Parachute Brigade but neither of these was ready for major airborne operations. The French 7th Armoured Division had been split up to conduct operations against Algerian guerrillas and tank crews, which had been converted to infantry, had to be retrained in mobile operations. The two British tank regiments had been dispersed to support reservist training and neither was fully equipped or manned.[48]

Either wilfully oblivious to its shortcomings or stubbornly holding to the view that 'it would be alright on the night', the British Cabinet gave its approval to Operation Musketeer on 15 August with a projected invasion date now of 19 September. The sense that this would probably not be the last postponement led to a report from the planners expressing their concern about deteriorating weather conditions in the Eastern Mediterranean after the middle of October which would result in unpredictable sea conditions. The plan was beginning to look unrealisable within the time frame and a general sense of uncertainty tainted with disappointment enveloped both the military and the government. Eden, however, urged the military to continue as planned. Then on 19 August, Keightley, the designate commander of operations came up with an amended plan which involved a massive aerial bombardment to destroy the Egyptian air force on the ground then attack Egyptian Armed Forces and Egypt's oil supplies thus avoiding a decisive battle near Cairo or a need to occupy that city. In this way, ground forces could be deployed directly in the Canal Zone by using Port Said as point of entry. This would mean that there would be no further postponement of the invasion date.

The bombing of Egyptian oil storage facilities was a crucial part of Keightley's plan which would go for the jugular in terms of the Egyptian economy and force early capitulation. Considering the centrality of this strategy, which had already been rejected by an ad hoc committee of civil servants, it is remarkable that, at this point there was so little high-level discussion of the consequences of such an act. When it came to the crunch once the bombing campaign had got under way, the idea was soon rejected on the grounds that it would irrevocably sour relations with other Arab countries. That would effectively lead to abandonment of the whole bombing strategy halfway through the campaign.

Task Force commanders, however, rejected the idea on the grounds that the R.A.F. lacked the resources to mount a prolonged air campaign given the distance of the target from air bases in Cyprus. Keightley and Stockwell took the idea to Eden in a private staff conference attended only by the Minister of Defence, the Secretary of State for War, and the Chiefs of Staff. Eden was deeply concerned by the prospect of further postponements which had now put the date back to 26 September but was reassured by the military that operations would still be possible right up until the end of October.

The next day an international conference met in London without prior consultation with the Soviet Union and in such a way as to guarantee an overwhelming vote of approval for measures agreed upon.[49] The meeting proposed the creation of an internationalised Canal giving Egypt assurances that it would receive appropriate financial benefits but Egypt and the Soviet Union rejected the idea. The Soviet Union had sent representatives to what it called an 'imperialist dominated' meeting. They protested that the conference should rightly have been held in Cairo and argued that the whole proceedings failed to protect Egyptian interests. The main criticism was that the position of the Western Powers was valid only if Cairo refused to reimburse the company's shareholders or interfered with the freedom of navigation in the waterway in violation of the 1888 Convention otherwise they had no legal case to intervene. Furthermore, they claimed that Britain, France, and the United States had deliberately confused the issue of nationalization of the Suez Canal Company with the problem of freedom of navigation in the waterway and that the London conference was a way of exerting pressure on Egypt to force upon it international control over the Suez Canal. The Soviet Union, however, had its own reasons for coming to London when Nasser had flatly refused to do so. It saw the crisis as a way of getting recognition as an important player in Middle Eastern affairs and while Britain and France could be seen to apply some form of logical argument for Nasser's removal through diplomatic pressure, the Soviets took every opportunity to increase tensions by emphasising the 'atavistic colonial practices' of the Western Powers and so, by pledging its support for Arab nationalism encouraged Egyptian resistance to Western solutions. They warned the Western Powers not to use force which might lead to 'a serious conflict which would encompass the whole of the Near and Middle East and, perhaps, go even further.'

Remarkably, however, Dulles thought he detected a certain Soviet willingness to work with the U.S. to impose their own solution. 'I feel that the Soviets would be open to making some kind of arrangement with us,' he told Washington, 'and perhaps impose a solution on Egypt...in a two-party affair with some downgrading of the British and the French'.[50] Clearly the Soviets were as enthusiastic as the U.S. to finally bring the French and British empires to heel and make way for their own imperial adventures. This partially explains Dulles' attitude to the Soviets here because one of his abiding traits had been his almost pathological hatred of communism and it is hard to see how else he could envisage working with the Soviets against U.S. allies.

The relationship Britain saw between oil, security and Suez was summed up by Ivone Kirkpatrick when he said,

> 'if we sit back while Nasser consolidates his position and gradually acquires control of the oil-bearing countries, he can, and is, according to our information, resolved to wreck us. If Middle East oil is denied to us for a year or two our gold reserves will disappear. If our gold reserves disappear the sterling area disintegrates. If the sterling area disintegrates and we have no reserves we shall not be able to maintain a force in Germany or, indeed, anywhere else. I doubt whether we shall

be able to pay for the bare minimum necessary for our defence. And a country that cannot provide for its defence is finished.'[51]

Eden wrote to Eisenhower again on 27 August this time emphasising the threat to the security of Middle East oil supplies and of Soviet influence spreading through all of Africa if it was allowed to get a foothold in Egypt. Eisenhower replied with a fairly unequivocal rejection of military intervention. He indicated a divergence of views with Britain by saying 'I must tell you frankly that American public opinion flatly rejects the thought of using force...I gravely doubt we could here secure Congressional authority [and] I really do not see how a successful result could be achieved by forcible means.'[52]

Much to Eden's chagrin, Dulles felt the need to clarify the U.S. position and came out with a blunt rebuttal of any suggestion that the U.S. would 'shoot its way out' of the problem and instead proposed setting up a Suez Canal Users Association to which all Canal dues would be paid initially before distribution in a manner as yet unspecified. This was not going to suit Nasser who hoped to use Canal revenues to finance the Aswan dam. Whatever Eden made of this it did not have much effect on his performance on 12 September when he faced a deeply divided House of Commons and threatened to take 'such steps as seem to be required' to protect British rights. He carried the day by a vote of 319-248. Robert Menzies, the 'tough, no-nonsense' Australian Prime Minister had gone to Cairo on 3 September to try and persuade Nasser to accept a compromise agreement but Nasser would not be moved while British military preparations continued.[53] 'The British and French', he said, 'are going to stay out there in the Mediterranean until they find a pretext to come in.'[54] A second London Conference convened on 19 September but was a huge disappointment for Eden and the French Foreign Minister Christian Pineau, whom Dulles found arrogant and difficult to work with which was a serious issue given that he already held animosity towards, and mistrust of, Eden. British and French distrust of U.S. intentions now began to colour their deliberations.

Dulles reported to Eisenhower on the increasing isolation of Britain and France from world opinion on Suez, but Washington concluded that talk of an invasion was all sabre-rattling and would remain so unless Nasser was to commit another significant act of provocation. It was part of Eden's plan that the mere threat of force would force Nasser to back down and come to the negotiating table but British war planners were getting increasingly nervous at the prospect of launching a massive attack that might incur significant casualties if the

Egyptians did not break swiftly. A protracted conflict was the last thing the country needed or indeed could afford. The whole operation began to smack of hubris with imperialist power expected to crush colonial rebellion despite the evidence of recent decades that had repeatedly seen that to be a redundant strategy. It was, however, a lesson that the ruling class in Britain had not yet fully assimilated.

The Soviet Union at this stage was taking note and assessing how best to benefit from the looming confrontation. It put its weight behind calls for talks while sending fourteen 'volunteer' canal pilots to alleviate the shortage that Egypt was facing after British and French pilots had been withdrawn. Improved relations with Egypt seemed to be an easy win with Nasser ready to stand up to western pressure and Britain unlikely to go off on a wild adventure but the Soviets were careful not to make the sort of commitment that might draw them in and erode their freedom of action.

There were two distinct levels of thought concerning the invasion. The political view was that diplomatic pressures and threats of military intervention would convince the Egyptian leadership that the cost of resistance was too high to bear and would force them to negotiate. For Eden, it seemed, the military threat was a concept; a piece to be advanced on the chessboard of international diplomacy. For the military, however, war was a reality and when they looked again at the invasion plans, the French, especially and despite their general enthusiasm for military action, began to illuminate flaws. In the first plan, the French had been given Port Said as an entry point and the British Alexandria. The level of resistance that the Egyptians might bring to the battlefield was hard to gauge. While the professionalism of the Egyptian army was not thought to be very high, their equipment had recently been upgraded and the terrain over which the battle would be fought was mired with difficulties. If the amphibian assault craft safely navigated the submerged reefs, if beaches were not heavily mined, if the Egyptian army failed to put up stiff resistance and if the parachute dropping zones were secured it still left the prospect of crossing the Nile at a time when its waters were high. If resistance continued as forces closed in on Cairo the number of civilian casualties would inevitably rise and become a political issue.

Mountbatten had prevailed upon Eden to reconsider the decision to attack through Alexandria which, he thought, would lead to large numbers of civilian casualties. Mountbatten was to change his advice on a number of occasions during the crisis, which did nothing to help Eden to clarify his own thoughts, and at this stage he may well have been influenced by analysis coming out of the French camp. Barjot had surprised even Beaufre on 24 August when his staff suggested that Port Said was now seen as a preferred entry point to Alexandria. This diminished the options but, in the process, reduced the time between receiving the final order to invade and actually doing so. Intelligence assessments showed that Egyptian defences had probably been strengthened in the Port Said area and the French feared that paratroop drops would meet fierce resistance there before they could be reinforced. Barjot may also have been influenced by wanting to coordinate more with the Israeli attack that he was aware of but of which others were not. This new plan had little to do with actually toppling Nasser and more to do with taking control of the Canal Zone but that might not be a sustainable objective if Nasser survived and rallied world opinion against the occupation. This was a clear deviation from Eden's objective which was the complete removal of Nasser from political leadership of Egypt but even the British Chiefs of Staff had not been made privy to this. Barjot was now immersed in tactical details and failed to grasp the strategic implications of the constantly evolving operations plans and widening rift between French and British objectives.

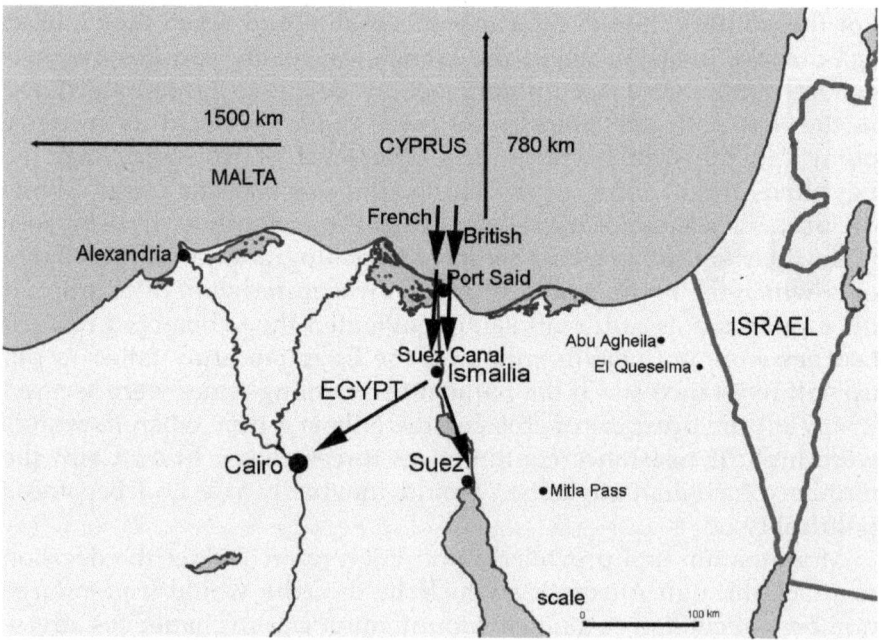

The Musketeer-Revise Plan

Stockwell opposed Barjot's plan, but Keightley saw merit in it. It placed great emphasis on the initial aerial bombardment to break Egyptian morale, which Eden still hoped would lead to Nasser's demise. There was some concern about what effect an extended bombing campaign against Egyptian infrastructure, with inevitable civilian casualties, would have on world opinion and the Chiefs were able to discreetly convey this whilst accepting the validity of the new plan now called Musketeer-Revise. It was noted that the bombing campaign would not break the Egyptian army and it would still have to be defeated on the ground if the Egyptian government held firm.

The problem for the planners was that British intelligence was unable to come up with a definitive assessment of morale within the Egyptian forces. That it would collapse if the Egyptians were subjected to intensive bombing was no more than conjecture partially based on wishful thinking instead of allowing for the worst-case scenario. Any stiffening of Egyptian resolve would subject British and French politicians to the pressure of public opinion which, in turn would test their commitment to each other. In this regard, the French, already embroiled in a war in North Africa, were much more confident of withstanding international disapproval and consequently adopted a more aggressive position.

Only the Chief of the Air Staff thought that the air campaign would be sufficient to bring Nasser down but by now the new plan, which was weeks in the planning, had government approval although it had not come to Eden's attention until days before it got the go-ahead. Whilst Keightley had used every device and argument at his disposal to persuade the Prime Minister, he was less than totally successful, but Eden allowed it to go before the Egypt Committee who approved it on 10 September. The view amongst task force commanders in the field was that an air campaign would not be sufficient to destroy the Egyptian army and any occupation force would be subjected to venomous guerrilla tactics by an enraged populace.

For the French the overriding consideration throughout the planning and execution of the operation would be speed so when Beaufre was told on 10 September about further delays he was furious as much because of the delays as by the news of the change of entry point and threatened to resign. When he was told that the aerial bombardment was now due to last up to eight days to destroy Egyptian morale before the main landings, Beaufre thought the British were now in the French equivalent of 'cloud cuckoo land.'[55]

In Israel, Prime Minister Ben-Gurion had responded to the supply of Soviet military equipment to Egypt by doing a deal with the French for eighty-two Mystère Mark IV jet fighters, 120 AMX tanks, forty Super-Sherman tanks and eighteen 105 mm mobile guns. U.S. Intelligence had continued to work closely with their British and French counterparts and so Washington was made perfectly aware of what was happening. It took a dim view since the French jets had been built with U.S. finance ostensibly for use only within the N.AT.O. Alliance. This deal initiated talks between foreign ministers to consider joint French-Israeli action against Egypt which proved fruitful but the Israeli Government would have to make the decision.

For months Israeli Intelligence had been sending up warnings about a possible attack on Israel by surrounding Arab countries, most notably Egypt which was being significantly rearmed, despite its own intelligence service saying that, 'In the current situation the Egyptian army is incapable of efficiently absorbing large amounts of sophisticated weapons.' An intelligence report concluded that of all Israel's enemies, the Egyptian soldiers were 'the worst.'[56] Israeli Chief of the General Staff, General Moshe Dayan, had made strong recommendations that Israel get in first with a pre-emptive strike to take the Gaza Strip and the Straits of Tiran. The Israeli Foreign Minister, Moshe Sharett, admitted that the threat had been exaggerated to support Israel's campaign for arms but the fear of some sort of aggression in the future was real. The real motivation for the Israelis was probably to extend its border with Egypt west across the Sinai Peninsula and to gain control of the Gulf of Aqaba, although the Suez Canal, itself, had no particular military significance for them.

In early September, Israeli forces had attacked Jordanian facilities near Hebron killing more than fifty in retaliation for Jordanian incursions inro Israeli territory. Britain reminded Israel that it was bound by treaty to go to the aid of Jordan in the event of war. This raised the nightmare possibility of Israel backed by France going to war with Jordan backed by Britain.

Meanwhile an Israeli delegation had gone to Paris to discuss a joint French-Israeli attack against Egypt but neither had the means to prevent retaliatory bombing attacks on Israeli cities. Only British heavy bombers, designed for war with the Soviet Union, could strike at Egyptian airfields and prevent their bombers from taking off and it was far from certain that the British would come on board to that extent. Further Israeli strikes against Jordan threatened to sour relations for good and precipitate a conflict far removed from the one planned against Egypt. Eden approached the issue by condemning the anti-Jewish bellicosity of the 'people in the [British] Foreign Office' and urged them to water down their public expression of loyalty to Jordan.[57]

Ben-Gurion was not averse to considering the French suggestion that Israel occupy the Sinai Peninsula and, in effect, make the Suez Canal an international waterway once again. After some reflection, he asked the French if Israel came on board with the plan might the French like to show their gratitude by building a nuclear reactor in Israel. This, of course, would give Israel a pathway to eventually joining the small number of countries armed with nuclear weapons. (Construction of the Dimona nuclear reactor in the southern Israeli Negev desert began two years later.) As part of the French initiative, Israel opened up a diplomatic assault on the U.S. for 'letting Nasser get away with [nationalisation of the Canal]' and Ben-Gurion instructed his military to formulate a plan of attack against Egypt to coincide with the U.S. Presidential elections in November. Military training, especially on the new French jets, was stepped up in Israel. The British were not willing to make any sort of deal with the Israelis but they would have little choice but fall in with any joint French-Israeli plan if these two countries went out on a limb and acted without Britain.

While still adhering to the fiction that they were pursuing a diplomatic solution, on 10 September, Eden and Mollet tried to justify their belligerent attitude towards Egypt on the grounds that Egypt was incapable of operating the Canal efficiently which would paralyse international trade through it but this was shown to be quite false. Nasser had never indicated that he wanted to restrict the passage of ships, indeed why would he? It would only reduce his revenues. Despite the British and French piling up ships at both ends of the Canal in the hope of illuminating the incompetence of Egyptian authorities to operate the piloting service, there was no logjam of traffic and no holdups. It was a significant embarrassment for them. For the Egyptians however, it became an economic issue. Because of the cost of employing pilots from across the world to replace those that had been withdrawn by Britain and France and to compensate for possible loss of revenues due to the reduction in traffic through the Canal the Egyptian government approached the International Monetary Fund (IMF) for a loan of $15 million.[58]

Eden and Mollet tried to speed up the diplomatic manoeuvres to exhaust that avenue towards a solution and give them a clear path for 'legitimate' military action but it still delayed their plans which now had to be further put back to 8 October. Even this date was too early when the U.N. refused to debate the issue before 5 October. In frustration at British prevarication, the French intensified negotiations with the Israelis. Both Pineau and Lloyd told Dulles on 5 October that they did not believe there was any peaceful way of resolving the Suez issue but Dulles called it an 'illusion' to think like that. Much world opinion was hardening against Britain and France for their outdated imperialist actions and the U.S. was increasingly worried that it would be seen as complicit and lose prestige in the eyes of Afro-Asian governments. Clearly any international opprobrium generated by Nasser's nationalisation action was evaporating and the U.S. now took urgent steps to distance itself from association with any action hostile to the Egyptian government.

The U.S. Ambassador to the Soviet Union, Charles Bohlen, informed Washington that the Soviets had warned France of 'dire consequences' if force was used to subdue Egypt. Beaufre responded with an assessment of the potential Soviet threat as being a naval blockade probably by Egyptian submarines and the potential of an escalating conflict with Soviet forces. He countered this by demanding 'all available resources' to achieve a quick victory after the invasion of Egypt.[59]

Serious concerns about the weather combined with U.N. moves were continuing to push back the invasion date. So much so that Keightley now brought out his Winter Plan that envisaged a landing sometime in the Spring of 1957. This did not at all suit the Joint Planning Staff, especially the naval representatives, and moves were started to reduce Keightley's input to the actual planning process and redirect his role more towards implementation. In particular the extended aerial bombardment was not welcomed since it deprived the other services of following up quickly before the Egyptians could recover from the initial shock.

By 5 October Israel had completed its own plans for Operation Kadesh (a biblical reference to the wanderings of the children of Israel in the Sinai Desert) and succeeded in provoking Jordan into a diplomatic row to divert world attention away from its real target which was Egypt. Their spat intensified and had the desired effect of making observers think that Israel was gearing up for action against Jordan. While Musketeer was getting their full attention, the French had given little thought to their previous option of combined operations with Israel but this was rejuvenated on 8 October by the French Minister of Defence who asked Barjot to see how it could be incorporated into a tripartite operation to include Britain.

The French had maintained a liaison team at the Israeli General Staff Headquarters. They had now been informed that Israel had stepped up its plan for a blitz-style attack against Egypt followed by a recall of troops home to counter the expected retaliatory attacks from Jordan and Syria. The Israeli Air Force would win air superiority and follow up with a continuous assault to encircle Egyptian forces in Sinai and take control of all strongpoints in the desert. The first ground attack would be by the 202nd Paratroops commanded by Colonel Ariel Sharon on the Mitla Pass in western Sinai to prevent Egyptian reinforcements getting through. The French were disappointed initially that the Israeli operation was designed to destroy only the Egyptian forces in Sinai and did not so as far as to move up to the Suez Canal itself and this would not have the desired effect of deposing Nasser which was a priority for them. At this stage, British military planners were not aware of the extent to which the French had been working with the Israelis.

Dulles had prided himself on his toughness and masculine vigour which U.S. politics generally considered to be vital traits in an effective Cold War policymaker but he blocked Admiral Burke's attempt to furnish the British and French with U.S. landing craft from the Sixth Fleet. He did, however, sanction the supplying of spare parts for French jets and U-2 spy planes supplied reconnaissance photographs of the whole Nile delta and continued to do so throughout the conflict. They also brought back high-resolution images showing that the number of French jet fighters in Israel significantly exceeded the number the French were permitted to transfer under the Tripartite Declaration and that large quantities of weapons were being loaded onto French and British ships in Toulon, Malta, and Cyprus.[60]

A build-up of U.S. military presence in the Eastern Mediterranean was called a 'dangerous provocation intended further to aggravate the situation' by Moscow since 'aggression in the area of the Near and Middle East touches on the security of the Soviet Union.' The Soviet Premier Nikolai Bulganin told Eden and Pineau that 'as a great power which is interested in the maintenance of peace [the Soviet Union] cannot stand aside from this question.' On 5 October, *Pravda* wrote that 'the position of the ruling circles in the United States gives no evidence of a peaceful and just approach to the solution of the Suez problem. [In contrast] the peace-loving socialist camp offered the Arabs disinterested and invaluable assistance in their struggle for complete independence.'[61] When Nasser staked his political future on nationalisation of the Suez Canal Company the Soviet Union had no choice but to back him. Just how far it might have gone is open to speculation but it was determined to use all diplomatic and moral pressure to prevent the Western Powers from crushing Nasser. It would do its utmost to transform the attack on Egypt into a political defeat for the Western Powers and Israel.

Chapter Three

THE SÈVRES PROTOCOL

'While our ultimate purpose was to place the Canal under international control, our immediate objective was to bring about the downfall of the present Egyptian Government.'
The [British] Egypt Committee 30 July 1956[1]

Strong diplomatic pressure was building at the U.N. for a negotiated settlement of the Suez crisis. Lloyd had presented a list of six principles for the operation of the canal and Egypt had raised no objections. The U.N. Security Council unanimously accepted the six principles. 'it looks like here is a very great crisis that is behind us,' said Eisenhower on hearing the news.[2] This was not what Israel, Britain and France, in particular, wanted to hear. They followed up the six principles with more conditions that they clearly expected Egypt to reject which stalled any progress towards an agreement. Dulles made it quite clear to Pineau that 'the views of the President and myself on [invasion] are basic and fundamental and I do not see any likelihood of their being changed after the U.S. Presidential election.'

'We are wasting our time talking to the Americans', said Pineau, '[Britain and France] should now go firmly ahead on our chosen path.[3] Eden returned from the Conservative Party Conference on the evening of 13 October to hear that the French had delivered 75 of the latest Mystère fighter aircraft to Israel without it being cleared with the UK or the Americans. Eden wondered if the French were inciting the Israelis to attack Jordan, which was a major British anxiety at the time. He gave no indication that he had the slightest inkling that the French were already deep in collusion with the Israelis over Egypt.

Despite maintaining a fiction for home consumption, Eden had hoped to limit British involvement in world affairs, whilst looking to the U.S. to fill the vacuum but, at the same time, the Americans were trying to scale down their own foreign commitments. This was a point that Eden never fully understood which caused him to rely on U.S. support for his actions towards Suez long after it was clear that it would not be forthcoming. It had now finally dawned on the increasingly ill and disillusioned Prime Minister that he was left only with the military option but no way of implementing it unilaterally.

This would all change on the very next day when Albert Gazier, Acting French Foreign Minister brought General Maurice Challe, the Deputy Chief of Staff of the French armed forces to Chequers and presented Eden with a plan of action which became known as 'the Challe scenario'. Britain, France and Israel were all open to discussion about military intervention in Egypt but there didn't seem to be sufficient cause to justify it. It was this problem to which Challe claimed to have found a solution. The French Ambassador was deliberately kept out of discussions and not told what the meeting was about. Challe laid out his plan which was that Israel should be invited to attack Egypt across the Sinai Peninsula and that France and Britain, having given the Israeli forces enough time to seize all or most of Sinai, should then order 'both sides' to withdraw their forces from the Suez Canal, in order to permit an Anglo-French force to intervene and occupy the Canal. They would take control of the terminal ports of Port Said and Suez, on the pretext of creating a *cordon sanitaire* between the belligerents thus protecting them from collateral damage. While it was the military threat of an Egyptian attack, with or without the involvement of other Arab countries, that worried Israel, the French saw Nasser as a clear threat to their control of Algeria by his encouragement of nationalist movements in that country. He had made his support of the rebels clear and the French Government blamed him for supplying them with weaponry and ammunition. For the French, the opportunity to get rid of Nasser was seen as too good to miss. For Britain it was simply a question of slapping down the upstart who had humiliated them.

The Eden-Macmillan dynamic would play a significant role in the development of British policy towards Suez. The two men had shared an uneasy relationship during the Second World War and continued to be burdened with what Matthew Jones called 'personal friction and mutual disregard.'[4] Macmillan was much more hawkish than Eden and looked on the Challe plan with favour saying, 'All history shows that statesmen of any character will seize a chance like this' and, according to Brendan Bracken, showed 'bellicosity beyond all description.'[5] Macmillan had a reputation for being 'unflappable' and had little time for Eden's 'indecisive tendencies and excitable temperament' but was careful not to let his personal feelings become public and prejudice his ambitions to succeed Eden as leader of the Conservative Party.

Eden seemed 'intrigued' by the Challe plan especially in view of the lack of support he felt he was getting from the U.S., but he demurred and asked for time to take it to his Cabinet. Lloyd returned from Washington with news that the 'extraordinarily naïve' statement by Eisenhower saying the crisis was over would make future negotiations with Egypt 'more difficult'.[6] Lloyd had been markedly less enthusiastic about the Challe initiative and had told Nutting that 'we must have nothing to do with the French plan' but was put under extreme pressure to come on board and reluctantly agreed.[7] Lloyd was far from being a dynamic personality. It had been his lack of knowledge of, or interest in, foreign affairs and his xenophobia that Churchill had found to be 'positive advantages' when he had appointed Lloyd to the Foreign Office in 1951.[8] Eden promoted him to the ministerial position at the end of 1955 possibly because of his almost total subservience to the Prime Minister who felt able to manipulate him in any way he wanted. Lloyd, himself, said that he had been over-promoted but there was never any question of disloyalty to Eden.[9]

Another factor that played on Eden's mind was that British military preparations, initiated as part of his overall strategy were becoming problematic with reservists, who had been called up from their civilian lives, frustrated at the lack of directive. They couldn't be expected to remain acquiescent for very much longer and the cost was not inconsiderable either. Any more delays would mean landings becoming too hazardous because of worsening sea conditions so reservists would have to be stood down until the Spring. Not least of the factors now influencing the Prime Minister was his belief that if nationalisation of the Canal was not reversed, by whatever means, within a short time, he would fall and his government with him despite his recent 'rumbustious and belligerent' speech that had gone down so well at the Conservative Party Conference. Believing that any chance of a negotiated settlement had all but gone, Eden now saw in the Challe plan a way out of his dilemma even though he had lingering doubts about the French military and saw no benefit in being seen to collaborate with the Israelis. When he intimated to his inner circle that the military option was now becoming his preferred one he was careful to avoid going into details over its implementation and as a consequence avoided awkward questions and was able to get a great deal of support for it.

Jonathan Pearson in his book *Sir Anthony Eden and the Suez Crisis* claims that before the meeting with Challe, 'there was very little evidence that [Eden] wanted to use force.'[10] The decision to do so, which the Challe initiative offered, was a high-risk solution to an increasingly high-risk situation. Up to this point, says Pearson, Eden, 'in line with his moral and political beliefs, as well as his experience', had attempted to bring the crisis to a peaceful conclusion. Because of Eden's sidelining of the Foreign Office and Lloyd's malleability, Britain did not have a viable foreign policy at the time, it merely had foreign relations which saw day-by-day reaction to events rather than the fulfilment of measured policies. Despite Eden's bellicose statements, his stated strategy in 1953 had been to maintain British influence in the Middle East, by harnessing nationalist movements rather than struggle against them. The British public, however, had been led to believe that its country was still a leading world power with the ability to create her own policy and act independently. The Suez Crisis would abruptly disabuse them of that notion.

There is some evidence that Eden had been made aware of Franco-Israeli negotiations as early as 20 September when Field Marshal Bernard Montgomery, the Deputy Supreme Commander of N.AT.O. mentioned it to him and again at the beginning of October, Eden's biographer, Alistair Horne states that the Egypt Committee discussed it on a number of occasions at that time. While these assertions are unsupported by documentary proof, it is undeniable that, at around the time that Musketeer-Revise extended the invasion date into November, the R.A.F. had started redeploying a number of bomber squadrons to Malta and Cyprus and the French had also moved aircraft to Cyprus on 18 October four days after the meeting with Challe.

It was a very uncomfortable position that Eden found himself in and must have contributed significantly to the deterioration of his health. The build-up of military hardware in Israel got from France might instead be used for an attack on Jordan, which Eden thought most likely, and Britain was legally bound to intervene on the side of Jordan if that happened. On the other hand, if Israel attacked Egypt while Britain and France were bombing Egypt it would look like collusion and that would have serious consequences for Anglo-Arab relations. At this point it was not clear whether Britain would end up fighting with or against Israel. The British First Sea Lord actually wryly pointed that if Britain allied with Israel who then attacked Jordan the U.S. might fulfil its treaty obligations to come to the aid of Jordan putting Britain and the U.S. practically on opposite sides.

When U-2 spy planes saw sixty French jets on Israeli airstrips Eisenhower was quick to tell Ben-Gurion on 15 October that he needn't think the U.S. would support him just because there was an election coming up. Ben-Gurion, however, was planning to gamble on Eisenhower not risking his Jewish vote in the U.S. If Israel struck just before the election, he surmised, the U.S. would have no choice but support it. The problem was that the French and British took the opposite view which was that U.S. support would be more, not less, forthcoming after the election and had made their own plans accordingly. The level of discord within the Anglo-French-Israeli alliance was breath-taking and did not auger well for future plans.

The next day Eden and Lloyd met their French counterparts at the official residence of the French Prime Minister, the Palais Matignon in Paris. The French, unaware that Eden had become enamoured of the Challe plan began discussions by flatly refusing to entertain any more negotiations with Nasser. Once again, they repeated all the arguments in favour of military intervention. To their surprise, the British were more amenable than they had anticipated and they felt sufficiently confident afterwards to assure the Israelis that Britain would not oppose a French-Israeli attack against Egypt and would feel obliged to intervene if military action took place around the Suez Canal. The British Cabinet was told on 18 October that an Israeli attack on Egypt was 'probable' but neither Eden nor Lloyd mentioned that the French and Israelis, with British approval and possibly participation, would shortly be negotiating the details of the attack in question. The meeting in Paris had, however, agreed that if Israel did indeed attack Egypt, Britain and France would intervene to protect the Canal but the Israeli Prime Minister David Ben-Gurion did not trust the British and their vague indirect assurances given in Paris.[11] Only eight years previously, Israel had been fighting an existential battle against Arab armies that had been commanded by British officers and since that time British policy in the Middle East had been anything but pro-Israel.

When Ben-Gurion first heard of the French plan, his first thought was to order his delegation to withdraw from negotiations with the French altogether. He insisted that Israel should not be the ones to launch the campaign and fill the role of aggressor, while the British and French appeared as 'angels of peace to bring tranquillity to the area.'[12] He feared that his country was being used by others for their own ends. He suspected that 'the English plot is to embroil us with Nasser, and in the meantime bring about the conquest of Jordan by Iraq' and that the French were acting merely to remove Nasser who they saw as a catalyst for revolution against French occupation of Algeria.[13] Despite the risk that Israel would 'mount the rostrum of shame so that Britain and France could wash their hands in waters of purity', he nevertheless agreed to lead a delegation to France to see whether a satisfactory agreement could be negotiated with the French and eventually with the British as well.[14] It would at least be an opportunity for Ben-Gurion to step up onto the world stage and be treated with respect by two major powers.

A meeting at Chequers on 21 October was attended by Eden, Lloyd, Macmillan, the new Minister of Defence, Anthony Head, the Lord Privy Seal, R. A. Butler and General Keightley. The meeting was told that Israeli leaders were due to arrive in Paris on the following day and it was thought important that Britain should be represented at the discussions implying that they would be attending as observers. It was agreed that Lloyd should attend under strict secrecy. When Nutting tried to get hold of Lloyd on the following day he was told that he was in bed with a cold and was incommunicado.

Ben-Gurion was not about to be taken for a fool, however. He deeply mistrusted the British and accepted a French invitation to arrive a day early for talks before the British arrived. This had the unfortunate consequence of Lloyd, arriving while the French and Israelis were deep in discussions, thinking that they had been colluding prior to his arrival which immediately put him on the defensive. He had come in expectation of simply filling in the details of the Challe plan but Ben-Gurion opened at Sèvres by objecting to the Challe scenario which made Israel appear to be the aggressor while Britain and France posed as peacemakers and he was doubly apprehensive about exposing Israeli cities to attack by the Egyptian Air Force. He then presented his own plan for the reorganization of the Middle East. He claimed that Jordan was not viable as an independent state and should therefore be divided between Iraq, who would get the East Bank, in return for a promise to settle the Palestinian refugees there, and Israel who would get the West Bank which would be administered as a semi- autonomous region. Israel's borders could be expanded up to the Litani River, thereby helping to turn Lebanon into a more compact Christian state and the Suez Canal area would be given an international status while the Straits of Tiran in the Gulf of Aqaba should come under Israeli control to ensure freedom of navigation. All this, of course, could only happen after Nasser had been removed and the threat of Arab nationalism destroyed. Britain would regain control of Iraq and Jordan with secure access to Middle East oil while France would consolidate its position in Lebanon and eliminate Egyptian interference in Algeria. Even the United States might be persuaded to support a plan that would check Soviet advances in the Middle East. The French were unmoved by Israeli fantasies that would require much time and effort to realise and reminded Ben-Gurion that time was short and a solution was required now.

The Israelis found Lloyd arrogant, antagonistic, aloof and snobbish and Lloyd in return thought the Israelis aggressive in manner and seemingly unwilling to believe anything the British said. While the Israelis wanted to discuss details of military action, the British seemed more concerned with seeking a diplomatic solution. Dayan thought that Lloyd's 'heart was not in it.'[15] If the Challe plan was to be the way forward, Lloyd insisted that Israel would have to make the initial attack and hold out long enough for Britain and France to deliver an ultimatum to them, for Israel to reject it and for the two co-conspirators to then seem to take time to consider their response and eventually intervene all of which was expected to take about three days. During all this time Israel would be exposed as the aggressor and subjected to intense international pressure to withdraw.

On the evening of 23 October when Lloyd had returned to London and Ben-Gurion had spent all day talking only to the French, he was seriously worried that the Soviets would intervene militarily in any Franco-Israeli-Egyptian war and that Israel would be the main (indeed sole) target of its aggression. In the absence of British delegates, the French and Israelis were failing to find common ground over their plans for the attack on Egypt and Ben-Gurion was so dispirited that he was ready to walk out but was persuaded to stay at the last minute. When news of the anti-Soviet demonstrations in Budapest came in, it was used by the French to convince Ben-Gurion that it represented an opportunity that should not be ignored. Pineau argued that Budapest could not have come at a better time for them to act against Nasser. Neither the Americans, preoccupied with a presidential election, nor the Russians, struggling with the Hungarian uprising, would do anything to help Nasser and a more favourable time would not come for France, Britain and Israel to take their own action to remove the Egyptian leadership. If anything, it meant that the Israeli attack should be made even sooner than planned. Britain, on the other hand, seemed to be quite disinterested in the Hungarian uprising which did not exert any significant effect on the development of the British policy. Ben-Gurion was persuaded to stay and continue negotiations.

Ben-Gurion wanted all three Parties to attack simultaneously after the R.A.F. had destroyed the Egyptian Air Force on the ground. Britain categorically rejected such an idea and insisted that Britain would only take such action as it could justify as defence of the Canal Zone rather than making an outright three-country attack on Egypt. He would not agree to that. The next proposal was presented by

Dayan who suggested an 'elegant compromise' providing for an Israeli retaliatory raid near the Canal, an Anglo-French ultimatum to Egypt to evacuate its military forces from the Canal Zone, an appeal to Israel not to approach the canal, and aerial bombardment of Egypt's airfields following the expected rejection of the ultimatum.[16] Britain argued that the initial Israeli action would be insufficient to warrant British military intervention. The French wanted to fly from bases in Israel and Cyprus to protect Israeli cities in the first two days of fighting, but Lloyd refused to allow the use of Cypriot bases which would have been obvious proof of collusion. However, he saw no reason to object to French warplanes flying from Israel.

British Canberra heavy bombers based in Cyprus were vital to any plan and so nothing could be done without British agreement, and it was the timing of British raids on Egyptian airfields that now became the focus of discussion. When the first day of talks ended, Lloyd flew back to London but Pineau, fearing that Lloyd would give a biased report to the Prime Minister followed on the evening of the next day to put the French and Israeli viewpoint directly to Eden. He emphasised Israel's intention to keep her forces for the purpose of permanent annexation of the entire area east of the line El Arish-Abu Ageila - Nakhl-Sharm el-Sheikh, in order to secure the long-term freedom of navigation in the Straits of Eilat. That would protect Israel from the scourge of the infiltrators and from the danger posed by the Egyptian army bases in Sinai. As a result, the meeting was reconvened on the following day without Lloyd. The French suggested a 'false flag' operation to simulate an Egyptian attack against Beersheba to justify Israeli retaliation, but Ben-Gurion would not hear of it. It was now that Dayan came up with his idea for the Israeli Defence Force (IDF) paratroops to drop on the strategic Mitla Pass, about thirty-five miles from the Suez Canal where there were no concentrations of Egyptian forces, and this together with an advance of a mechanized brigade would constitute 'a real act of war' and thus provide the pretext for intervention by Britain and France thirty-six hours later. Pineau included in his summing up of the meeting a call for Britain and France to support or at least to commit themselves not to show opposition to Dayan's plan which would address Israel's demands as 'her share in the fruits of victory.'[17]

Pineau was right not to trust Lloyd who had told the British Cabinet that he 'was doubtful whether Israel would launch an attack against Egypt in the immediate future' but he had more confidence in Eden who, however distasteful he found dealings with the Israelis, approved the plan.[18] Lloyd made it clear in a letter to Pineau, however, that

Britain could not be seen to have asked Israel to take any particular action and should be portrayed as simply responding to events. Any hint of collusion with the Israelis would have been particularly difficult to explain to the Arab oil-producing countries and could have serious consequences for Britain's oil imports. Lloyd did not attend the final day of talks sending Patrick Dean, an Assistant Under-Secretary at the Foreign Office instead. Dean's brief was to make it abundantly clear to France and Israel that there would be no British military action unless the Israelis had advanced beyond their frontiers and a case could be made that there was a clear military threat to the security of the canal. If there was no agreement on this point, Britain would not participate in any military contingency plan.

As the Sèvres negotiations reached their climax, Eisenhower and Dulles became concerned by a number of developments but had little hard intelligence to inform them. The tension on the Jordanian-Israeli frontier was clear, as was continuing Israeli mobilization and the large numbers of French jets being flown into Israel. If the Franco-British military activity in the Mediterranean was more than an exercise, it had ominously coincided with the termination of regular high-level communications with Washington by Paris and London and a sizeable growth in Israeli-French diplomatic radio traffic. All the evidence, such as it was, pointed to collusion between Israel and France but the level of British involvement was unknown. It is indicative of the relationship that existed between the U.S. and the two great European states at the time, and surprising in view of the way that power shifted seismically afterwards, that the U.S. should have been treated with such disdain. Despite the U.S., along with the Soviet Union, having been instrumental in the defeat of Nazism, the deeply-embedded imperial mindset of Britain and France was proving to be remarkably resilient. Again, in the light of the way that Middle East politics evolved, it is no less surprising to see how U.S. foreign policy in 1956 treated Israel as something of an untrustworthy pariah.

Ben-Gurion finally gave his approval for the IDF to take action if Israeli airspace could be defended until the Egyptian airfields were put out of commission. Pineau returned from London to report that Eden had seemed to accept most of Israel's conditions and had given approval of Dayan's plan.

- Israel would decide how precisely to initiate hostilities in Sinai
- Israel had to carry out an operation that would look like a real act of war so that the French and British governments could argue that the Canal was in danger.

- The air forces of France and Britain would go into action not more than 36 hours after Israel launched its attack.
- On the day after D-Day, the French and British governments would send two somewhat differently worded messages, to be called an appeal rather than an ultimatum in order to preserve Israel's good name.
- To reinforce the air defence of Israeli cities in the period between the opening of hostilities and the allied intervention, France undertook to station fighter bombers in Israel but these planes were to be given Israeli Air Force markings to conceal their true identity
- Finally, D-Day was to be Monday, 29 October 1956, at 19.00 Israeli time.

Dean arrived late in the afternoon to be confronted with Dayan's six points and two more conditions submitted by Ben-Gurion which were,

- In return for an Israeli pledge not to attack Jordan, the agreement should explicitly commit Britain to refrain from activating the Anglo-Jordanian Treaty if either Jordan or Iraq attacked Israel
- He wanted the British and French governments to note Israel's territorial demands, even if they could not officially support them[19]

Dean reiterated Britain's position making it plain to the Israelis and the French that British forces would not move unless the Israelis had advanced beyond their frontiers against Egypt and presented a clear threat to the Canal. Ben-Gurion took the initiative in suggesting to the French that a document be drawn up, which became known as the Protocol of Sèvres, to summarize the decisions that had been reached and that this document should be signed by the three parties and be binding on them. By 19:00hrs on 24 October the document written in French was ready for signing but this took the British completely by surprise with them not having taken any part in the drawing up of the agreement and indeed having no idea that one had been drafted at all. After lengthy discussion with the other British delegates, Dean initialled the document making it clear that, at this stage, it was simply a record of discussions and would still require approval of his government.[20] After the British had left, the French and the Israelis signed a second document agreeing that the French air force could use Israeli airfields, and the French navy could use Israeli harbours. Eden did not know the second agreement existed.[21] This plan enabled the UK to go to war against Egypt behind the back of her American ally and was the cause of high, avoidable Israeli casualties in the first military operation of that war, the Israeli parachute drop at the Mitla Pass.

Even Israeli military commanders in the field were unaware of this conspiracy and were essentially kept in the dark as to the intentions of their political commanders. The document set out in precise detail the plan of the three governments to attack Egypt which would serve as the pretext for an Anglo-French military intervention. The British copy of this signed Protocol was destroyed on British Prime Minister Anthony Eden's orders, the French copy was apparently lost, and the Israeli copy was kept under lock and key in the Ben-Gurion Archives in Sede-Boker until 1996. Numerous memoirs by people involved at the time have subsequently combined to give a detailed and authoritative account of the three-day Sèvres conference that preceded the signing of the Protocol.

The Protocol document is a most illuminating piece of evidence since it lays out in precise detail, and with a precise timetable, how the joint war against Egypt was intended to proceed and shows foreknowledge of each other's intentions. The central aim of the plot which emerged clearly and unambiguously from all the records of the discussions surrounding it was the overthrow of Nasser. There does not seem to have been very much debate over what might happen in Egypt if and when Nasser fell. Presumably Eden and Mollet thought that they still had enough influence in the Arab world to ensure that any administration that came in to take over from a disgraced Nasser would be malleable and could be coerced into working in harmony with the West. It was a glaring illustration of just how out of touch they were with the way the world was changing and it was also reflected in how invasion plans, especially those of the British, showed that the military chiefs were unable to see beyond a D-Day scenario. It is remarkable that this view should have been allowed to persist without being challenged given how much support Nasser actually had in Egypt, support that had only been heightened by his stand on Suez.

Eden was very uncomfortable to learn that the meeting at Sèvres had been recorded in a formal document and was seriously worried about the possible consequences. He ordered Dean and Sir Donald Logan to return to Paris the next day to persuade the other parties to destroy their copies of the Protocol. Pineau demurred and added that Ben-Gurion was already on his way back to Israel with his copy. In an attempt to maintain security and prevent any rumours propagated as a result of their visit, the British pair were then locked in one of the reception rooms in the Quai d'Orsay until late afternoon when Pineau informed them that not only would he refuse to destroy his copy of the agreement but that he had contacted Ben-Gurion who declined to destroy his copy also. When Eden was informed he ordered the original and English translation of the document made in the Foreign Office to be delivered to him but, whether by accident or design, within days, rumours of the meeting at Sèvres were circulating in Paris.

Eden reluctantly admitted that war was the price Britain would have to pay in order to get rid of Nasser and it was clear now that this could only be done in alliance with Israel. His desire for Nasser's elimination clearly clouded his better judgement if he had ever thought that the Challe plan was sophisticated enough to convince international observers that it was anything but a blatant, transparent and clumsy subterfuge. His attempt to round up and destroy all the copies of the Protocol was a clear effort to expunge the war plot from the historical record. Neither the British nor the French Ministries of Foreign Affairs were informed about the Sevres meetings in which only the highest-level government officials had participated. The timing of events agreed at Sèvres meant that hostilities would begin with the Israeli invasion on 29 October, the issuing of the ultimatum on the 30th, an Anglo-French air bombardment on the 31st, followed by an airborne invasion on 5 November and an amphibious landing on the 6th. Eden now staked his whole political career on this and by now he was showing signs of extreme nervous exhaustion.

It had been Ben-Gurion who saw the agreement as a major achievement and it was he who had proposed the drawing up of a document signed by the representatives of the three countries concerned. It represented, for him, a military pact with two great powers against a common enemy and gave him some sort of guarantee against betrayal by 'perfidious Albion'. In the final analysis, the Protocol of Sevres was thus a monument to French opportunism, Eden's duplicity, and Ben-Gurion's paranoia.[22]

Chapter Four

22-24 OCTOBER

'Tonight at 7.00 p.m. at the latest, we want to respond to the call of the Budapest University students. Let's make a free, truly democratic, independent university life! Everybody should come!'
Call to students at Szeged University 16 October 1956[1]

Few events during the Cold War have received as much attention or generated so much criticism as the Soviet Union's crushing of the Hungarian revolution.[2] While the U.S. struggled to justify its passive response to communist aggression, it found itself confronted by a second crisis in North Africa where Britain's deluded leaders, vainly trying to prove that they still wielded imperial power, threatened to drag the superpowers into a second confrontation. This was at a time when U.S. President Dwight Eisenhower was preoccupied with the upcoming presidential election in which he hoped to win a second term in office. Rather than alienate voters by any talk of war, the U.S. administration's response was to render covert assistance to the Hungarian uprising and secretly discuss plans threatening the use of tactical nuclear weapons to interdict rail and road connections into Hungary by a 'surgical nuclear strike limited to Lvov...and selected passes in the mountains of Russian Ruthenia and western Romania' to destroy Soviet supply routes into Hungary.[3] Eisenhower's strategy, characterised by his trademark cautious approach to decision-making, was essentially to 'keep the pot boiling' without letting it boil over. The question which remains unanswered is whether the U.S. betrayed the Hungarian people by promising much and thereby stoking the fires of revolution but, in the end, delivering little. It is of profound importance given the death toll during those fateful weeks in October and November of 1956.

The decade since the end of the Second World War had seen the Western press and public opinion embrace a doctrinaire view of the superiority of democratic government over communist rule and saw the U.S. media, in particular, adopt an almost evangelical tone in its belief that Soviet Bloc countries were enslaved communities. Given the opportunity, they said, any one of them would jump at the chance to cast off the communist yoke and rush into the arms of the free world. Experience should have taught them otherwise. When Yugoslavia and Albania moved away from direct Soviet rule they had remained stubbornly communist. The keen observer could see that there were other ways that a country might wish to develop politically outside the influence of the two dominant factions and the rejection of communism would not be automatically followed by an eager application of capitalist doctrine. The brutal division of Europe between East and West agreed at Yalta was merely an expedient for a particular purpose, i.e. to win the war, but none of the signatories could have believed that it was a long-term solution. Simple answers offered up to complex problems, whilst not losing their appeal to the scribes of the rightist media and its gullible readership, were beginning to look a little over optimistic. A more nuanced view of the revolutionary potential within the communist bloc accepted that communist regimes could withstand immense internal revolutionary pressures without crumbling unless outside support was available to the rebels right from the start. Both of these concepts, especially the idea that the U. S. as the world's dominant superpower could dictate either independently or in collusion with the Soviet Union the trajectory of global events, would be challenged by what was to come in Hungary in 1956.

A study prepared for U.S. Army Intelligence in January 1956 had concluded that Hungary was 'singularly unpromising' for U.S. military or paramilitary special operations. Its assessment of resistance organisations in the country at the time, however, showed that peasants were particularly unimpressed by communist culture and were vocal in their opposition to the government. The whole communist youth programme had stayed equally unsuccessful in capturing hearts and minds with apathy and criticism widespread among students who showed their contempt by wearing American-style ties, chewing gum, listening to American jazz, reading and distributing western paperbacks. Industrial workers seemed universally unhappy with working conditions, food shortages and levels of pay. It was they who were considered the most active and dangerous opponents of the regime and they were the ones who were particularly closely monitored by the Hungarian and Soviet security services. In the community as a whole, passive resistance was widespread and manifest itself in absenteeism, a poor work ethic and in some cases deliberate small-scale sabotage. The removal of Nagy from power a year earlier had been seen as a singularly ill-judged move that was widely unpopular. When, in 1955, the Soviets made a promise to have all their troops removed from Hungary it was accompanied by a crackdown on potential troublemakers.[4] The report offers no evidence for the existence of active resistance groups in the country or even of any signs of an organisation that might try to create and organise them. Partisan activity was considered unlikely but there was a report of five men who tried to break into an ammunition storage facility at Erdotelek. Neither was there any evidence of an organised underground movement. Any reported incidents of active resistance were of a spontaneous nature in response to particular circumstances.[5] The political character of the coming revolution would be largely determined by the Revolutionary and Workers Councils, which sprang up spontaneously in different parts of the country. Whilst populations of east European countries under communist control were expected to grow increasingly restive and, indeed, would be encouraged to do so by the U.S., that country had made no plans about how to respond to precipitate mass, violent demonstrations simply because none had been anticipated.

A seemingly innocuous and quite unremarkable expression of student dissatisfaction in the distinguished university of Szeged was, within weeks, to have a quite disproportionate effect on the whole of Hungary. It was here at the start of the Autumn term in 1956 that officials rather than the students themselves had raised expectations and an awareness that change was possible with the deprivations of war now some years in the past. Student curricula were modified to allow a greater choice of subjects and the idea of student exchanges with western countries was mooted. Youthful desire for greater freedom took this as a sign to express their own frustrations and asked why it was that all students were obliged to study the Russian language which seemed to have no great value to them and was actually a yoke put round their necks by the regime to mollify their Soviet masters. Once the idea that change was not only desirable but possible it was not long before other aspirations surfaced. Why, asked the students, were they obliged to spend so much time on National Defence training? The sense of impending change in the air amongst young people who had known only war and Soviet occupation was so powerful that delegates were sent to other universities to spread the word and organise a new student organisation, MEFESZ (*Magyar Egyetemisták és Főiskolások Szövetsége*), independent of the Communist Party.

Official support came from the Hungarian Minister of Education himself who, on 19 October, announced the ending of the compulsory study of Russian and a promise to look sympathetically at the other student demands. By this time, though, the movement for change had taken wings becoming more organised, more radical and more politicised. Students marched through the streets on the following day full of good humour and eager to 'free their spirit' as one put it to an accompanying western journalist, and 'throw off the shackles' of bondage.[6] They held a meeting at which every new demand encouraged ever greater ambition and inevitably attention came to focus on the government and the occupying Soviet forces. Such ideas had powerful attraction and appealed to almost all who heard them. There was little expectation that anything much would be achieved very quickly, of course, and even less appreciation of what a political minefield they were entering but that did not matter. The sense of adventure and the prospect of greater freedom gripped the movement right from the start but it was still a great surprise to see how popular the ideas were and how quickly they spread and motivated other students across the country.

In the industrial town of Miskolc, the already prevalent atmosphere of political dissent and support for Nagy proved to be fertile ground when the seeds of change settled there and took root. Students and lecturers at its technical university already had close connections with the industrial workforce through evening courses. In the Dimavag iron and steel foundry, a meeting was held on 21 October at which a workers' council was established. On the next day, students met to discuss joining the MEFESZ and over the next couple of days news began to filter through about events in Budapest.

22 October
In Budapest, students were already enthused by the Szeged action and agitated to set up their own branch of MEFESZ. Officials became concerned and tried to head off any disturbance by calling a meeting of students and workers on the evening of 22 October to debate the issue in the hope that sufficient numbers of party loyalists would turn up to support the status quo but they totally failed to appreciate the strength of feeling that had been aroused. Students went round appealing to workers and by the time the official meetings began at the Technological University of Budapest there were more than 5,000 people there.

János Dabasy was a third-year student from Győr, at the university in 1956. He lived in the Castle district of the city which had never been renovated since the devastation wrought by the war which had destroyed many of its historic buildings. It was, said Dabasy, a wasteland of rubble and ruins, mostly deserted, a deathly quiet place.[7] Of the meeting, he recalled 'fierce political debates and discussions [that] went on late into the night, the students never tiring, everyone eager to have their opinions heard.[8]

Students in Hungary were considered to be an elite but they shared the grievances of the wider population. The meeting started off quietly with discussion of issues, such as the cost of textbooks and the quality of food and housing but soon the situation in Poland came up which was seized on and expanded into a wider debate about democracy in Hungary. Eventually the meeting agreed on a list of demands to be put to the government which were encapsulated in a sixteen-point resolution calling for, amongst other things, the immediate evacuation of all Soviet troops, election of all party officers by secret ballot, a new Government led by Imre Nagy, the dismissal of criminal leaders of the Stalin-Rákosi era, general elections by secret ballot to elect a new National Assembly, and recognition of the workers right to strike. The speed with which demands multiplied and intensified in such a short time was indicative of the deep dissatisfaction within the Hungarian population, especially in Budapest. When the students went to local press and radio stations they naively expected that their resolution would be enthusiastically printed and shared with the public and so it was with some surprise and anger that they were met with resistance. They asked for their resolution to be read out on the evening news broadcast but the news censors wanted a number of points removed first. The students would not compromise but could not force the issue since the radio station was protected by a platoon of soldiers who had just arrived. Faced with this show of force, after a day of high excitement and anticipation that was now spent, the students dispersed quietly.

According to Soviet Lieutenant-General Yevgeny Malashenko, who led the operational section of the Special Corps Headquarters in Hungary at the time of the rebellion, plans (codename Volna) for dealing with a potential Hungarian insurrection had been formulated as early as 20 July 1956 in collaboration with the ÁVH. There had been rioting in Poznań a month earlier which had been easily supressed but there was a sense of unease in both Hungary and Poland that more trouble lay ahead. At first Mikhail Suslov and Mikoyan had been despatched to deal with what Moscow saw as a deterioration in the authority of the Hungarian Communist Party but they seemed to misunderstand, or refused to acknowledge, the origins and true nature of the revolutionary movement in Hungary despite their long association with the country and its recent history. They thought the trouble was being stirred up by a small coterie of writers and intellectuals failing to realise that frustrations ran very much deeper. Suslov reported back to Moscow that 'the mood of the workers and peasants is healthy [and] there are no conversations about a 'crisis' in the party leadership'.[9]

When the Volna plan was drawn up it was acknowledged that Soviet troops would be sufficient only for the protection of main targets and could not be relied upon for the maintenance of order if there were mass protests. The Hungarian authorities, however, assured them that their police and security forces would be perfectly able to do that themselves. There was every confidence in both Moscow and Budapest government circles that these forces were quite adequate to deal with any trouble that might arise.

As part of the plans, maps were drawn up marking out the departure points, routes and times of arrival of units into the capital as well as around forty buildings that the Soviet forces would be required to protect. After Rajk's funeral on 6 October the build-up of popular feeling against the ruling party became apparent but Malashenko maintained that the Hungarian authorities did not pay it sufficient attention with the result that 'the incompetence of the party and state leadership became completely obvious to the opposition'.[10] Gerő, in fact, had told the Soviet Ambassador in Budapest, Yuri Andropov, that after 6 October, authority of the party leadership had been dealt 'a massive blow' and conceded that Rajk's funeral was likely to provoke 'even greater insolence' on the part of opposition forces, who would now 'openly demand the return of Imre Nagy to the Politburo'.[11] Malashenko had placed all of his troops on alert when he became aware of the demonstrations planned for 23 October but he was candid when accepting that what actually took place went far beyond anything he had anticipated.

23 October
On that day the Polish paper *Sztandar Młodych* published an editorial entitled "Long live the Hungarian comrades!" which went on to say "Hungary and Poland are at the forefront of the de-Stalinization process and the restitution of popular power." Overnight the Hungarian students had broken into the room in the university were there was a duplicating machine and had made their own copies of the sixteen-point declaration (see appendix 2) and the next morning were distributing copies at factory gates and in city streets posting them on lampposts, trees and shop fronts. They called for demonstrations and

got support from schools, factories and even from officer cadets at the Pétőfi Military Academy in Buda. 'It was a beautiful autumn day, mild for the time of year with gold and red autumn leaves drifting, a hot wind blowing from the direction of the blue mountains of Buda and something holiday-like in the air,' said Irene Korponay in the early afternoon of 23 October, 'the streets were already packed with people. I had never seen so many on the streets at that hour, as if all work in Budapest had come to a standstill.'[12] The streets became crowded with hundreds of university students led by their professors all waving flags. Workers drifted out of factories to join in. Students from the Eötvös Lorand University in Pest had organised their own march and joined the main group in Bem Square.

The Hungarian Communist party was led by a hard-line fraction led by Gerö but as a very weak Stalinist dictatorship it had failed to make clear choices. It had allowed meetings of the Pétőfi circle of several thousand people in the middle of Budapest, organised national funerals for Rajk and others executed by the regime which degenerated into demonstrations of hostility towards it. Gerö had no sense of incipient unrest when he went off for a week's holiday in Yugoslavia and had just returned in a good frame of mind but his mood soon darkened as officials brought him up to date with events in Budapest. He met other party leaders in an atmosphere that one described as 'in a turmoil of confusion, fear and hesitation' and became increasingly infuriated that things should have got so out of hand and called for a ban on all public gatherings and demonstrations.[13] Supporters of Nagy saw this as a chance for him to seize the moment and rehabilitate his political career by standing with the demonstrators. It was tempting to think that he could use the movement to implement his own much less radical version of reform but, for him, there were too many of the sixteen points that went way beyond what he was willing to concede. His own concept of progress was for a slow, gradual programme of reforms. Anything else was entirely against his character. He also half suspected that Gerö might have engineered the disturbances to draw him out in support so that Gerö could then denounce him to Moscow and get rid of him once and for all.

KGB Chief Ivan Serov and commander-in-chief of the Soviet forces in Hungary, Mikhail Malinin, and a number of armed KGB personnel and seven KGB generals had arrived on 23 October. The KGB played an important role in Soviet military operations not by participating directly in combat assignments but in the implementation of punitive actions. According to Russian historians, the Soviets had decided as early as 20 July to set up an armed division tasked with 'restoring public order in Hungary through military occupation'. The plan code-named

'Wave', drawn up after the Summer disturbances was to be launched with the password 'Kompas'. It was within the framework of this plan that the KGB personnel had been sent.

The Budapest Chief of Police, Sándor Kopácsi, had been called in to discuss the planned demonstrations at the office of the Interior Minister, László Piros who was in 'a nasty mood'.[14] With Piros was Serov, a 'crafty-looking little man with blue eyes, blond hair, and an air of self-importance'. Kopácsi asked Serov what action the police were to take if planned demonstrations went ahead despite the ban. 'You are wrong to reduce a political problem to the dimensions of a police matter' Serov replied. 'If fascists and imperialist groups dare to go onto the streets in Budapest,' he added, 'the time has come to give the Fascist underworld a lesson.' Ágnes Ságvári who at the time was a shorthand typist at Party Headquarters on Akadémia Street said that Serov 'participated with absolute sovereignty over the proceedings'.[15] Kopácsi argued that the demonstrators were not fascists but students, the sons and daughters of workers and peasants. Serov flew into a rage at Kopácsi's defence of the demonstrators but went on to demand that Gerő lift the ban and allow the demonstrations to go ahead. It was clear that Serov was engineering a confrontation.

News of the lifting was broadcast on the radio and the numbers of demonstrators grew throughout the day as something of a carnival atmosphere developed with speeches, singing and much shouting of slogans against the Soviet occupiers. Marchers proudly wore red, white and green rosettes of the national flag. Later in the afternoon more workers joined in. István Pálos was an apprentice tool maker in the Buda district. When a friend told him about the march his reaction was that they were crazy to even think about it in a city where 'You couldn't even cross the street in the wrong way, because the police would brutally stop you.'[16] When a crowd of marches passed by his place of work, however, Pálos and the other ten people in his workshop were caught up in the moment and joined them despite the fear that the security police would turn up and arrest them. He recalled Hungarian flags waving from balconies and windows of apartment buildings all the way to Bem Square where a huge crowd of 20,000 or more, including the 800 cadets from the Pétőfi Academy, rallied next to the statue of Josef Bem, a Polish General who had helped lead the Hungarians in 1848. Once there, they laid a wreath and heard hear the President of the Writer's Association, Péter Veress, read out the Sixteen-Point Manifesto and demand the return to power of Imre Nagy.

Members of a large literary group, the Pétőfi Circle, formed a second demonstration and congregated at the statue of their inspiration, the poet Sandor Pétőfi, who had also died fighting for independence in 1848. Here they read out inspirational lines from his works 'Arise, Hungarians! Shall we be slaves, or shall we be free?'[17] This branch of the revolutionary movement had evolved out of the Bessenyei Circle that had previously been little more than a mildly reactionary debating society. This new manifestation burst onto a wider stage in March 1956 under the leadership of men such as Hegedüs and began to forge a new more reformist movement of Budapest intellectuals that was structured horizontally as opposed to hierarchically as would have been the case with more traditional communist models. These, mostly professional, people had found it the most difficult to adapt to communist rule. Many had tried to flee the country which could result in a shooting at the border or a heavy prison sentence if caught. The U.S. Central Intelligence Agency (CIA) Chief in Vienna reported that at least one of the Pétőfi Circle meetings was attended by a CIA agent in June 1956 when participants demanded the resignation of Rákosi.

Although the Pétőfi Circle debated Nagy's 'renewal of Socialism' enshrined in his 'New Course' philosophy in a favourable light, he, himself, was never directly associated with them but he was admired as someone who 'defended himself against vile slanders'.[18] He repeatedly refused to address their meetings which began to attract delegations from across the country giving it something of a national character. It was really only after the demonstrations on the night of 22 October that members sat up and took notice of the strength of feeling around them. They reacted swiftly and had brought out their own manifesto which was rather less radical than the Sixteen Points Resolution and the leadership tried to negotiate with both the student movement and the government from a central position but their moderation alienated both sides and they found themselves increasingly redundant as a force before they had even begun.

Moving on from the Bern Memorial, demonstrators, of whom students were now no more than about a fifth, moved to the Parliament building on the Pest side of the river tearing down Soviet flags and Red Stars from public buildings along the way and repeatedly shouting 'Russkik haza!' (Russians go home) and "Oltsák el a csillagot!' (Extinguish the star) in a rhythmic chant. It was at this point that the demonstrators created one of the most potent symbols of the revolution by cutting out from the centre of the green, white and red Hungarian tricolour flag the Communist hammer and sickle leaving a gaping hole in its place.[19]

In Parliament Square the crowd set up another repetitive chant this time calling the name of Imre Nagy. Nagy appeared on the balcony and spoke to a crowd which had grown dramatically to almost a quarter of a million people but, at a moment when the revolt could have gone either way, it was unfortunate for him and for the movement as a whole, that he proved to be an uninspiring orator. It was really the first time he had ever been called to address a public gathering, let alone a crowd of this magnitude, having hitherto limited his speech-making to closed meetings in which debate was constrained by the deathly, invented, bureaucratic parlance of Soviet communism.[20] Nagy's first reaction to the insurrection had been to follow the party line and reject the more radical demands of the protestors. For instance, he vehemently opposed any idea of creating a new role for trade unions beyond that of implementing government policy. When he had met the leading demonstrators at midday, he had urged caution and refused to endorse the student demands fearing that if he showed any support for the movement it would give Moscow an excuse to have him arrested. All through the day he resisted calls to lead the rebellion and only agreed to speak to the crowd at the behest of the Politburo itself who thought he might be able to calm the situation down.

When Nagy emerged to see the thousands upon thousands of faces all focused on him and eagerly calling out his name, he appeared to become 'tense and stupefied'.[21] He disastrously misjudged the mood of the crowd and aroused immediate anger by opening his address with the single word 'Elvtársak!' (Comrades). 'Nincs elvtárs!' (We are no longer comrades), the crowd roared back. He tried to argue the case for negotiation and urged the demonstrators to go home but he was unable to deviate from the tedious, functional language of the smoke-filled, claustrophobic backroom party debates and quickly lost his audience who became restive and agitated. His unemotional detached address to the crowd was totally at odds with the excitement and expectations that had been whipped up during the day and after no more than about ten minutes he went back inside the building leaving the crowd deflated and hugely disappointed.

Another group of demonstrators had congregated around a massive bronze statue of Stalin, the 'symbol of [Soviet] tyranny and political oppression'[22] in Felvonulási tér ("Marching square") which, according to the young police Lieutenant Kiss who had been sent to keep control with a party of twenty-five soldiers, was 'thick with people'.[23] The statue stood 26 feet tall on a 13 feet-high limestone pedestal on top of a 20-feet high tribune altogether rising to a height roughly equal to a six-storey building. It had been made out of the melted-down statues of Hungarian heroes and stood on the site of Regnum Marianum, a wonderful church that had been built in 1931 but blown up on the orders of Rákosi on 23 September 1951. Around the statue's neck had been hung a placard appealing to departing Soviet soldiers to take him home with them. Ropes and steel cables were strapped to the statue and tied to tractors and lorries in an attempt to pull it down but its massive bulk defied them.

Nothing daunted workers brought oxy-acetylene welding torches and proceeded to cut away part of the legs. Steel hawsers were again strapped to the statue and fixed to a diesel truck that strained to dislodge the massive bulk. While officials in Party offices watched from their windows afraid to intervene the truck heaved and skidded burning rubber on the cobblestones sending up clouds of bitter smoke. Men piled onto the truck to add weight and give it more traction and eventually the edifice wobbled and fell leaving only a huge pair of boots on the plinth. Irene Korponay who was there described a huge crowd cheering and screaming leaving her 'emotional [with] a choking sensation in my throat'.[24] People hammered at the statue in an iconoclastic fervour, decapitating its head, and hacked at the bronze for souvenirs. The broken and battered head was then dragged through the streets and left outside the National Theatre in the city centre. It was a stunningly bold and irreversible statement made in the heat of emotional fervour and that statement would be clearly heard in the Kremlin. For the people of Budapest it was an unequivocal sign that the revolution had become a reality and that doors had opened into a future that was as unknown as it was terrifying. Suzanne Budaházy was there and recalled the sensation: 'It's like, something had got to change now,' she said 'because when that head hit the concrete after that, you either all die, or you get rid of the Communists!'[25]

The city streets were now full of people shouting slogans, raiding bookshops and burning Marxist and Stalinist texts. Buildings that housed organisations with connections to the Soviet Union were broken into and ransacked. Where pictures of the Soviet leaders were found, they were added to the flames. A crowd went to the main police station and demanded that prisoners be released. Yet another band, mostly students, had gone to the radio station in Sándor Bródy Street to demand that the Sixteen Point Resolution be broadcast to the nation. There were already over 200 soldiers and State Security ÁVH personnel in the station armed with machine guns. A small delegation of twenty students was allowed into the building to talk but when they failed to come out again the crowd suspected foul play by the authorities and started pelting the building with stones. Very quickly the mood of the crowd darkened but feelings were still restrained being manifest in shouting and gesticulations rather than in any threat of an escalation of violence. The station's director, Valéria Benke, told the crowd that she would broadcast the sixteen points if the crowd agreed to settle down but when the people in the flats around the radio station building turned on their radios and heard only music, the protestors realised they had been duped.

Gerő made a radio broadcast at 20:00hrs which was expected to address the student demands, but all hopes were dashed when it turned out to be no more than a 'snarling and aggressive' attack on the demonstrators in which he roundly condemned them as mere puppets who were being manipulated by 'bourgeois reactionaries' and 'enemies of the people'.[26] Whether by design or accident, his uncompromising, belligerent and ill-judged speech was the 'fuse that set off an explosion' infuriating the crowd who now tried to force their way into the building where they were met with fixed bayonets by a cohort of security police.[27] There were soon casualties with several people killed on both sides. The body of one protestor was draped in a Hungarian flag and raised up above the crowd further incensing them. Was Gerő's speech all part of Serov's plan to incense the demonstrators and ignite a brutal confrontation? Whether it was or not, that was the result.

What happened next was told by Ottó Szirmai, the Party Secretary in charge of Hungarian Radio, who would later be sentenced to death by the Kádár government, István Angyal, József Teuchert, the writer László Gyurkó, historians Péter Gosztonyi and Miklós Kovács who all made statements to the effect that the first shots were fired at an unarmed crowd. A telegram sent to the U.S. State Department by Spencer N. Barnes, U.S. Chargé d'Affaires in Budapest, stated that, 'the Hungarian troops refused to shoot at the unarmed crowds; Russian-speaking men wearing ÁVH uniforms opened fire'. There is speculation that these were KGB agents who had arrived only that day. At his trial. Szirmai said that the crowd had been warned to disperse or they would face gunfire. When the crowd refused to budge, the ÁVH troops in the building were lined up ready to fire but refused until their officer called them cowards and threated to shoot them if they did not obey the order. Szirmai made one last plea for the crowd to disperse telling them to 'leave the vicinity of the Radio building, because once the shooting begins, you will have no escape'. Gyurkó later wrote, 'The soldiers did not want to fight'. Angyal, who was on the street outside the Radio building said 'the first volley of shots, which came from the weapons of the ÁVH inside the building, was fired at about 01:15hrs.'

The noise attracted more of the demonstrators from other parts of the city. Cars were overturned and set on fire. A Hungarian motorised unit was called up from Piliscaba to help quell the riot but refused to act against the demonstrators and when their commander, Colonel János Solymosi, stood atop one of the tanks to address the crowd he was loudly cheered. His men came out of their tanks and mingled with the crowd. Solymosi was shot dead on the command of a captain of the security forces.[28] Word of the violence had spread and workers from the industrial suburbs, who were much more militant than the students, had arrived.

At this point shots were fired back into the building from the crowd and a firefight began lasting half the night. After dark, the mild day had turned into a bitterly cold night as some protestors were able to gain access to the radio station through the attic of a neighbouring building and by next morning they had taken complete control of the building, now aflame and heavily damaged by gunfire, but sixteen of their number had been killed in the effort. In homage to the U.S. backed Radio Free Europe, they renamed the radio station 'Radio Free Kossuth' but their broadcasts of seditious material were blocked.

It is important to look at how the protestors were able to acquire so many weapons so quickly. It is inconceivable that, unarmed, they could have broken into heavily protected armouries and overpowered soldiers there so weapons must have been provided by someone. It may have been workers from the munitions factories in Csepel, or a group of demonstrators who had attacked an army recruiting centre, occupied the police station and seized the arms that were there. One protestor said 'No one asked why you came or went. They gave out arms to whoever wanted to fight. When the person was tired she left her combat position and went home keeping her weapon or not.'[29]

Kopácsi claims that a passing motorised army detachment of Hungarian recruits newly arrived from the countryside, appalled at the shooting of unarmed civilians had handed over weapons and ammunition to the crowd. It is the case, however, that after the rebellion had been put down not a single soldier was put on trial for supplying revolutionaries with weapons. One compelling scenario is that weapons were deliberately handed out by provocateurs, who had been infiltrated into the factories and protest movements weeks or months before, and then distributed to the crowd. The writer Gyula Fekete claims that at around 19:00hrs just off 60 Andrássy Street (ÁVH headquarters) he went to a phone booth to make a call and was shocked when, opening the door of the booth, a large stash of weapons fell out. Then he went to another booth, which he didn't even open, since he could see that it too was full of weapons. The inference is that hardline Stalinists Gerő and Rákosi, with the connivance of the Soviets, had planned to exploit the July disturbances as an excuse to crack down on the growing number of 'reformists' rallying around Nagy and were waiting for the right moment to ignite a mass movement against the government. Nagy had been warned ten days before this that a conspiracy was working against him so that he could be drawn out and destroyed. According to this theory, the rebellion would have had to be incited to violence in order to justify the crackdown and this had been brought about by first herding the protestors into Sándor Bródy Street and then firing on them indiscriminately. At this point weapons would be produced as if from nowhere and many in the crowd, seeing dead and dying citizens all around would have been quick to use them against the troops inside the radio station.

Gerő called Andropov, who had been touring the city during the afternoon to gauge the level of unrest and had been jeered at by the crowd. Gerő had become increasingly nervous during the day. He urged Andropov to ask Moscow to send troops. He then reported to his masters in the Kremlin when Khruschev told him to come immediately to Moscow for talks but Gerő told him that the situation in Budapest was grave and he could not leave. Andropov then came on the line to Moscow and told Khruschev that Gerő had requested troops be sent although Gerő, torn between panic and reticence to admit just how bad things were, had apparently been afraid to say as much directly to Khruschev when they had talked. Adropov then asked Lieutenant-General Lashchenko, commander of Special Forces in Hungary, to despatch Soviet troops into the city since the situation in the capital was 'extraordinarily dangerous' but Lashchenko had no confidence that his troops were qualified to conduct what was essentially a police action and replied that it was the task of the Hungarian security service to maintain order and anyway only the Minister of Defence in Moscow had the authority to send his troops into something like this.[30]

Khruschev was not willing to make a decision before discussing the issue with the other Soviet leaders in the Presidium of the Communist Party of the Soviet Union Central Committee which was still coming to terms with the erstwhile alien concept of collective leadership after Stalin's iron rule. A meeting was convened and Khrushchev's report on Hungary created a sense that the government there was in danger of being overthrown by popular revolt. His solution was to send troops and he was supported by his Minister of Defence, Georgy Zhukov who had been on the phone to Andropov also and called for the imposition of martial law in the whole of Hungary. Vyecheslav Molotov, who had recently been removed as Foreign Minister, as Khruschev pursued his policy of de-Stalinisation, warned that Hungary would fall apart if a solution involving Nagy was pursued but he was not able to garner enough support to challenge the decision.

Only Soviet Deputy Premier Anastas Mikoyan preferred to apply the solution that seemed to have worked in Poland and called for restraint by allowing Nagy time to restore order and suggested that troops should only be sent as a last resort. Soviet power, he believed, was overextended within eastern Europe, especially with unrest in Poland as well, and some sort of compromise might have to be considered if the Hungarians proved incapable of restoring order by themselves. Nagy, he said, was the only hope of achieving this. The meeting was not willing to make any admission of Soviet weakness and saw no merit in Mikoyan's argument but Khruschev, who would stand or fall depending on the outcome, hoped that a peaceful solution could be found along the lines of that he had so recently achieved in Poland. He was by far the most powerful member of the Politburo, but he was vulnerable to criticism since it could be argued that it had been his 'secret speech' in the first place that had given the Hungarian rebels the idea that reform was possible.

His decision was to send Mikoyan and the ultra-orthodox Mikhail Suslov to Budapest. Serov, whom Hegedüs referred to as the 'chief executioner', and the jowly, balding, overweight Deputy Chief of Staff M. S. Malinin had already gone to make one last effort to bolster the Gerő regime and restore order but if that failed then Mikoyan was to replace Gerő with Nagy. There was a confidence that Nagy might have enough popular support to be able to quell the unrest and resolve the situation along the lines of the solution arrived at in Poland. He had resisted the temptation to join those who were trying to improve Soviet-U.S. relations after Stalin's death and his many years living in the Soviet Union together with his impeccable communist credentials meant that he was generally thought of as being a steady hand at the helm despite having been sacked from the post of Chairman of the Council of Ministers in April 1955 for 'rightist deviation' and replaced by Rákosi.

Khruschev again called Gerő later that evening and agreed to send troops if he received a request in writing from the Hungarian government. When Gerő pointed out that there was no time for such niceties, Khruschev suggested to Gerő, in a way that invited no dissent, that the request come from Hegedüs on behalf of the Party and furthermore that a new administration, more amenable to Soviet sensibilities, needed to be elected to run the country and, significantly, one that included Nagy in high office.

At a previous meeting on 20 October, the Presidium had already discussed the events in Hungary and while Mikoyan and Zhukov were asked to consider the withdrawal of troops and KGB advisers from the country, military preparations for intervention had, in fact, already begun. Judging by the minutes of the Presidium meeting of 23 October it is not clear just how much of this was known to Khruschev. The official order did not reach the meeting until well after the 2nd Mechanised Guards Division, which had been on alert since the crisis in Poland on 19 October, was mobilised. In order to execute its orders all that was required was the simple expedient of substituting Hungary for Poland as the target. The 128th Artillery Division and the 23rd Mechanised Division were readied in support and special forces were prepared for action. As a result, the first mechanised columns of Soviet armour were able to respond quickly and they arrived in Budapest at 02:00hrs on 24 October just five hours after history records the mobilisation order as having been issued which would not have been possible had they not already been on the move.

Soviet military presence in Hungary at the time comprised 20,000 combat troops and 600 tanks of the 2nd Guards stationed at Cegled, fifty miles southeast of Budapest, and the 17th Guards, forty miles to the southwest. However, on 23 October, only 700 soldiers and 50 tanks were mobilised at key locations around the capital as a token show of force which. it was hoped, would be enough to intimidate the demonstrators and restore order. Soviet commanders on the scene had received no rules of engagement or orders beyond that.

A new Hungarian administration was formed during the night and, with Khruschev's approval, by next morning Imre Nagy reluctantly found himself as the new President of the country. Being well versed in the machinations of communist politics, he suspected that he was being lined up by Gerő as a fall-guy and refused to be the one to sign the request to the Soviet government for troops to be sent. Never one to go against the wishes of the Party, however, he had been left with no choice but accept the post which was announced on the radio at 07:15hrs. According to one observer, Nagy had become 'a moral prisoner of his own loyalty which [never left him].'[31] He found himself fallen between two stools. On the one hand, he had some sympathy with the demonstrators' demands but on the other he was a servant of the ruling party. Mikoyan and Suslov hoped that Nagy would not show any weakness but as an insurance against that, they made sure that the hardliners were not far away. Shielded now somewhat from the wrath of the protestors, Gerő was made First Secretary of the Central Committee and Hegedüs became First Deputy of the Council of Ministers leaving Nagy as the titular head of the government but one that was, to a large extent, kept isolated from his supporters and out of touch with events around him by an ÁVH detachment.[32]

The American response to the events in Eastern Europe in the autumn of 1956 ended any illusions that there still existed a 'rollback and liberation' policy, repeatedly stressed in public and private, of seeking to contain and reverse Soviet domination of Eastern European countries. The policy had relied on clandestine actions to strengthen governments supporting the American position in the Cold War and could have been applied to Hungary as a way of indirectly undermining Soviet power in Eastern Europe. U.S. policy during the Polish and Hungarian crises was driven by the fear of the revolts spreading into an all-European conflagration and that it would bring Khrushchev down and his policy of detente with the West and his programme of de-Stalinization, seemed to make him the statesman with whom the American government would find it easiest to work. Eisenhower had taken office as President of the U.S. in 1952 with a promise to follow an 'explosive and dynamic' policy of liberation in its dealings with the Soviet Bloc which made his administration seem more belligerent that they really were but in its first real test it had backed down from intervention to support the anti-Soviet East Berlin uprising of 1953.[33] Official policy was transformed later that same year in the National Security Council by abandonment of any ambition to support aggressive liberation of East European countries under the Soviet yolk. Secretary of Defence Wilson said the American people were 'sympathetic with the people of any land that are trying to throw off tyranny and oppression and assert their freedom [but] when it comes to intervention, that is a much more difficult thing'.[34]

However, all U.S. Foreign Service posts in Eastern Europe were instructed to be particularly on the alert for any information related to Hungary. The Vienna Station, in particular, was instructed to devote extra attention to the gathering of political intelligence on the Hungarian scene. This meant that by the time of the unrest in Hungary in October, Washington would have been quite well informed about what was taking place. The Eisenhower administration, however, never made any plan for what U.S. policy should be in the event that either the Polish or the Hungarian Communist regime lost control. They showed little interest in making contact with dissident movements and seemed to have had little understanding of the relationship between the various factions inside the Hungarian Government. It was as if domestic argument between what they saw as committed communist factions could have no relevance for foreign relations.

The danger of a nuclear confrontation ruled out the forceful liberation of Eastern Europe, and Eisenhower was firmly convinced that any military confrontation with the Soviets would quickly escalate into a nuclear one. His experience as leader of Allied forces in Europe at the end of the Second World War, when it had seemed as if the Nazis were willing to see the whole of European civilization destroyed rather than accept defeat, made him fearful that the Soviets might take a similar approach and precipitate another global war. It is estimated that in 1956, the U.S. had over 3,500 nuclear warheads, the Soviets more than 400 and Britain about 20. The reliance on the nuclear deterrent by both sides had brought a significant shift in the balance of power. The smallest miscalculation could now escalate into a major incident. For the threat of nuclear weapons to be effective their use could not be ruled out and the levels of animosity prevalent between the communist and democratic regimes allowed for a great deal of uncertainty as to just how any situation might develop. The Korean War had first raised the spectre of nuclear conflagration and now only a few short years later, another situation had all the potential to raise the stakes again. All official U.S. government aid to Hungary therefore was channelled through the International Rescue Committee (IRC) and restricted to non-military supplies such as food and medicines.[35]

The U.S. Democratic presidential candidate, Adlai Stevenson, claimed that events in Hungary had taken the U.S. by surprise but that was hardly credible. Dulles had prepared a speech on 18 October in which he intended to speak about 'the rising tide of protest against the ruthless domination of the Kremlin' and the willingness of the U.S. to 'exert a contagious influence [to] build up a steady pressure for freedom'.[36] It was, however, something of a shock, and here Stevenson might have been closer to the truth, when Khruschev had led a delegation to Warsaw on 19 October which indicated the level of Soviet concern over events in Poland. Eisenhower responded by speaking to the press of a Polish 'burning desire to live in freedom', but the inadequate level of U.S. interest and knowledge of events was exposed in a meeting of the Intelligence Advisory Committee, appearing to be getting its information from newspapers, which merely noted the development of an 'apparent' crisis in Polish-Soviet relations. Had the U.S. administration known about the divisions within the Soviet Presidium they might have been able to do more to support Mikoyan's position but all their decisions at this stage were based on guesswork.[37] The State Department's general view had been that any armed uprising in the Soviet Bloc was doomed to failure, and little would be gained by antagonising the Soviets by encouraging dissent to the point of insurrection.

Dulles, whom Eisenhower would call 'one of the truly great men of our time', would go on to appear on the news programme 'Face the Nation' on 21 October and spoke optimistically of what he saw as the apparent beginning of Poland's return to independence through internal dissent. However, he offered significant, if inadvertent, support for Soviet interference when asked about the government's view regarding the movement of Soviet troops in Poland. Dulles said that the movement of troops was a matter which perhaps could not be challenged as a violation of international law because the Soviets had a treaty which purported to give them that right. He did say, however, that he did not want to give the impression that the U.S. was indifferent to what is going on but actions in these situations had to be judged very carefully, which was political parlance for doing nothing about it. He did not expect the Soviets to use 'mass military means' to halt Polish democratization, but if they did, the West would avoid any military interference. The U.S. approved of the Polish move toward independence, but 'the last thing the Polish people want', he said, 'would be for any outsiders to attempt to hurry the process.' When asked what the U.S. reaction would be, he warned, somewhat disingenuously, that 'meddling and interference' in the affairs of other countries was often counter-productive.'[38]

It was as clear a message as political protocol allowed but Radio Free Europe and the Voice of America propaganda organs continued to give the impression that the U.S. was serious in its efforts to restore independence to the Soviet satellites. After January 1956, the Soviet Union had tried to prevent knowledge of Khruschev's 'secret speech' leaking out and it was the Voice of America, on the authority of the head of the CIA Allen Dulles, the brother of John Foster, who had broadcast it in full across the airwaves in Hungary. These broadcasts as a whole had fostered in the Hungarian opposition, generally unaware that this was just so much empty propaganda rhetoric, a sense that the U.S. was 'just waiting for the moment' to intervene and help the country to win its freedom.[39] When it became clear that this was not the case, the high esteem in which Soviet Bloc opposition movements had previously held RFE began to evaporate and proved to be very much a 'shooting itself in the foot' incident for the CIA.

In Hungary, the U.S. 30-strong diplomatic mission was housed close to Parliament Square where much of the fighting had taken place and had to contend with periods during which encrypted communications with the outside world were severed. Staff continued to compose telegrams even though they were unable to transmit them until 29 October and then only through their embassy in Vienna. However, RFE stations in Munich were picking up transmissions from Hungary sent out from radio stations that had been taken over by revolutionaries and this would have fed back into the White House so Eisenhower had some idea of what was going on at the time but was getting this information from a biased source. CIA agents inside Hungary working out of Vienna Station were also getting information out on a regular basis. Edwin Wailes had been appointed to head up the Budapest mission in July but by 24 October he was still not in place and it was led by the 'timid, cautious, weak and soft' Spencer Barnes whose butler, apparently on his own initiative, had actually draped a white flag outside his window at the height of the disturbances on 23 October.[40]

The *New York Times* journalist James Renton summed up the view of the Soviet and East European analysts at the State Department as follows:

'It is generally agreed here [the State Department] that the prudent thing for the United States Government to do is to watch developments closely and keep quiet, clearly not an aggressive policy in line with 'liberation'; but in view of the meagre first-hand information available, the apparent solid Communist nature of both of the new regimes and the complete lack of a prepared Western counterforce in the area, there was little else the United States could do at this point in the crisis. The feeling that the Soviets had suffered a setback, no matter what the final outcome, strengthened the tendency not to act. Why should the United States risk getting involved in a volatile situation, which it had no direct means to control, and thereby give the Soviets a scapegoat to heap the blame on and a pretext to justify more drastic action?'

In the provincial town of Győr, meanwhile, demands had already been raised for liberalisation of the regime and the withdrawal of Soviet troops from the country but there was little public display of unrest until 24 October when a group of more than twenty people marched through the town carrying the Hungarian flag and calling for 'freedom' but at the same time being careful to swear allegiance to the ruling Communist Party. A CIA agent in the town reported that Red Army soldiers there had been ordered to 'keep out of everything'. Ambassador Thompson in Vienna had forbidden any of the Embassy's staff from even approaching the Hungarian border but Peer De Silva, the Vienna CIA Station Chief, recorded that 'within hours we had a number of Hungarian-speaking sources moving into Hungary.'[41]

In Miskolc, the local communist newspaper launched a virulent attack on the Party leader Gerõ and declared themselves to be supporters neither of the government nor of the Party. After hearing his speech on the radio they had been awakened during the night by the rumble of Soviet tanks heading towards the capital. At the Dimavag works, students and workers met to draw up their own sixteen-point plan for reform of the government. The Hungarian government's response was to call to arms communist supporters and pro-government factory workers in a counter-revolutionary movement promising to send them weapons but, fearing that the guns might fall into the hands of the rebels, they were never sent until Mikoyan quickly stepped in and arranged to have the guns delivered in armoured vehicles to ensure that they were not intercepted.

24 October Hungary

The Soviet Operation Wave got the 'kompass' codeword at 21:00hrs on 23 October when four large formations crossed the Hungarian border from Carpatho-Ukraine and at 00:35hrs on 24 October. Units arriving from Romania also crossed the border. A special army corps commanded by Laschenko set off in the direction of Budapest at 22:00hrs. According to the report of the British ambassador to Hungary, on 22 October a Soviet armed column was advancing from its base in Szombathely (Western Hungary) in the direction of Székesfehérvár on the road to Budapest. It is reasonable to assume that this was in response to reports that a large demonstration was planned for noon on 24 October in Budapest and it is certain that Gerõ must have had early warning of this before making his incendiary speech the night before knowing that Soviet armed forces were already on their way to defend him. Soviet forces had been stationed in Hungary since 1945, living in villages built especially for them. Their children mixed with locals and Soviet military vehicles were a common sight throughout the country. These forces did not require permission from the Hungarian government to move towards the capital which they did at speed and without infantry support.

In the early hours of a foggy 24 October, Operation Volna was activated when Soviet troops crossed the Hungarian border at Csop, Beregovo, and Vylok without incident but in Budapest tensions were exacerbated at the sound of Soviet tank tracks lumbering over cobblestones on the city streets. János Dabasy remembers coming across a Soviet tank in the street in the early hours and, employing the Russian he had been forced to learn at school got into conversation with the crew who seemed friendly enough. The writer Stetson

Kennedy observed 'wild excitement' in the morning light as crowds containing many women 'lost all reason' in what he described, with a lavish measure of hyperbole, as 'a state of mass psychosis'.[42] Barricades manned by armed groups were hastily thrown up at the Móricz Zsigmond and Széna Squares in Buda and at the Baross and Borosos Squares in Pest. The first Soviet T-34 and T-54 tank units that entered the capital had been told that they were being sent to quell a fascist uprising, but they had orders not to open fire. Tactically, they had been trained to fight along the lines of the Second World War combats but at the last minute their orders were changed and they were to apply techniques that had come to the fore during the events of East Berlin in 1953. This basically meant exhibiting technological superiority in a demonstration of overwhelming force to scare and disperse the supposedly poorly armed and poorly organised opposition. The first tanks entered the capital in darkness travelling at full speed and, contrary to orders, firing their machine guns at any building that was showing a light. They began what started out as an act of intimidation, but which soon turned into a suicide mission in their open-topped vehicles.[43]

Radio broadcasts coming from the basement of the Parliament building sent out the following message 'Reactionary fascist elements have launched an armed attack against our public buildings. They have also attacked our police detachments. In the interests of public order, it is forbidden to hold any assemblies, meetings, or parades. The police have been ordered to apply the full force of the law against any persons who do not obey this decree.' There was no mention of Soviet tanks. This was news to police chief Kopácsi, who had received no prior warning and thought the statement had been drawn up by someone who 'knew nothing about the state of public opinion or the capabilities of the so-called forces of order.'[44] His building was under siege by armed protestors and he had no intention of putting his police officers onto the streets. Another provocative government broadcast described 'gangsters who have invaded factories and public buildings, murdering civilians, soldiers and members of the security police.'

Tanks were quickly stationed to protect the Soviet Embassy, the Ministries of defence and ÁVH headquarters. They anticipated meeting little real resistance in a police operation to put down student demonstrations but immediately many found themselves in an urban guerrilla war against a determined and inventive enemy. The appearance of the tanks had galvanised resistance within the population which at first was manifest by unarmed crowds blocking the streets but behind the peaceful protests other groups were preparing a different response. It is a matter of conjecture as to what extent rebel certain groups had been primed to act to take advantage of the situation but there is no evidence that the actual revolt itself was brought about through intervention by Western agents. Once it broke out, however, there is some evidence that covert support was rapidly infiltrated.

There had been a number of post-war moves to instigate an anti-communist propaganda war in eastern Europe. In 1949, a group of prominent American businessmen, lawyers, and philanthropists, including Dulles and Eisenhower, had launched the National Committee for Free Europe (NCFE), which was, in reality, an innovative psychological warfare project undertaken and funded by the CIA. The Committee took to distributing leaflets over Hungary using balloons, one of which was entitled *Manifesto and Twelve Demands of the National Resistance Movement* and contained twelve demands of the government including free speech, freedom of religion and free trade unions.

Despite official denial, throughout the early 1950s, plans were made to obstruct communist bureaucracies in a policy of 'aggressive rollback' and to induce the satellite regimes not to fight alongside the Soviets in the event of conflict breaking out. It was proposed to organize, train, and equip organizations that would be capable of protracted resistance and even though mass uprisings and 'premature rebellions' were not encouraged, there were guidelines given for creating unrest.[45]

Ever since the last shot was fired in the Second World War, the top U.S. priority in its covert operations in eastern Europe was not to reverse Soviet territorial gains, or to bring down Soviet rule there but simply to gain intelligence about Soviet military activities and provide early warning of any Soviet preparations for a military move against the West. The support of resistance movements in eastern Europe, however, was still seen to be an important covert objective but choosing which movements to support proved to be problematic. The Polish *Wolnosc i Niepodlenosc* (Freedom and Independence army, WIN) that received significant U.S. support was later found to have been controlled by the Polish Security service from the start.

The first significant signs of popular revolt in Hungary were in 1950 when a fledgling underground youth organisation calling itself the 'Fifth Group of the Patriotic Association of Hungarian Boys and Girls' accused the Hungarian government of high treason. Another rather more militant group, the White Guard started collecting weapons with the ultimate aim of overthrowing the government by force. There is no evidence to suggest that any of these organizations ever made contact with officials of the U.S. Legation in Budapest and neither got very far before being crushed by the Hungarian security forces.

The Eisenhower Administration never quite abandoned the idea of using covert operations to try to undermine east European communist regimes. A Volunteer Freedom Corps made up of Soviet Bloc exiles was created by the CIA to undertake missions behind Soviet lines in the event of war. In early 1956, it supported a major new covert effort called Operation Red Sox/Red Cap run by Mike Ray and Charlie Katek, which had mustered 5,000 Czech, Hungarian, Polish, and Romanian recruits out of refugee camps in western Europe and had been formed into paramilitary units trained in camps near Munich by the Gehlen organisation, an ex-Nazi intelligence outfit that had been taken over by the CIA.

According to William Corson, a large team of Gehlen-trained Hungarian agents were sent into Budapest right at the start of the uprising and Steven claims that another group of Soviet Bloc exiles of the CIA's 'private army' went in under the orders of Dulles.[46] Malashenko would later say that during the revolution 'armed groups were often led by people who knew the art of street fighting'.[47] All this is discounted by De Silva, who ran the CIA Vienna Station and who is on record as saying that 'CIA activities in Hungary during the Revolution consisted only of intelligence gathering and not covert operations... There was no intelligence impetus given to the Revolution; it was spontaneous in every respect, although clearly the Hungarians hoped for U.S. help.[48]

As for the CIA plans to undermine Soviet rule in eastern Europe, arms caches had been secretly stored in Hungary and other East European countries. Frank Wisner, the CIA's Deputy Director for Plans (Operations) had flown to Vienna, where he was contacted by many of the émigrés who had been trained by the CIA to go into Hungary. They asked for permission to retrieve what they called the caches of sterilized arms which were waiting for the Red Sox/Red Cap forces but when Wisner signalled to Washington 'We must give them antitank weapons and expert cadres to lead them. Now now now! before it's too late!" he was rebuffed with the reply that it was 'too dangerous [and] could rebound in the voting booth.' According to Clare Boothe Luce, the U.S. Ambassador to Italy, one CIA agent who appeared at the Embassy in Rome on 29 October was distraught, explaining that he had been led to believe that once the Hungarians' will to resist had been demonstrated, the U.S. would provide the Hungarians with tangible support, specifically "small arms, bazookas, and antitank guns but there had been no indication whatsoever that there were Western agents out in the streets funnelling weapons or supplies to the rebels. The Joint Chiefs of Staff looked briefly at a plan to bomb railroad junctions used by the Soviet invasion force but it was knocked back and Eisenhower refused to authorise an airlift of arms. Officially the CIA admitted to having only a single officer, Geza Katona, in Hungary between 1950 and 1957 and who did not engage in operational activities during the uprising.

Rebels, who appeared to be operating without any sort of centralised leadership had acquired weapons and, relying on local knowledge, harried the Soviets where they could employing hit-and-run tactics that the invaders found hard to counter and who were not prepared to risk losses by sending infantry into the streets for hand-to-hand combat. A hallmark of the uprising would be continuous improvisation and the way in which in a matter of a few days, and in sone instances in a matter of a few hours, a leadership group emerged which commanded the respect and cooperation of a community or a group and which set up contact with similar organizations in other parts of the country and the way that guerrilla tactics were so quickly and efficiently employed. Some, however, would come to be ashamed of 'shooting at bewildered Ukrainian peasant boys' instead of 'the real enemy' who were well out of sight.[49]

As the conflict developed, the main rebel fighting groups consisted of 'people [who] got together, fought [and] went home 'in ever-changing formation. Although there was 'no organisation [and] no discipline... there was astonishingly good teamwork.'[50] Fierce street battles erupted where guerrilla groups would sometimes prevent the free movement of Soviet tank units but in other places barricades were breached and the defenders were scattered into the narrow back streets.

Lacking infantry support, the leading tanks, lumbering along the narrow streets, made easy targets for protestors hurling Molotov Cocktails from the windows of buildings lining the streets. (A Molotov Cocktail is a glass bottle filled with petrol and sealed with a cloth wick. The fuse is lit, the bottle is thrown and as the glass breaks the petrol ignites and spreads flames. They were first used by Finns during their war with the Soviet Union in the winter of 1939/1940). The T-54 had the word 'petrol' helpfully written on the fuel caps. The lack of infantry meant that it was relatively easy for protestors to rush the tanks, unscrew the fuel caps and deliver their deadly cocktails directly into where they would do most damage. Many tanks went up in flames and the escaping occupants were shot down. Iron bars that were used by tram drivers to operate track points, and carried as standard equipment on all trams, would be jammed into the tracks of the tanks to disable them. At the Kilián army barracks, where many of the insurgents' weapons had come from, Hungarian conscripts and officers had joined the protestors and were even instructing them in the use of the more sophisticated weapons.

Elsewhere when the tanks were met with unarmed protestors, the Soviet commanders refused to fire on them. In emotional scenes, they were embraced by the crowds who believed that they had come to support the uprising and Hungarian national flags were draped over their machines. There were even reports of Soviet soldiers who joined in with the crowds and helped to persuade others to do the same. Often where Soviet forces appeared to be friendly, however, it was the case that they had been sent out on reconnaissance to ascertain the position and strength of the rebels and so they were careful not to give any excuse for confrontation. In other situations, they would send in armour and observe where the heaviest fire came from. Malashenko ominously records that over 300 captured protestors were interrogated to extract information. By noon armed groups were all over the city centre with gun battles raging but reconnaissance had done its job and the positions of strength of the insurgents had become known.

At 07:45hrs on the morning of 24 October, Nagy had spoken on the radio, which had earlier called for the population of Budapest to 'receive our [Soviet] friends and allies with affection' and the government declared a state of emergency.[51] He blatantly ignored the reality of the situation and said that the Hungarian government had invoked the Treaty of Warsaw and appealed for support from Soviet troops to help restore order signing a decree establishing a military tribunal authorized to pass immediate sentence on anyone who put up resistance. 'Summary jurisdiction would be applied throughout the country to acts calculated to overthrow the People's Republic', he said and 'crimes in the categories coming under summary jurisdiction [were] punishable by death.'[52] By now, Nagy had lost much of his popular support and was seen by the demonstrators as someone who had betrayed the uprising. In a third speech on the radio later that morning, he seemed to distance himself from the decision to impose martial law by saying that the positive action that the students had begun was being abused by the 'bandits' to foment turmoil and shoot people and that he was offering an amnesty to anyone laying down their arms by 13:30hrs, a limit that was later extended to 17:00hrs. There was an inconsistency about the messages that the people were receiving from the authorities which did little to give them any confidence in what they were hearing.

Mikoyan and Suslov had arrived at Communist Party headquarters on Akadémia Street in armoured vehicles in the early afternoon having been forced to land well away from Budapest and driven fifty miles in the fog which enveloped the capital. Serov, Malinin, and a number of armed KGB personnel and seven KGB generals had arrived on the previous day. On the way in Mikoyan and Suslov had witnessed the crowds and mayhem that had erupted but, not wishing to jump to conclusions before finding out more, their first reports to Moscow were not particularly alarmist. They first met Nagy privately and told him that all the trouble in Hungary had begun during his Premiership and they made it quite clear that it was his responsibility to find a way to restore order in the country. They then went into a meeting with the Minister of Defence and a group of Central Committee members in the afternoon. Gerő was quick to deflect criticism of himself by implying that he had the situation well in hand and gave them the impression that it had been Nagy who raised unnecessary concern by exaggerating the level of the opposition and underestimating the strength of government forces.

While the meeting was in progress, a Hungarian border guard armoured company turned up outside ostensibly to provide extra security for the Soviet delegation but an ÁVH contingent was already in place there. The KGB agents inside the building, clearly under orders to protect their charges and quite unaware of the exact circumstances into which they had been catapulted, reacted in a way that may have been second nature to them, but which was staggeringly alarmist to their hosts. They believed the Hungarian security forces to be already in the building and so they surmised that those outside driving up in armoured vehicles bearing a Hungarian flag must be rebels. Opening fire without hesitation they killed at least fourteen of the border guards before they realised their mistake. It is not hard to imagine the wave of shock that rippled through the Hungarian government building. As chaos reigned, another incident, one of many, took place on the same day at the Party Headquarters on Köztársaság Square, where the Hungarian tanks (with Hungarian flags), arriving under orders to defend the Party building, were fired upon from the windows. Thinking the building had been taken over by rebels, they returned fire before withdrawing.[53]

At 17:00hrs the Soviet delegation received erroneous reports from the Hungarian secret police that all insurgencies had been crushed and demands for the removal of Gerő had been suppressed. Arrests of the leading demonstrators were under way, they were told, with some 450 people already in custody. Nagy agreed to the use of more Hungarian military units, militia, and ÁVH units to lighten the burden on Soviet troops and to emphasize the role of the Hungarians themselves in the 'liquidation of the riots'. The Soviets thought that it had been a big mistake not to arm government supporters sooner and not to have given the order troops to fire on protestors right from the start. Hungarian leaders who had been most responsible for the oppression in the years since the war, were hastily taken out of the firing line and shipped off to Moscow. This might have been the Soviets' first mistake since the presence of hardliners in the Hungarian government might have coalesced more with the Kremlin approach and contributed to an earlier clampdown and a suppression of the uprising before it could gain traction.

Mikoyan's reputation was on the line to some extent given that he had been the only one of the Soviet leadership to oppose Soviet military intervention on 23 October. His position in the Kremlin hierarchy was far from secure and he was lucky to have avoided elimination by Stalin, being saved only by the dictator's death in 1953. His current status was very much reliant on support from Khruschev. It was Mikoyan and Suslov who had engineered the removal of Rákosi during the July disturbances and the current leadership had been installed with their blessing which would put them in a very uncomfortable position if things went wrong now. Mikoyan had now put his faith in Nagy to bring the country back in line and he was under no illusions that Moscow would accept nothing less than the resumption of total Soviet control of the country in one way or another.

Incredibly, Nagy told the Soviet delegation that he thought his speech outside the Parliament buildings on the previous day had been well received and it was only small groups of fascists who had tried to shout him down. The crowd, he said, had dispersed peaceably at the time, but began to regroup in various places in the city and only then had the serious violence broken out. The Soviets assured the Hungarian leadership that their role was to give all assistance required in such a way as to be 'without friction and for the public benefit', referring especially to the participation of Soviet troops in restoring order. This was met with the full approval of the Hungarian leaders, especially Hegedüs who called the rebels 'fascists' who must be suppressed 'bloodily' if necessary.[54]

Amongst all the painfully convoluted political language that often seemed to cloud rather than clear the atmosphere, the Hungarian political leadership at this time was mired in acrimonious argument about who to blame and what to do. Gerő came out as the main target for their anger for his abrasive speech that had so angered the crowd.

Beyond that it was a choice between negotiation or confrontation. There was general agreement that the Hungarian forces had been failed by the political leadership for lack of clarity in both objectives and methods. Malashenko would criticise the Hungarian authorities for not being united in their struggle and was quick to see that the Hungarian People's Army was not resisting the uprising with conviction not least because they 'did not receive orders…for decisive action.'[55] With hindsight, they thought that imposing a curfew would have kept many people off the streets and allowed the troops to seek out and destroy the pockets of armed resistance.

By midnight the Soviet delegation was still not clear about the position with a great deal of contradictory information coming into the Ministry of Defence where they had set up their headquarters. The Buda area, they thought, was relatively calm with most of the remaining rebels in the centre of the city. The Defence Ministry was in melt-down with contradictory orders going out to units that may or may not have defected, may or may not be where they were supposed to be and may or may not have weapons or ammunition left. The Soviets were unimpressed by the way that students had taken over the radio building against armed security forces. Serov, in particular, was so incensed that he immediately phoned Moscow, even before 'knowing any of the real facts' to express his deep dissatisfaction at the way the situation had been allowed to get out of hand.[56] When one Soviet officer asked Suslov why they were being shot at if they had come to give help, he was quietly removed. They received demands from all quarters for help but, in a city of more than a million inhabitants, the 6,000 Soviet troops were far too few to respond to the myriad security crises that existed in government buildings, police stations, weapons storage facilities, railway stations and even the private residences of government officials. To use troops for even half of these tasks would leave none to crush the insurrection. The position and strength of Hungarian security forces was barely known so it was quite impossible to organise an effective security strategy. The Soviet commanders did what they could. A night-time curfew was imposed. They recorded twenty of their troops dead with forty wounded. When it quickly became clear to the Soviet military that Hungarian army, police and security organisations were unreliable, all joint operations were cancelled. The Soviets had little confidence in the Hungarian army that had twice within living memory faced Soviet forces on the battlefield. There was a strong anti-Hungarian feeling and a sense that they were now preparing once again to oppose them as allies of the West.[57]

Zhukov reported to the Presidium that Soviet forces had entered Hungary and taken control of Debrecen, Jázbrény and Szolonk. Mechanised forces supported by fighter aircraft, he said, had advanced and, in cooperation with ÁVH personnel, taken control of Szeged and Kekcskemét. In all more than 1,000 tanks had been deployed. Bomber aircraft were on standby.[58] If the U.S. claimed to have been taken by surprise by events, the Soviet Union's actions testify to them being no better prepared. It is indicative of an intelligence failure of some magnitude that their agents inside the country did not give adequate warning of what was to come. It may be that the uncertainty which had pervaded the Soviet Politburo since the death of Stalin had left a vacuum where vigilance should have been as leaders constantly vied for position and paid insufficient attention to other issues. Complacency cannot be ruled out either as a contributing factor to the lack of urgency displayed in the first days of the crisis. Khruschev chose to deflect blame by raging at the ineptitude of the Hungarian authorities whom, he said, had been on holiday while all this trouble was brewing. His own understanding, based on reports, was that the trouble in Hungary had been stirred up by intellectuals and writers and was supported by students but the population as a whole had reacted passively to everything and had not been hostile toward the Soviet Union. He 'recommended' that the situation in Hungary not be covered in the Soviet press for the moment and asked the meeting to think about the problems in Hungary in greater depth especially the question of how to raise living standards. Factory employees refused to work because basic economic and social issues had not been resolved and unrest occurred in Hungary and Poland, he said, because the standard of living is much lower than for instance in Czechoslovakia. It was his view that the people would not listen to the BBC and Radio Free Europe if they had full stomachs.

24 October Suez
In Paris, Ben-Gurion had emerged from the Sèvres conference on 24 October confident that the news from Hungary would lessen the risk of Soviet intervention in Suez and would also divert U.S. attention from the Middle East. Eisenhower and Dulles were in full campaign mode and having to tread carefully with how they responded to the Soviet action in Budapest. They would not, thought Ben-Gurion, want to be seen by their electorate to be risking involvement in any kind of overseas adventure. The Middle East may well have been of great geopolitical significance to U.S. business and the Pentagon but for the U.S. person-in-the-street military intervention thousands of

miles away in a situation that seemed to pose no direct threat was not a vote winner.

Eden had taken his plans to the British Cabinet where a majority of members had shown a willingness to back force against Egypt without being given any precise details of what had been agreed at Sèvres. Indeed, they were not even told that the Sèvres meetings had taken place at all. Such information that they had been given clearly showed that the military action they were being asked to condone would be in alliance with the French and Israelis and they were fully aware of the risks involved with being seen to have colluded with Israel but on the other hand they had been persuaded by Macmillan's assurances that the U.S. would remain indifferent to any British involvement in the attack on Egypt. The British Cabinet had given Eden permission to go to war, but the circumstances were such that leading figures in the Cabinet, whose opinion gave weight to the decision, were later accused of misleading them and the U.S. would be no less critical when they learned the truth. After this date, Eden became even more secretive and further restricted the distribution of documents pertaining to Suez. People close to Eden now thought him on the verge of a breakdown.

The Israeli leader saw this as his chance to bring the British on board with his accelerated timetable. Eden had insisted that after the Israeli attack at Mitla no British or French troops would be deployed in action until both Israel and Egypt had rejected a ceasefire. If the Egyptians delayed making a response for whatever reason then the Israelis would be left out on a limb while their allies marked time. Now Ben-Gurion suggested that he was willing to accept this as a condition if the French were allowed to provide the Israeli Air Force with another two squadrons of Mystère IV jets and one squadron of F-84 Sabrejets all with French pilots and ground crews. Another condition, of course, was that the attack would go in before the U.S. election.

Chapter Five

25-28 OCTOBER

'Budapest was elegant and beautiful. The tall houses had the silkiest colour, burnished by the centuries. The beautifully landscaped parks were full of flowers in season. The elaborately designed bridges connecting Pest and Buda were lit up at night, the reflection of their lights swam in the dark water of the Danube like thousands of floating stars.'[1]

25 October Hungary
The general strike of workers in Budapest was almost total. Revolutionary district committees appeared in places such as Újpest where the first workers' council in Budapest was created in the factory of Egyesült Izzó and later in the heavy industrial complex of Csepel. Many striking workers had acquired arms. In the provinces, revolutionary committees composed of delegates from the councils of workers, soldiers and peasants took power and sent delegations to the Nagy government which tried to placate them with new promises.

On the morning of 25 October, Soviet tanks resumed their patrols of the main squares in Budapest. Reinforcements had been sent to the city overnight, but they seemed to have learned nothing from the previous day's action. Tanks and heavy armour had been trained to destroy cities by incessant bombardment before the infantry, trained in urban warfare, moved in to secure the ground but the fighting in Budapest was nothing like that. Now the Soviet commanders were under instructions to bring the city to order not destruction. To foolishly expect soldiers to become policemen overnight was a grievous mistake that would be echoed down the years that followed. Buoyed with the successes of recent days, students set off on a march from Kossuth Lajos Street and were joined along the way by workers who had been unable to go to work because of transport disruption. There has been a suggestion that demonstrators had not gone out with the intention of going to Kossuth Square but had been surreptitiously guided there by provocateurs from five different directions simultaneously.

By the time they reached Blaha Lujza Square they were 1,000 strong and blocked the streets so that the Soviet tanks could not get through but there was no aggression and the situation remained peaceful as demonstrators, who had been forced to learn Russian at school, chatted amicably to the tank crews. Hungarians climbed aboard the tanks and draped them with Hungarian flags. The Budapest Chief of Police, Sándor Kopácsi, later wrote that he had watched the huge crowd making its way along Tanács Avenue – with three Soviet tanks laden with demonstrators and Hungarian flags at the front – among them many women and children. The implication here is that the Soviet tanks had appeared to be friendly to create a sense of security among the crowd, but were, in fact, deliberately shepherding the crowds into the square.

Growing in size by the minute, the whole throng then moved off towards Kossuth Square and the Parliament buildings. Many more people from buildings and offices round the square joined in. Soviet tanks in front of the Parliament remained passive as the younger demonstrators climbed onto them. More Hungarian flags were hung over the gun barrels again in a friendly atmosphere as demonstrators pleaded their case denying that they were fascists and that they were seeking peaceful reforms of government.

When it was clear that the reports of reduced tensions had been a gross exaggeration, inevitably it was Gerő who was now right in Mikoyan's firing line. He tried to deflect blame by pointing at Nagy for going soft on the demonstrators, but the Soviets were losing patience with the constant bickering. It was Gerő, said the furious Mikoyan, who had 'stampeded [the Soviets] into an ill-advised commitment of Soviet troops through an exaggerated and distorted picture of the situation.'[2] It was time for decisive action. The choice between Nagy and Gerő was not a difficult one to make but Nagy was warned in no uncertain terms where the red lines were. He argued that the government had to take the initiative and take control of the agenda which was fine but he was told to go so far and no further in placating the rebels. There would be no more talk of Soviet troops leaving unless and until it had been cleared through Moscow. Nagy negotiated for the removal of a number of hard-liners from the government as a condition of taking responsibility. Gerő pleaded that he had the full support of Khruschev himself, but his chance had gone. He was replaced by the 'tall, brown-eyed forty-four-year-old with a self-effacing smile', János Kádár[3] who was seen as a product of the working classes and somewhat more acceptable to the protestors, but it was Nagy in whom Mikoyan placed his greatest hopes. Kádár, like Nagy, was warned to keep a firm grip on things but he had some leverage with the protestors having expressed a measure of support for changes in the government. Arrested on Rákosi's orders, imprisoned and tortured in the purge that had followed the Rajk trial, he had long been a vocal critic of the ÁVH. In November 1954, he had been released with all his front teeth broken and on the verge of a nervous breakdown. He was, however, still a loyal, long-time member of the Party and knew where his duty lay.[4]

Given his new responsibilities, it is clear that Nagy then failed to make the most of his opportunity as probably the most acceptable bridge between government and rebels but that was perhaps not an indictment of his will but more a consequence of his character. Rather than take a proactive stance, he remained in relative isolation throughout the day racked with indecision. His speech to the crowd on 23 October had markedly wounded his reputation with his critics and his elevation to Prime Minister when he didn't have a strong power base in the government left him with responsibility but little authority. He did not, however entirely lose the support of the people, many of whom still believed that he alone was the one leader who could be trusted. Ferenc Fehér called him inexhaustible, imperturbable and determined in his endeavours to find consensus between rival factions.[5] Mikoyan's assessment of him as weak and vacillating can also, from another perspective, see him as a man always willing to listen and learn and, where necessary, alter his views. The turbulence of events that confronted Nagy continuously in ever changing ways over the next days proved to be an enormous challenge that even the most rigid doctrinaire communists in the Kremlin found difficult to address with a constant viewpoint. The wonder perhaps is not that Nagy struggled to cope but that he continued to survive in his role for so long.

It could well be argued that the single most important factor that influenced the trajectory of the whole revolution was the weakness not of Nagy but of the Hungarian Communist Party as a whole because of factional in-fighting. The Party had never been firmly in control of the country right from the start of Soviet rule. Its founders had been Soviet 'puppets' with little public support who had relied heavily on a Soviet presence in the country to underpin their authority and who had never developed the sort of organisation within the population that was fundamental to authoritarian control. This had resulted in many important positions within the government, armed forces and security services being filled by 'unreliable' people who would prove to be sympathetic to a reformist movement.

Serov and Malinin who had witnessed street fighting in the city, arrived at the Hungarian Ministry of Defence in a foul mood. While the Soviet delegation was in discussions with the Hungarian political leadership, Serov's fury knew no bounds when he got wind of the fraternising going on between Soviet soldiers and demonstrators in Kossuth Square. He was obviously not used to such an appalling lack of discipline and ordered the commanders to immediately clear the area around Parliament using any means necessary. Ferenc Szűcs, who was an Agriculture Ministry employee at the time, says that during the morning employees in the building were told to vacate all offices facing the Square and congregate in a large room in the basement. Kopácsi was told by a frantic colleague that there were ÁVH snipers on the roof of the building, but he knew that they had also been in place when Nagy made his speech to the crowd the day before and that had gone off peacefully enough so that might not be such an ominous portent.

Estimates of numbers in the square vary widely but there were certainly several thousand covering more than half the open space. There were no speeches and no attempts by demonstrators to enter any of the buildings and the crowd milled round apparently unsure why they had come to this place which lent weight to the idea that they had been shepherded there. Inevitably, the usual anti-Soviet and anti-Gerő chants started up and the national anthem was sung in an atmosphere devoid of menace. One version of what happened next was that the Soviet tanks on Akadémia Street and Vértanúk Square fired into the crowd, but it does not mention shots being fired from anywhere else. Another version has it that shots were fired from the Ministry of Agriculture building into the crowd with no mention of firing from the Soviet tanks. Research by the distinguished Hungarian military historian Miklós Horváth suggests that Soviet tanks fired into the crowd, but Hungarian border guard units at ground level fired too while there may also have been salvos coming from the Ministry of Agriculture. Tank and armoured car crews around the Parliament and from elsewhere fired back at the building apparently in defence of the crowd. Volleys of shots were fired at the defenceless, unarmed crowd from different locations and directions simultaneously which suggests that they started in response to a single command.

The Hungarian Justice Reparations Commission in 1991 concluded that both Soviet and Hungarian units were responsible for the killings. Modern research has shown that shots came from the roofs of the Ministry of Defence, the Ministry of Housing and Public Construction, and the building of the Parliament cafeteria. The crowd panicked and fled the square. Many protestors fell and were trampled while others, especially those up on the Soviet tanks became targets and were quickly picked off by snipers. Firing continued for about fifteen minutes then stopped. People who had taken shelter and the lightly wounded now tried to escape while others went out to aid the wounded who were laid or crouched on the square crying for help. At this point the firing started up again and more were shot down. The British Embassy reported that the dead were taken away by twelve trucks and the official British report put the number of dead anywhere between 300 and 800.[6]

Fighting in other places was now vicious with no quarter given on either side but these incidents were far from the norm in the experience of the vast majority of the population. It is true, however, that surrendering forces on both sides were shot under their white flags and at least one ÁVH officer was captured and hung upside down from a tree where he was beaten and spat on before being killed. One witness describes a man being set upon on the corner of Lenin Boulevard and Aradi Street and hanged from a tree with a crude placard placed round his neck saying, 'This is the fate of every security policeman'.[7] The Reuters news agency even described the security police as being 'killed like dogs' by the revolutionaries but it is now recognised that the frequency of such incidents was greatly exaggerated by the press for dramatic effect and by the Hungarian government for propaganda purposes.[8] It should not be taken as read that any such atrocities were carried out by any other than a small number of revolutionaries and criminals acting out of the most bestial motives. These executions were 'foreign and unacceptable' to most of the revolutionaries.

Besides the killing of soldiers and rebels, civilians also fell victim to the revolution which fuelled the outrage felt by the population at all the violence they were experiencing and had experienced for years under the communists. Suzanne Budaházy recalled an incident where Soviet tanks had fired into a crowd at Móricz Zsigmond körtér causing multiple casualties. A young boy, Öcsi Schäffer, took a piece of shrapnel in the throat. 'It had struck with such force that it had taken off the back of his head.'[9] His body was driven round Budafok district on the back of a truck with the driver telling everyone 'This is what the Communists did to us – let's do something about it!'

Of the many Hungarian soldiers who had defected a number were shot by Soviet forces and again the government distorted the picture for propaganda by claiming that they had been killed by their fellow countrymen in acts of terror. There were also well-documented cases of cold-blooded executions by Soviet forces which in some cases were investigated and the perpetrators condemned to death. Malashenko wrote that 'Officers and soldiers fulfilled their combat duties; they did not wonder whether their actions were legitimate; they did not question orders'.[10]

Fearful of attack from above the streets, Soviet tanks fired indiscriminately into residential buildings killing innocent residents. The gates of the city's prison were opened and up to 5,000 inmates released. Barricades of ripped-up paving stones, burnt-out vehicles and whatever else came to hand were quickly thrown up on all the main entry points into the city to prevent Soviet reinforcements from entering. ÁVH offices were ransacked with files thrown onto heaped bonfires. Many buildings in the city had been damaged with some lying in ruins. Tramlines had been buckled, telegraph wires were sagging from toppled poles and burnt-out cars, lorries and Soviet tanks were a common sight. Citizen militias carried guns with even young children draped with belts of bullet. The bodies of dead civilians and Russian soldiers lay on the ground some sprinkled with lime to hide the smell. Tony Ámon was eleven at the time and remembered that 'Beneath the disinfectant [the Soviet] faces appeared smooth and boyish. In their uniforms and capes, they looked like children in fancy dress who had fallen asleep, exhausted after playing a wonderful game.'[11] Soviet soldiers were stuck inside their tanks for days afraid to come out and running short of food and water. In a hellish parade, some T- 54 tanks were seen dragging dead Hungarians behind them as a warning to other insurgents.

The rebel groups, growing stronger by the hour since news of the Parliament Square massacre went round, captured new strongholds that offered reasonable defensive characteristics such as Zsigmond Móricz Square in Buda or Tzoltó Street where there was a dense concentration of narrow roads that were hard for tanks to penetrate. The strongest of the rebel positions were the Corvin Cinema and the solid old Kilián Barracks, where Colonel Pál Maléter, the commander of a Hungarian armoured division had been ordered by the government to secure the premises which had been heavily infiltrated by demonstrators led by László Iván Kovács. Maléter had been captured by the Soviets during the Second World War and ended up fighting with partisans against the Germans in Transylvania. When he arrived, he saw a fierce battle raging around the Corvin Cinema with, in his words, kids lying dead in the street. He lined his five tanks up outside the barracks and the Soviet tanks retreated after which he sent his men to recover the wounded off the street. He then contacted his commanders with a simple message that, as a result of the killing of students by Soviet tanks, he was 'going over to the insurgents.'[12] When word of his defection got round he became a national hero of the revolution.

The Corvin group was led by 24-year-old worker from the Budapest suburbs Gergely Pongrácz. Under him they began attacks on Soviet tanks using underground passageways for swift movement. Behind that in the area of Ferencváros, a group led by the small, stocky Auschwitz survivor István Angyal and Per Olaf Csongovai included one Russian and twenty ÁVH personnel who had gone over to the insurrection. In what became the biggest battle so far, they knocked out three tanks within a couple of hours and captured another two, along with an armoured car. After the Soviets were driven off in disarray, the Corvin group found themselves in possession of heavy armour and equipment, and a large supply of fuel in a solid defensible position.[13]

A telegram composed by the U.S. Embassy, but not delivered until four days later, said '…dead and dying Hungarian women and men lay everywhere on the street…mowed down by Soviet tanks.' While the U.S. State Department heard nothing from its diplomats, they learned much from the press who reported 'massive loss of life' forcing the Eisenhower administration to respond with its first criticism of the Soviet action, thinking that Moscow should at least suffer some world moral condemnation for the deed, but privately believing that the revolt would be quickly put down.[14]

U.S. Ambassador Bohlen sent a telegram from Moscow to the State Department that was misleading in a number of respects. 'In view of [the] appeal by Nagy for Soviet troops there is not on the surface at least, any open differences between [the] Hungarian and Soviet Governments' he wrote. It was Gerő who had begged Andropov for troops and there was clear water between Nagy and Moscow. Dulles followed up on this theme by suggesting that Nagy and the Soviets were aligned against the Hungarian people which was not a particularly accurate assessment and certainly not one that the U.S. administration should have used as a foundation upon which to build its response.[15]

Both the British Embassy and then U.S. Legation buildings had been surrounded during the day by protestors. The British Embassy had actually been fired on. The Hungarian National Council in New York called on Dulles and Henry Cabot Lodge, the U.S. Ambassador to the U.N., to raise the situation in Hungary at the U.N. but the U.S. did not want to open themselves up to the charge of using the issue for domestic political reasons. At first they chose to wait for more information and get more support before making any public response to the call but now Dulles told Lodge that the level of Soviet military action could leave the U.S. absent from such 'great moments [in history when], these [Hungarian] fellows are ready to stand and die and we are caught napping and doing nothing.'[16] They knew full well that any U.N. proposition would be vetoed by the Soviets but they saw an opportunity to score diplomatic points and show some solidarity with the 'enslaved' peoples of the Soviet Bloc. They wanted to make a joint approach with other countries which would take some time to organise. It was clearly more important for the U.S. to score points off its main rival rather than do something positive to bring the tragedy of the Hungarian people to the world stage. To embarrass the Soviets, the U.S. could suggest sending U.N. observers to Hungary but of course the Soviets would never agree to that. In the eyes of the Hungarian rebels this was weak to the point of useless.

Eisenhower was deeply upset by the crushing of the revolt, and he was not deaf to public opinion, but he had also concluded that there was little the U.S. could do to help the rebels short of risking global war. It is worth looking at the arguments that supported Eisenhower's assumptions at the time. It was a time when the ravages of the Second World War were still evident and the images of the Hiroshima and Nagasaki destruction were powerful symbols. Fear of another war in which nuclear weapons would be used by both sides was prevalent in a much wider sphere than the White House. Richard Davis of the State Department's policy planning staff produced a paper warning that U.S. intervention, multilateral or not, would lead to 'a major crisis with the Soviet Union and possibly the outbreak of general war.' The Joint Chiefs discussed the risk that 'serious [political] defeat [of] the Soviets could conceivably result in precipitous action on their part.' Dulles knew the Soviets must not be put in a position where they 'could not retreat,' and looked for 'a tolerable way for the Kremlin to pull back,' and was advised by diplomats this would only happen if the United States paid 'a fair price at the proper moment.'[17]

Diplomatically, the options were anything but clear cut. Sending a message that the U.S. would 'under no circumstances...consider military action' risked giving the Soviets *carte blanche* to do whatever they wanted to resolve the crisis but the merest suggestion of U.S. interference might be a first step on a very dangerous path given a lack of certainty over how the Soviets would react to such an attack on their prestige.[18] Eisenhower had put out a statement 'deploring' the use of force in Hungary which had been used not to protect Hungary against armed aggression from without, but rather to continue occupation by the forces of an alien government. This, however, was not followed up with any degree of vigour and proved to be the last statement he made along those lines. The President put out statements 'earnestly [hoping for] restoration of law and order and eventually sent in $20 million worth of food and medical supplies but he patently did not order American forces worldwide onto a higher state of alert, did not make a big thing about sending a squadron of bombers over to England, did not send U.S. troops in West Germany into demonstrative manoeuvres near the Austrian or inter-German borders, did not send warships into the Adriatic and did not offer to go to Budapest in person to meet the new leaders. Ambassadors could have been instructed to impress upon their Soviet colleagues that the Soviet occupation of Hungary was totally unacceptable. He did not do any of these things that could have sent a strong message to the Soviets without precipitating a violent reaction from them. Was it the proximity of U.S. elections or was it perhaps a certain war-weariness from Eisenhower's experiences of leadership during the Second World War that saw so many of his men die that stayed his hand? At best, Eisenhower's response beyond this time could be categorised as 'cautious' and at worst 'craven.' His choices became further complicated, however, when it became clear that the CIA-administered Radio Free Europe broadcasts to Hungary had become much more aggressive in tone and seemed to be encouraging the rebels to believe that Western support was imminent, and even giving tactical advice on urban guerrilla warfare.

In the southern half of Hungary very little actual fighting took place essentially because the Revolutionary Councils there were unable to secure weapons. In Pecs, although student demonstrators had come out into the streets, there was little unrest as local ÁVH forces clamped down hard on dissent, ordering a curfew and locking up a number of prominent activists. When news of events in Budapest filtered through, it was the workers who then took up the cudgel calling for strikes in the mines and factories. During a meeting held in the town square on 25 October the students found their voice and elected a MEFESZ Committee which immediately called for the removal of the university authorities. The workers elected a revolutionary committee and the strength of feeling on the streets caused the ÁVH to falter even as it tried to break the strikes and force the workers back into the factories. About a third of the ÁVH force gave up and joined the protestors.

There were three distinct insurgencies, the students and intellectuals who were idealistic, the much more heavily armed factory workers who wanted better conditions, and a large part of the Hungarian army itself. At no time did significant numbers of Hungarian army personnel fight alongside the Soviet forces in a coordinated effort. Indeed, right from the start large numbers of them went over to the insurgents or simply passed their weapons on to them. Many of the junior ranks were from peasant or working-class communities where grievances against the government were widespread. The Ministry of Defence was, on more than one occasion, forced to broadcast appeals to Hungarian soldiers who had become 'separated' to report back to their command. The refusal of many Hungarian forces to actively oppose the insurgency was a powerful factor in legitimising the revolt in the eyes of the population. It was the case, however, that where military personnel joined the ranks of the revolutionaries they subsumed themselves to civilian control. The three groups did not always see eye-to-eye and were not always on the best of terms. The factory workers were distinctly more rough-and-ready and threatening and more motivated than the army or the students by a brutal spirit of revenge. It was a common hatred of the communist regime that brought them together and, for the most part, held them together in their crusade.

The Revolutionary Councils included representatives of all segments of the population. In Debrecen, the council had 100 members, of whom 60 per cent were workers, 20 per cent university students, and 20 per cent representatives of the armed forces. The councils of Győr and Eger consisted of workers, peasants, soldiers, and intellectuals, while half of the twenty-eight members of the council of Jaszbereny were peasants. From the very start of the revolt, these Councils had the support of much of the armed forces, police and some even had radio stations, Free Radio Győr and Free Radio Pétőfi were allowed to broadcast the aims of the revolution such as complete independence and freedom for Hungary, a protest to the United Nations against the presence of Soviet troops and the intervention of the U.N.

In Salgotarjan also it was the workers who led the rebellion since the town did not have a university but, ironically, it was the action of the local ÁVH who alerted them to what was going on elsewhere in the country. In an aggressive move to pre-empt disturbances in the town, their men took up positions at all public buildings and transport hubs and the first agitators were hauled off the streets and thrown into prison. Soon there were meetings of workers with Revolutionary Committees, set up in the town's steel works and glass factories, calling for strikes. By 25 October most of the factories were at a standstill. Crowds marched through the streets tearing down Soviet insignia and besieging the local police station where political prisoners were released. By now the local ÁVH had recalled its troops and awaited instructions from Budapest.

In the small town of Mosonmagyaróvár, near the Austrian border demonstrations had taken place involving all ages within the community. On 26 October a noisy crowd surrounded the ÁVH station and demanded that it lower the flag depicting the red Soviet star. Without warning Lieutenant József Stefko ordered his men to open fire on the crowd with machine guns and hand grenades. Amongst the fifty-two men, women, students and workers killed were children and even an 18-months-old baby. Eighty-six were wounded. The crowd returned with guns and, together with insurgents from the nearby town of Győr, laid siege to the building. Of the four ÁVH members who were taken captive, two were badly injured and were taken to hospital but the other two were 'beaten until their bodies were bloody objects. Then they were split into pieces as if this had been the work of wild animals.'[19] On the following day, a group of Western journalists crossed the border from Austria and were taken to Mosonmagyaróvár where they saw for themselves the scores of wounded men and women and children, and the fifty or so bodies laid out in the town's mortuary. Photographs of the scene were published in newspapers throughout the West. Terrible violence broke out elsewhere in the provinces. At Miskolc, the whole staff of the regional administration was killed to a man. When the commander of local forces tried to negotiate, he was tied to a car by the neck and dragged through the streets.[20] Terror, once unleashed by a movement with deep grievances, and allowed to flourish without restraint can feed on itself and escalate with unimaginably horrific consequences. As a consequence, Communist Party organisations everywhere collapsed. In order to survive persecution, leaders sided with revolutionary elements and themselves became 'preachers of anti-democratic slogans'.[21]

Tensions in the capital had not abated. In Széna Square, a busy transport hub, a group of rebels had created a redoubt using overturned tramcars as barricades. Their numbers fluctuated as people came and went but were never more than about 500. One eyewitness claimed that most of the fighters there were teenagers with some as young as twelve.[22] György Szabó was a rebel leader in Győr, a 'drab and depressing city, grim, grey and sooty.' On his way to Budapest to deliver medicines, Michael Korda described a bunch of ÁVH officers he came across there, 'swarthy, robust fellows, wearing shiny ankle-length black leather trench coats, with a submachine gun hanging from the back of their chairs, or a pistol on the table in front of them [and] women, heavily made up, wearing black berets, in high heels and stockings...they did not look like student revolutionaries.'[23] At one point Szabó refused to let five truckloads of young boys go to

Budapest to fight. 'I did not want it on my conscience that I allowed youngsters to go to their deaths' he said. The one truck that did get past him returned empty, but with a black flag inside it. In the city, if a man wanted to fight, he simply got hold of a gun, went to Széna Square, stopped at one of the street corners and fought. At first, they had only a few infantry rifles and a few machine-pistols we got from the Hungarian army but later they captured machine guns from the Soviets and then got hold of an armoured car with a heavy machine-gun. The leader of this group was János Szabó, an untidy 'fifty-nine-year-old man with huge side-whiskers, sporting a gunbelt and wearing a wide-brimmed hat'.[24] Although totally uneducated and almost inarticulate Uncle Szabó, as he came to be known by worshipful followers, was a man of extraordinary leadership qualities. He had fought in the Red Army during the Russian Civil War in 1919. At one time he had been a personal chauffeur to Nagy. 'The Russian soldiers that we kill are as much heroes as we are. It is the crime of the leaders which makes us fight against each other', he said.[25]

His acute ability to improvise led to a number of unconventional methods that were supremely effective against the lumbering Second World War Soviet T-34 tanks. The drivers were easily confused by strings of kitchen pans filled with water that would be suddenly lowered on a cable in front of them inches from the turrets. When the tanks slowed or stopped suspecting that they were explosives fighters would hurl Molotov cocktails and grenades from the windows above. Bricks covered with wooden paving from a distance looked like landmines which again caused the tanks to slow right down with catastrophic consequences for the crews. The destroyed tanks were useless as fighting machines but were extremely useful as barricades. Szabó would be arrested and executed by the Hungarian government months later.

Mikoyan and Suslov had agreed a number of measures such as wage rises for the workers but they were having second thoughts about the suitability of Nagy who had barely slept for three days and was constantly being undermined by Gerő who still hung around the government offices. Nagy had alarmed the Soviets by going on the radio and, in his deathless prose style, suggesting that talks were ongoing regarding the withdrawal of Soviet troops on the basis of 'proletarian internationalism'. Mikoyan was open to Nagy's idea of bringing non-communists into the government to appease the rebels, out of the 'utmost necessity' but Suslov was going to take some convincing of that. While conciliatory moves such as this might have had some positive effect in the early stages of the revolution, things had now gone way beyond that point but Nagy refused to acknowledge it. Mikoyan thought Nagy to be 'an honest man but sometimes easily swayed by others'.[26] He had become worried by Nagy's apparent mood swings, no doubt exacerbated by his lack of sleep, and what appeared to be mere opportunistic initiatives. Nagy was warned not to make any further references at all under any circumstances to the idea of Soviet troops being withdrawn from Hungary. Another major problem for Mikoyan was that the revolution was spreading well beyond the capital now where security forces had been denuded having had most of their men hurriedly brought into Budapest.

Moscow was getting very nervous and saw the situation slipping out of control. The revolt in Hungary, which had turned out to be much more intense and widespread than anticipated, had preoccupied them and Gomułka had taken advantage by consolidating his power in Poland. Their forces in Hungary in support of the Hungarian army and AVF should have been sufficient to quell the unrest but with so many of the Hungarian forces refusing to act and, in many cases, actually joining the rebellion, it was becoming clear that if the Soviets wanted to restore order by militarily means, they would have to rethink their strategy and definitely bring in reinforcements.[27] Decisions made in the Kremlin were hampered by the lack of clear intelligence about what was actually happening on the streets of Budapest. Indeed, the authorities in Budapest were having similar problems. What was clear, though, from reports coming in was that by the evening of 25 October, 31 Hungarian soldiers were dead with a similar number wounded and, equally worrying, 175 had disappeared from their ranks presumably having gone over to the rebels.[28]

26 October Hungary

Notes from the Session of the CPSU CC Presidium on 26 October showed that Mikoyan was coming under criticism for his 'improper and ill-defined position' which was not helping the Hungarian leaders put an end to their 'flip-flops'. Molotov wanted the meeting to instruct Mikoyan how to 'act accordingly'. There was little sympathy with Nagy whose weakness was becoming apparent. If pressure could not be brought to bear on him to restore order with a military crackdown, it might be necessary to restore Hegedüs to the leadership.

For the first time, on 26 October, the full scale of the rebellion was becoming clear to both the U.S. and the Soviets. If the Soviets allowed it to escalate and saw the levels of violence reach even greater heights the U.S. would come under increased pressure to take measures to assist the Hungarian people and both sides would be dragged unwillingly into dangerous territory with the increased risk of a direct N.AT.O.-Soviet confrontation. It was with this knowledge that the NSC met on the morning of 26 October. Eisenhower told them that it was a 'dangerous moment' for the Soviets and for world peace.[29]

It was agreed to send a clear message to Moscow. In a speech in Dallas the following day, Allen Dulles made it clear 'beyond a possibility of doubt' that the U.S. had no intention of intervening in either Poland or Hungary and neither country would be welcomed into the N.AT.O. fold if the Soviets lost control.[30] Washington was perfectly aware that if the Soviet Union calculated that a consequence of going easy on Hungary was that it ended up as part of N.AT.O. it would be a serious threat in Soviet eyes to their own security and could well have repercussions well beyond Hungary. For many historians, this became a significant factor in how the U.S. responded but, in reality, the idea of Hungary joining N.AT.O. had never even been on the agenda of either Washington or Moscow and could not be taken seriously. A CIA request to airlift weapons into Hungary was firmly and loudly dismissed by Eisenhower. An American military response was once again definitely ruled out. U.S. power in eastern Europe had found its limits and they had been reached with temerity and caution without a shot being fired. The only hope that something positive could come out of the situation was the rather humble aspiration that a guarantee to Moscow of U.S. non-interference might persuade the Soviets to deal more leniently with its satellites in the future and slowly allow them a degree of independence. Whatever the merits of such a stance it was hardly one of which a superpower might want to boast.

27 October Hungary

Budapest radio broadcast to the city on the sunny morning of 27 October with a rallying call for peace in the streets. It urged the people to recapture a spirit of togetherness in which the fear of death would no longer torment them. The fourth morning of the revolution was quieter than the three that had gone before but much of the city lay in ruins. Gaping holes scarred the streets many of which had been stripped of paving stones that were now strewn across the road where barricades stood or had been smashed through. Amongst this devastation, however, that spoke of a broken society and hopeless destruction was a true sense of the togetherness that the radio had advocated but it was not manifest in quite the way the authorities had envisaged.

Cart-loads of fresh produce were piling into the city from the surrounding farmlands and was being distributed freely to the population. Newspapers, some of which were new and had sprung up overnight printed on single sheets began circulating but their message now was one of support for the uprising. There was criticism of the privileged lifestyle of some communist party leaders. The printed word acquired an unprecedented force and popularity and where there were too few copies to go round their contents were read aloud to groups gathered in the street. Posters were stuck on trees and shop windows denouncing Rákosi and demanding reform. Irene Korponay saw a Hungarian army truck that had stopped in the middle of the street with a young captain standing on top of it reading aloud a proclamation of the Revolutionary Council of the Air Force, which demanded the complete withdrawal of the Soviet Army.[31]

In Mosonmagyaróvár, where the massacre had taken place the day before, the population was still seething with hatred for what had happened there. Togetherness was not a concept that was uppermost in their minds. A crowd surrounded the hospital where the two wounded ÁVH soldiers had been taken the night before. One had died in the night but the other, Lieutenant Stefko was still alive after undergoing overnight surgery. The hospital staff were unable to prevent him being taken out on a stretcher, fully conscious, into the crowd where he was spat on and cursed. His body was thrown to the ground, beaten and trampled then hung upside down from a tree.[32]

Outside the exchanges between armed groups and military units, mob violence in the early days of the revolution took two distinct forms. There was the hunting down of members of the hated ÁVH which Fehér called a fascist action since it is an indiscriminate act against a category of person in which the level of individual guilt is not examined. Then there was retribution against ÁVH officers who committed acts of terror against unarmed civilians as in the massacre of unarmed demonstrators at Mosonmagyaróvár. Both are seen as examples of how normal law-abiding and sympathetic people who feel terribly wronged can collectively act in barbaric fashion in a time of war and in the absence of legitimate authority.

Nagy formed a new Cabinet casting out Hegedüs and a few other hardliners and bringing in a number of Social Democrats and non-communists still believing that this would be enough to quell the riots but with more than 300 civilian deaths it was going to take rather more than a shuffling of the cards. The people were going to settle for nothing less than a new deck. Mikoyan complained that he did not become aware of the political changes until after they had been made and decided to confront the Hungarian politicians with 'hard facts'. He echoed Andropov by saying that the withdrawal of Soviet troops would inevitably mean the arrival of western forces. A strict curfew must be imposed immediately. The counter-revolutionaries must be separated from the mass of people, who would be placated by a number of concessions. The rebels would then be 'ruthlessly destroyed'.[33]

After a relatively calm morning in Budapest, Hungarian tanks, acting in accordance with a Soviet battle plan, were sent to smash resistance at the Corvin Cinema and Kilián Barracks. The idea was for three T-34s to approach from Nagyvarád Square and three T-54s from Kálvin Square before lining up in front of the cinema to pound it. Another ten tanks were to follow with infantry. These Hungarian infantrymen would then launch an assault but when they were ordered to advance in open-topped Soviet armoured vehicles their commanders would not allow their men to go into the battle in 'open coffins'. One of the Hungarian commanders, Lieutenant-Colonel Lázló Tóth, then pointed out that the tanks did not have any radios so it would be impossible to coordinate the attack. 'This is a completely unprepared operation which risks the lives of the men at stake and has no hope of success,' he told the newly installed Minister of Defence, Károly Janza.[34] Colonel András Márton also refused saying 'I will not lead units to the slaughterhouse even if they string me up.' In the end no Hungarian troops took part in the operation. Furthermore, because of the access points the tanks would have to approach in single file. Despite all objections, Janza sanctioned the attack but with modified last-minute orders. The first three tanks moved in to carry out reconnaissance and when they did not return, three more went in after them. One hour later two returned, one of which was badly damaged. Three were left burning in front of the cinema and a fourth was 'shot to pieces'. Maléter called Janza and asked, 'Is this how the government makes political concessions?'[35]

Morale within the Soviet force was declining by the hour. With all the heavy firepower at their disposal, they were taking casualties and making little progress against the committed resistance of an enemy that seemed at times to be little more than a disorganised rabble. Soviet commanders were acutely aware that their troops were being asked to fight in conditions for which they had not been trained and operating in circumstances for which they themselves lacked a strategy. They could see no way of turning the tide and blamed the politicians for allowing the situation to slide out of control.

The western press was in Budapest in force and constantly making grossly exaggerated claims in their reports that Soviet forces were deserting to the rebels *en masse* and even fighting amongst themselves. Mikoyan, however, continued to tell Moscow that morale was good and Soviet troops were performing well but it was clear to them that tank crews were exhausted and running very short of supplies and getting only minimal support from the Hungarian army. The intervention of Soviet troops to prop up the Gerő regime had been an operational disaster They had quickly succumbed to major logistical problems and, despite Mikoyan's assertion, morale had plummeted. There were multiple instances, such as at Győr and Veszprem where Soviet commanders had simply refused to take action against demonstrators. Troops had been misinformed about the true nature of their mission and many were disturbed at having to confront unarmed crowds. In other cases, guards had to be placed on unreliable units to prevent them defecting to the rebels. Newspapers of the free press began to appear in Budapest, while radio broadcasts from Western Hungary indicated that most areas of importance had fallen to the insurgents.

Spencer Barnes at the U.S. Embassy called on Washington to 'lead the case in the U.N. and use all its influence to mobilise world opinion [against the Soviet Union]'[36] while Dulles clarified his own position by saying that he was not 'one of those who believes we should be hindered by undue caution'.[37] In the early afternoon, in New York the U. S., Britain and France formally asked the U.N. Security Council to discuss Hungary but there was little enthusiasm to go beyond that. There was hardly any confidence that Nagy, whom the U.S. saw as a communist dupe, would bring the country out of its nightmare. Eisenhower and Dulles, now into the final days of campaigning for the presidential elections wanted to make it crystal clear in a message delivered to the American public but shouted loud enough to be heard in the Kremlin, that whilst they firmly supported independence for the Soviet satellites, they did not seek to draw them into any sort of western military alliance against the Soviet Union.[38] This supine U.S. position had come out of Eisenhower's profound belief that U.S. intervention in Eastern Europe risked nuclear war and this rendered his administration effectively impotent militarily and it became a question of how to maintain a non-interventionist stance without looking weak and the only way open at the time was to wage a propaganda campaign against the Soviet Union. The NSC suggested that 'as a matter of high priority [the U.S. should] exploit fully throughout the world propaganda opportunities afforded by recent events in Poland and Hungary.' Unfortunately, such opportunities would be swiftly eroded by events in Egypt that gave the Soviets ample ammunition to return fire in this regard. Eisenhower's frustration boiled over when he said 'what a great tragedy it is when the whole Soviet policy is collapsing, the British and French doing just the same thing in the Arab world.' The British Ambassador in Moscow reported that the

Soviets regarded Suez as 'a heaven-sent distraction from Hungary [and an opportunity] to recover their moral standing by posing as the champion of the United Nations and of an Arab country.[39]

Had the Hungarians waited a few days until after the U.S. presidential election things might have been different but right at this moment militarily, diplomatically and politically, Eisenhower was constrained by public opinion and had few cards to play. Soviet-U.S. trade was minimal so no pressure could be brought to bear in that sphere. Military intervention of the sort advocated by the Pentagon, blind to political niceties, right at the start of the revolution would have involved western forces traversing Austrian territory in blatant violation of its neutrality which would have done little to authenticate U.S. credibility as a bastion of democracy. The idea of using the Hungarian crisis to begin constructive talks to advance an atmosphere of détente in the new post-Stalinist Kremlin apparently never made the agenda.

While the U.S. had done much to encourage revolt in the Soviet Bloc they had not expected it to happen so soon and had done precious little to prepare for it. Even now they misread the situation by refusing to give any sort of support to Nagy, whom they disliked and distrusted, at a time when he seemed the only hope of compromise. Bohlen had mistakenly told Washington that it was Nagy who had signed the request for Soviet troops in the first place. There was never a serious effort by Eisenhower's administration to make a deeper study of Nagy's position probably because the lack of real-time intelligence allowed their ingrained prejudices against him to persist. They considered him to be hand and glove with Moscow. Unfortunately, the fact that he shared a number of the goals of the revolution escaped them entirely which closed any door that might have been prised open to influencing the revolution through covert support for his position. Radio Free Europe broadcast a message to the Hungarian people denouncing Nagy as a Stalinist 'Trojan Horse' who was acting out of self-interest and not on behalf of the Hungarian people and would break the revolution from within.

This moment had given the U.S. an opportunity to act even within its own stipulated limitations. Washington knew enough about what was going on to know that Nagy had survived the first four days of revolution and it seemed as if he had two options available to him. He might insist on retaining the Communist monopoly over state power but at the same time try to distance Hungary from the Soviet Union, along the Yugoslav model, or he might attempt to diminish communist control in a way that was acceptable to Moscow. In either case he would have benefitted from some level of support from the U.S. on the world stage.[40]

Unfortunately, the performance of the Hungarian representative at the U.N. gave little cause for hope. In the U.N. Security Council the Soviet intervention in Hungary was discussed under article 34 of the U.N. Charter. The mood of the meeting was struck when Hungary's representative, Péter Kós, a citizen of the Soviet Union, protested against holding the discussion in the first place and the Soviet delegate tried to deflect accusations by erroneously claiming that Hungary had failed in its obligations to 'extirpate fascist movements'. The Soviet and U.S. delegates exchanged acrimonious jibes but eventually calm was restored and the debate closed.

Late in the day Nagy went into a meeting with Mikoyan and Serov who by now were completely frustrated with his efforts to find a political solution to the crisis. This time he took with him Kádár, a man whom Nagy said had been 'born sitting on the fence'. Both Nagy and Kádár argued strongly for a ceasefire and amnesty followed by top-level talks on the future role of the Soviet forces in Hungary. The Soviet emissaries agreed to seek Kremlin approval for the deal but in the meantime, had a plan to break the revolt with one final military action. Mikoyan and Suslov then returned to Moscow taking Hegedüs and Gerő with them.

28 October Hungary

Sunday 28 October was a day on which many Hungarian funerals took place and huge rallies were held in western capitals in support of the revolution. Public emotions were running high. Nagy was taken completely by surprise when he heard about the Soviet plans for a major assault on rebel positions. For a man who had spent his life immersed in communist plots and machinations he had shown himself to be incredibly naive and trusting in negotiations with Mikoyan and Serov. He had gone to bed convinced that his arguments had prevailed, and Moscow would agree to a ceasefire and a programme of limited reforms but when Janza sought his approval for the fifty or so Soviet tanks, supported this time with artillery, to attack the rebel Corvin and Kilián strongholds he was soon disabused of that notion. Smaller units were also preparing to attack lesser targets at Boráros Square and Tzoltó Street but Hungarian forces were now reluctant to take part. When he heard that the Soviet tanks were in position and ready to attack, Nagy refused to condone the action and threatened to resign if the plan was carried out. He made clear his position to Andropov and finally to Khruschev, who tried to mollify him believing that Nagy was his last chance of finding a united Soviet-Hungarian political solution. The Soviet leader would agree to a ceasefire but only if he could get the rest of the Council of Ministers approval. Serov raged at Mikoyan for failure to 'isolate the battlefield' by blocking off all main roads into the city along which he believed armed groups were coming in from other cities.

Getting his Ministers to agree was going to be no easy task for Khruschev, with a number of ambitious members eager to use the situation to undermine his position and it required several hours of acrimonious debate which included contributions from Mikoyan and Serov. Molotov bemoaned the fact that the initial messages from Mikoyan and Suslov had been reassuring about the strength of the Hungarian government, but it was becoming clear that the influence of the Hungarian Communist Party on the masses was weak.[41] It was hard work to get the Council to think about how to move forward instead of spending precious hours arguing about whose fault it all was. It took the intervention of Suslov, who had just flown in, to persuade them that the situation was getting worse by the hour with Soviet troops having squandered what goodwill or effectiveness they might have had four days earlier. The choice was becoming polarised into compromise or defeat. The option of successfully crushing the rebellion seemed to have gone.

For the Soviets this was a humiliation. Militarily they had failed to restore order and politically they had achieved the opposite by hardening the will of the protestors and driving them to adopt a more resolute position. For Moscow it was a situation without precedent and one that they had, to some extent, brought upon themselves after Khruschev's January speech had given hope of some relaxation of despotic rule. Two factors played into their hands, however, and subsequently had a big influence on their decision-making during the following twenty-four hours. There was every chance that the crisis bubbling up in Egypt might divert world attention away from eastern Europe giving them a freer hand to respond in Hungary and the U.S. administration had made it perfectly clear, despite its vow made in 1952 to bring an end to the 'despotism of godless terrorism' in its foreign policy, that they were not interested in becoming embroiled in a spat with the Soviet Union on the eve of the presidential elections. Having chosen deterrence over intervention, the U.S. was about to come to terms with the limits of its power as the Soviets had just done but not in the same way. Ironically, for a country like the U.S. that had vowed to roll back communism, the more the Soviets had failed to deal with the Hungarian revolt, the more the U.S. reiterated its position of 'active non-interference.'

It would, however, have been the optimum moment for U.S. intervention. The Budapest Legation was having trouble getting its cables through to Washington but in one written on 28 October, and probably received in Washington the next day by way of Vienna, it said that, if the U.S. stepped up the rhetoric and marshalled international opposition then the Soviet leadership 'might be willing [to] extricate themselves from [the] present situation through an armistice followed by negotiation.'[42] The Hungarian rebels, too, might have been persuaded to drop their more extreme demands and settle for an international guarantee of the withdrawal of Soviet forces. The two things that mitigated against this was the growing tensions in Suez that had started to take up much of Eisenhower and Dulles' time. Washington's handling of the Hungarian crisis amounted to little more than a 'wait and see' strategy. Gaza Catona, who worked at the U.S. Legation in Budapest later said 'the biggest problem we had was probably that there was no one in Washington who could give us immediate responses. When we recommended that certain Presidential pronouncements be made, or suggested various courses of action, there was no timely answer.'[43]

The other was the unfortunate perception of Nagy as a puppet of Moscow and one who could not be relied on to seek a middle way, despite his claiming to have agreed a Soviet withdrawal. There is some truth in the suggestion, however, that whatever Nagy may or may not have been willing to do as a leader, he had made no move up to this point to approach the U.S. for any kind of support and his administration was still substantially composed of Moscow hard-liners who constituted a bedrock of communist control that would have been resistant to any U.S. initiatives. The U.S. Legation actually contacted the Hungarian government with a proposal for a ceasefire but it was rejected out of hand by an administration that felt it was regaining control of the situation.

The rejection of Hegedüs was interpreted as the Hungarian people showing disrespect to the Soviet Union. Voroshilov thought Mikoyan and Suslov had been particularly weak and categorised their performance as rather less effective than that of the CIA. He favoured imposing a government on Hungary that could be relied upon to take orders from Moscow but Bulganin and Kaganovich thought that would drag them into a full-sale occupation of the country. Kaganovich said that the counter-revolution must be suppressed by making concessions to the workers and peasants and crushing the centres of resistance, but as a bare minimum, the Hungarian government must show friendship with the Soviet Union and be seen to assist the Soviet troops otherwise they would step in and appoint a government that would. Almost as an aside, and oblivious to the irony of his remark, Khruschev mentioned that he thought that the British and French were getting themselves into 'a real mess' over Egypt.[44]

Meanwhile in Budapest, the Soviet force opened up on Maléter's position but it was a half-hearted effort and soon the confrontation once more petered out into a stalemate which saw a Soviet withdrawal. The Soviet commanders in the field now came out openly to condemn the Hungarian forces for failing to act decisively and the Hungarian politicians for vacillating and giving them no consistent strategy to follow. In reality nobody had any idea how to deploy the Soviet tanks units which had proved to be quite unsuited to urban warfare once their primary tactic of intimidation had failed so abysmally. The Soviet casualty list told a sorry tale and all the while the revolution had grown stronger and stronger. Hungarian resistance fighters, whose exploits had been lauded across the Free World's press and cinema screens, became instant heroes on the international stage.

Nagy eventually got approval from Moscow and a ceasefire was announced just after noon. He continued to call for order and went on to say that an agreement had been reached by which Soviet forces would withdraw from Budapest and pledged that the ÁVH would be disbanded but Russian units conspicuously remained in the capital and although ÁVH power was scattered it was not destroyed. Revolutionary councils were hastily set up throughout the country many calling for withdrawal of Soviet troops from Hungary and the establishment of a multiparty system with guaranteed rights. While the people wondered whether this was a plot to disarm them before a resumption of attacks, Nagy continued to argue for the removal of opposition within his Cabinet so that he could implement the necessary reforms.

It was on this day that Major-General István Kovács, Chief of the Hungarian Army General Staff, was told by the Soviets that he was to make preparations to take full control of security in the country because the Soviets were about to withdraw in two phases but no plans were put to him until the following day. The first plan was to withdraw troops in non-combat situations initially and they would be followed later by those still fighting at the Corvin Cinema and Moszka Square. In the event it happened the other way round.

Khruschev was preoccupied with a rather tricky issue that threatened now to embarrass him. On 23 October, he had called on the Hungarian Council of Ministers to send a written request to the Soviet government to 'kindly' send troops to Budapest to 'liquidate the disturbances there and restore order' but none had arrived.[45] With the Hungarian situation coming up for debate in the U.N., this now put him in an uncomfortable position of seeming to have authorised an illegal aggressive invasion of another country. He turned for help to the 'taciturn and reserved'[46] Andropov who had been one of his more trusted sources of intelligence during the previous days and one who had not recognised a single one of the revolution's demands as legitimate. Andropov suggested to Nagy that he sign a backdated telegram requesting Soviet assistance, but Nagy bluntly refused to do so leaving Andropov with no choice but to pressure Hegedüs into putting his name to the forged document. The following note was duly delivered to the Kremlin on 28 October but dated 24 October,

> 'On behalf of the Council of Ministers of the People's Republic of Hungary I appeal to the Government of the Soviet Union to send Soviet troops in order to put an end to the riots that have broken out in Budapest, to restore order as soon as possible, and to guarantee the conditions for peaceful and creative work.'[47]

Suez

On 25 October, Jordan had announced that it had joined the Egypt-Syria military alliance and on the same day Israel had called up 10,000 reservists. Keightley ordered a practice drill in Malta to embark troops. French paratroopers had been sent forward to Cyprus and its fleet was on the move. In response, Egypt moved forces into the western desert but suffered a setback when the Soviet Union, anxious to avoid losing any in combat, had ordered that forty-five of their jets that had been sent to Egypt were to be relocated to airfields in Saudi Arabia. At this point, the risk of Soviet aircraft, probably with Soviet pilots given that few Egyptian airmen were qualified to fly them, engaging with British and French fighters with inevitable casualties threatened consequences that the Soviets were not willing to contemplate. Whatever was going to happen would not involve these prized assets.

It was on 25 October, the day after the signing of the Sèvres Protocol, that Keightley altered his plans again or rather cancelled the Winter Plan and reverted to Musketeer-Revise. With Israel now in the mix, there was an added impetus and confidence of working with a proven military ally despite the extra burden of coordination. The French and Israelis had already made extensive plans for dual collaborative action weeks before the French had brought the British into a tripartite agreement.

In London, Without giving anything away about the secret Sèvres agreement, Eden told his Cabinet that 'in the event of an Israeli attack on Egypt, the government should join with the French government in warning both belligerents [to agree to a ceasefire] British and French forces would intervene to enforce compliance.'[48]

The Cabinet voted to approve Musketeer-Revise on 25 October. Washington had been kept in the dark about preparations in Britain and France and their intentions in the Middle East but the Israeli mobilisations, which were far in excess of routine drills, unnerved Eisenhower who sent a message to Ben-Gurion urging caution. The response he got cannot have been very encouraging because on 28 October he went public with his concerns and warned of a grave threat to peace. Ben-Gurion was now forced to address the warning but claimed that all Israeli moves were purely precautionary prompted by Arab troop movements all along its borders. Dulles called in Abba Eban, who at the time was Israeli Ambassador to both the U.S. and the U.N., and gave him the opportunity to justify what amounted to a full mobilisation of Israeli armed forces at a time when the U.S. estimated that external military threats to Israel were low. Eban, who had been out on the golf course, was invited to come clean but all he could offer were bland reassurances that he had no knowledge that his government was planning unilateral military action. Notwithstanding Eban's assurances, the U.S. State Department ordered the evacuation of all diplomatic staff from embassies in Syria, Jordan, Israel and Egypt.

The next day Eban was called in again and given an opportunity to clarify what was going on to Assistant Secretary of State for Near Eastern Affairs William Rountree. Eban defended his government by saying 'Israeli mobilization has been purely precautionary and protective…the United States need have no concern…no danger has arisen from Israeli defensive measures. The American press is distorting the situation by saying there is a danger.' It was therefore a huge embarrassment for him when Donald Bergus, the head of the Bureau of Near Eastern Affairs' Israeli-Palestinian office entered and passed a note to Rowntree who read it aloud saying that there had been 'a massive eruption of Israeli forces around the Egyptian boundary and a parachute drop deep into Sinai.' Rowntree suggested that Eban might 'want to get back to your embassy to find out what is happening in your country.'[49]

The Soviet Union, meanwhile, had been kept well informed about the tripartite conspiracy by their agents in France, Egypt and Israel the most important of which were army reserve Colonel Israel Beer, who became Ben-Gurion's personal secretary, and Ze'ev Goldstein, an official of the Israeli Ministry of Foreign Affairs and a veteran of the Red Orchestra spy network of Second World War fame. The Soviets also had an Egyptian spy, Sami Sharif, Nasser's future chief secretary.[50]

Chapter Six

29 OCTOBER

> Imre Nagy's group wanted the Revolution the least of anyone, because it ruined everything. They were reformers, not revolutionaries: they did not create the Revolution, they did not push for it, they did not want it. It saddened them. Imre Nagy did not know what to do with it. It was completely against his character, plans, and purpose.
>
> Major-General Béla Király[1]

Hungary
Described by a Polish journalist as a 'tall, flushed, black-haired [man] with a repulsive face...a Tyrollean hat, a coat thrown over his shoulders like a cape...a revolver at his belt and wearing black riding breeches' a new popular hero now emerged as a player in the Hungarian drama. Cast by the Soviets as a leader of the counter-revolution in an effort to discredit him, the swashbuckling and flamboyant József Dudás, had become the leader of one group of revolutionaries, albeit one of a political rather than an activist nature, and became another legend of the revolution for whom his supporters 'lived and died.'[2] His reputation rapidly grew through his frequent press conferences to which the foreign press was invited in his 'revolutionary headquarters' with the result that, eager for sensational stories, correspondents promoted Dudás in their despatches as one of the main rebel leaders. He described his policy as 'shooting the bastards and trying to defend the decent people.'[3] He even printed his own newssheet, *Magyar Függetlenség* in which he denounced the government and called for his own National Revolutionary Council to be the sole representative of the nation's freedom fighters and be allocated six seats in the Cabinet. A day earlier he had, as self-styled leader, demanded to meet Lieutenant General Petr Laschenko, commander of the Soviet Special Corps and be

recognised as the alternative to Nagy's government. That approach did not get him far with the Soviets who saw him as a political adventurer but it was recognised at the time that Dudás' group was not actively fighting the Soviet forces which rather weakened his claim to represent those who were. Nagy agreed to meet him after he had walked into the government building with a cohort of supporters and laid a machine gun on the table. It made everyone nervous, but Nagy refused to take him at all seriously. Dudás, however, would go on to play a significant role during the coming days.

The ceasefire was holding on 29 October apart from a few minor skirmishes such as when some Soviet forces, short of food, had started looting and were engaged by Hungarian National Guards. Estimates put the total Hungarian dead at around 1,000 and Soviet troops at 500. Food shopping once more became possible as shops had plenty of produce. In Budapest there was a feeling within the population that they had won some sort of victory. However, there were still a lot of weapons in the hands of the revolutionaries and Nagy was warned that he had to ensure the safety of the Soviet forces by persuading the people to remain calm during the Soviet withdrawal. His plan to achieve this was to set up a new National Guard made up of army, police and insurgents. This was organised by former Budapest police chief Sándor Kopácsi and put under the command of Major-General Béla Király, to rid the city of troublemakers, criminals and adventurers but it would be an uphill struggle for the government to regain the confidence of the people.

Nagy also had to contend with the opprobrium of the U.S. administration who continued to oppose him by instructing the newly appointed Ambassador Wailes to shun him by not presenting his credentials upon arrival and thus destroyed any hope of direct communications between Nagy and Washington. This denied Washington the opportunity to pass on to Nagy an authoritative and high-level message without fear of interception or misunderstanding and to get a realistic appraisal of Nagy's position and strategy to oppose Soviet occupation. When Nagy had officially ordered that all Soviet troops evacuate his country and had simultaneously requested U.S. support in achieving that objective, the Eisenhower Administration dismissed him as incompetent and untrustworthy. Again, we are left with the clear impression that the U.S. was doing everything it could to avoid any sort of confrontation with the Soviet Union and Moscow was not slow to recognise this. The Soviets could go ahead with their invasion confident that the U.S. would not interfere militarily. By the time that the U.S. State Department changed its mind on 3 November and asked Wailes to go ahead and present his credentials, it would be too late to influence events.

Expectations had been aroused to such a pitch and public debate freed up to an extent unprecedented under Soviet rule that Nagy's typically belated and half-hearted measures were simply not going to be enough to satisfy the appetite for reform that the previous few days had whetted. However, he opened his door to one and all and listened patiently to demands that he knew full well would never be countenanced in Moscow. Eventually the days of anguish and the sleepless nights overtook his better nature and later in the day he railed at a delegation of intellectuals calling their ever-changing demands 'worthy only of hotheads' and told them it was not their job to formulate policy but to implement it.

Getting support for his National Guard, however, was going to be every bit as difficult as all the other things Nagy had tried to do over the previous week. The army bristled at the thought of sitting down and discussing policy with the more violent insurgents. Even Maléter, who had now been promoted to General and made Minister of Defence, could not stomach that. On the other side, far from showing willingness to compromise, the rebels were maximising their demands. The character of the reformers had changed from the early days. Gone were many of the students and intellectuals and taking over were young, impoverished, uneducated factory workers who had little to lose and much to gain. Furthermore they came from groups that had little or no connection with each other and who jostled for influence making it almost impossible for the government to find a representative body with whom they could negotiate. It became a crucial issue now for Király to prevent the 'troublemakers' from whipping up violence again and destroying the delicate balance that had been achieved. The one thing that would derail the withdrawal of Soviet forces and bring them back with a vengeance was another breakdown of order on the streets. The level of extreme but relatively rare violence inevitably had a huge interest for foreign journalists and disproportionate influence both within and without the country. 'The Hungarian Revolution was not characterised by brutality' claimed Király but lynchings had taken place and those responsible should not be allowed to violate the 'purity' of the revolution.[4]

In Moscow, British and U.S. diplomats met the Soviet leaders briefly as they all attended functions on the diplomatic circuit. A smiling Khruschev seemed eager to put on a brave face and show that the Soviet Union had not been particularly discomforted by recent events in Hungary. The U.S. Ambassador, Bohlen, had an important carefully worded message, that Washington had prepared for him, which had to be made clear to the highest levels of the Soviet government. Just in case they had been distracted and failed to get the message from either Eisenhower or Dulles, he took Zhukov aside and told him that the U.S. does not see Hungary as a potential military ally for the U.S. It is significant that both Eisenhower and Dulles thought this point so important that it had to be repeated several times. It puzzled the Soviets, who had not considered it remotely likely that Hungary would join N.AT.O. and the assurances may well have had unintended consequences if Moscow surmised that the U.S. did 'protest too much' to hide deeper ambitions. Zhukov got the point, but his reply gave Bohlen the impression that the Soviet withdrawal of forces from Hungarian soil was not quite what it seemed to be. It might not be quick and it might not be absolute.

In Hungary, the ÁVH had been dissolved, revolutionary committees had been elected in many businesses and government agencies. The Soviet withdrawal plan was put into operation at 20:00hrs on 29 October. Hungarian forces were ordered to replace the departing Soviet troops at all the areas where rebels were still fighting but great effort was to be made to try and persuade the rebels to disarm when it was clear to them that the Soviets were really going. Just as Soviet forces were leaving Budapest, Israel launched Operation Kadesh to create a military threat to the Suez Canal by seizing territory in proximity to it; to break the Egyptian blockade of the Strait of Tiran by capturing Sharm al-Shiekh; and to 'confound the organization of the Egyptian forces in the Sinai and bring about their collapse.'[5]

Suez

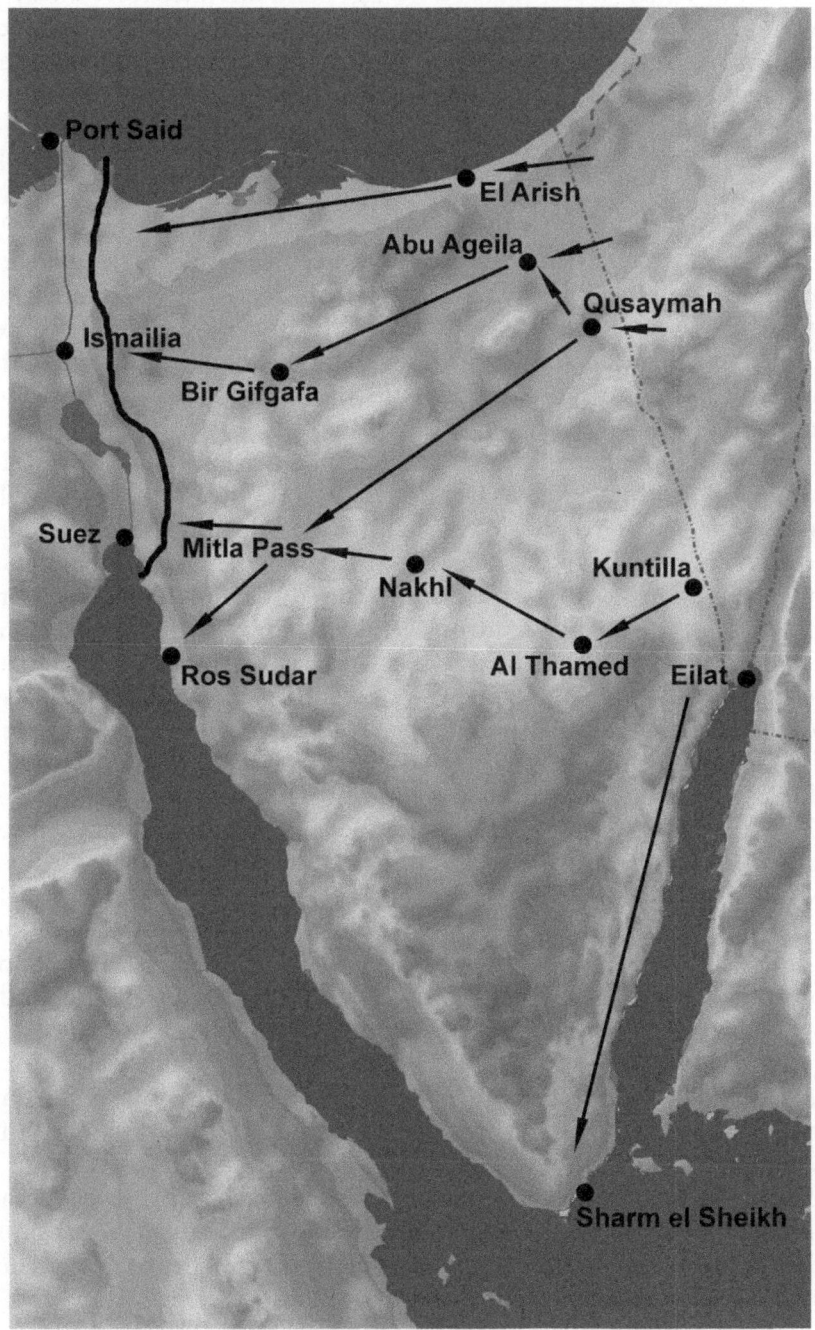

Map of Sinai showing the extent of the Israeli advance by 2 November

There were few avenues of advance across Sinai available to the Israeli forces all of which were guarded by Egyptian advance forces. Key to Egypt's defence strategy was Abu Ageila close to the Israeli border on the central route across the desert. Militarily, the Sinai Peninsula forms three distinct regions. The northern coastal sector has open stretches of loose sand and sand dunes making many areas impassable for vehicles. The only route across this section was vulnerable to choke points that slowed down any movement of forces. The southern half is mountainous, barren, and desolate. The central area, however, is an arid limestone escarpment with patches of loose, heavy sand alternating with hard, rocky surfaces. Its surface is cut with numerous, deep, dried-up watercourses and steep hills of jagged stone. This area had the best-surfaced road in the entire peninsula going through Abu Ageila, Bir Gifgafa, and ending up in Ismailia, after crossing the Suez Canal at the Firdan bridge.

As part of Operation Kadesh another called Operation Steamroller swung into action. Sixteen Israeli DC-3 Dakota aircraft under the command of Major Ya'acov Aviyashar had flown from Tel Nof airfield at low-level under Egyptian radar. They carried men of the 1st Battalion (sometimes referred to as the 890th after the 890 soldiers who first manned it) of the 202nd Paratroop Brigade led by Lieutenant-Colonel Raful Eitan towards the Mitla Pass which was a series of narrow passages cut through the Heitan/Jebel Giddi Massif (Pilgrim's Way) an otherwise impenetrable barrier to mobile forces. Meteor and French-built Dassault Ouragan fighter-bombers flew alongside the DC-3 Dakotas, with the paratroops on board, at 100 feet across the desert while Mystère jets harassed the nearby airfields to prevent Egyptian jets taking off to intercept. Reconnaissance had shown tents and vehicles at the Mitla Defile, which was the easiest terrain to defend and where the Israelis had planned to drop. The area was guarded by two battalions of Egypt's desert Frontier Force. By now, however, the Egyptians' communication with headquarters in Ismailia had been severed in the most novel way. Four Israeli P-51 Mustang aircraft had flown low over the desert and cut through the telegraph wires with their propellors. It was decided to drop some way east of the 24-kilometre long Mitla Pass at a place known as the Parker Memorial and approach on foot but a navigation error put them about eight kilometres adrift of even that.

They marched for two hours in darkness and arrived at Jebel Heitan. Here they were reinforced by another parachute drop from French Nord Aviation Nord Atlas 2501 transport aircraft of eight jeeps, mortars and other weapons, ammunition, water, food, and medicine. They dug in amidst minefields and sporadic Egyptian probing attacks and waited

Anti-government protests in Budapest 23 October 1956.

Anti-Soviet protests in Budapest 25 October 1956.

Protests outside Hungarian Communist Party HQ, October 1956.

Hungarian Rebel Leader Pal Malater.

Hungarian communist leader Mátyás Rákosi.

Imre Nagy at his trial in 1958.

Kossuth Square.

Soviet T-34 tank outside Kilian Barracks.

Hungarian insurgents.

Hungarian revolutionaries.

Hungarian revolutionary.

The head of Stalin's statue torn from its pedestal.

Soviet BTR-152 troopcarrier on fire in Budapes.

Murder of Hungarian secret policeman.

President Nasser announcing the nationalisation of the Suez Canal.

President Nasser and Anthony Eden.

President Nasser and Dwight Eisenhower.

President Nasser and Nikita Khrushchev.

Blockships in Port Said.

Royal Navy Fleet Air Arm Hawker Sea Hawks FGA4 Fighter Jets of No. 800 Squadron on the deck of the Centaur Class Light Fleet Aircraft Carrier HMS Albion.

British protests against the Suez invasion.

Israeli Commander Moshe Dayan.

Israeli scout tank in the Sinai.

Damaged Egyptian tank in the Sinai.

for the rest of the 202nd coming overland. These reinforcements, however, were getting into serious trouble with vehicles getting stuck in the sand. Sharon had been promised French front wheel drive trucks but they had not shown up in time.

During the first night, while the paratroopers dug in at the Mitla Pass, the Israeli 38th *Ugdah* (division) under Colonel Yehuda Wallach was to advance through Umm Qatef and capture Abu Ageila supported by the 4th Infantry Brigade which would advance on the southern flank through Qusaymah to approach from the south and the 9th Brigade would prepare for its long and arduous journey toward Sharm al-Shiekh. Egyptian tanks had been withdrawn from Abu Ageila leaving it with anti-tank guns and artillery as its only defence against the Israeli armour. The main body of Sharon's 202nd Brigade had made a feint move towards the Jordanian border on the previous day to confuse observers but was now forging ahead across the Sinai at full speed along the relatively unguarded southern Kuntilla - al-Thamad - Nakhl route to reinforce Eitan's men who were pinned down by Egyptian artillery of the 2nd Infantry Brigade and by strafing air attack by Mig17s.

As a consequence of Dayan's decision to commit the whole of the 202nd, the IDF's most effective fighting unit, to what was essentially a political tactic to create a pretext for British and French intervention the main attack would be undertaken without them. The problem for Dayan was that he had to commit to the Mitla Pass attack in order to trigger the Anglo-French ultimatum but was then forced to hold off his main attack for 48 hours to allow the ultimatum to expire before the Egyptian airfields could be bombed and it was only after that bombing that Ben-Gurion would give permission for Dayan to unleash his whole force. Dayan, however, was not about to leave his men at Mitla cut off and at the mercy of Egyptian counterattack and ordered the 82nd Armoured Battalion of the 7th Brigade to break through at Qusaymah and move at top speed up to Mitla before waiting for any authorisation from Tel Aviv. When attacked by Israeli forces coming out of the morning sun on 29 October, Egyptian forces at Qusaymah had quickly abandoned their defences and retreated to Umm Qatef as they had been instructed to do if confronted by far superior forces. This gave the defenders at Abu Ageila advance warning of an attack. The Israeli Southern Command, Colonel Asaf Simhoni, had worried that the Egyptian force at Qusaymah might have been stronger than he had been led to believe and, not wanting to hold up the whole plan, he had attacked early to make sure of success. An attack on Qusaymah would be most effective with Israeli forces attacking with the rising sun behind them so it was launched a full 24 hours earlier than planned.

As part of the political subterfuge, Simhoni had been given orders not to move any forces into Sinai for the first forty-eight hours of the war but he was not told why. He thought that Dayan's orders must have been a mistake so, on his own initiative, he had attacked Qusaymah only hours after the paratroop drop at Mitla.[6] In Cairo, Nasser seemed unconcerned, thinking that the Israeli action was a diversion from the main action to come. The first reports coming to him indicated that the Israelis had been beaten and Egyptians were engaged in mopping up operations. It was soon clear to him, however, that this was entirely false and the Israelis were mounting a serious offensive and he ordered reinforcements to Sinai.

Every year the IDF would go on to conduct a major map exercise involving an attack against Abu Ageila and use the 1956 experience as an example of what not to do. In contrast, the Egyptian military leadership would come to characterise the battle for Abu Ageila as a showpiece of Egyptian heroism in which Egyptian officers and soldiers held out for four days against several Israeli attacks some which they had to face in fierce hand-to-hand night combat.

Before the attack, Dayan had held the fighting spirit of the Egyptian army in low regard. 'There is no need to fear that Egyptian units who will be bypassed will launch a counterattack or cut our supply lines', he told his forces before the attack.[7] To Dayan's great surprise, the first attack on Abu Ageila from the south was repulsed. He blamed this on the early warning the defenders had got when Qusaymah was attacked prematurely. For political reasons, Dayan was frustrated by not being able to explain to his field commanders why the drive into Sinai had to be delayed and it brought a great deal of criticism for being 'over-cautious', not something any Israeli commander wanted on his CV. Knowing that his 202nd was sitting out in the desert at the mercy of Egyptian aircraft, Dayan instructed the Air Force to maximise sorties over Mitla to protect them as much as possible. His 7th Armoured Brigade was split up, some to protect Sharon's flank as he advanced and others to speed ahead to Mitla. Because of this when the attack on Abu Ageila was resumed it was weakened by the absence of the 7th leaving a single tank company.

Israeli forces were now becoming dangerously spread out in central and southern Sinai without having taken any important position or destroying any enemy forces. By early evening of 30 October, the Egyptians were becoming acutely aware that a major Israeli force might be surrounding Abu Ageila. Israeli forces were moving through the Daika Pass threatening to cut off Abu Ageila from Ismailia and al-Arish. By 07:00hrs, the Israelis had seized the important crossroads at Abu Ageila and effectively surrounded the Egyptian forces but their forces were extremely low on fuel and ammunition and would have found it extremely difficult to sustain a defence against a coordinated counter-attack from two directions. An aggressive, synchronized attack by Egyptian units from al-Arish and Ruafa Dam in conjunction with the Egyptian Air Force might well have destroyed them. The Israeli commander Lieutenant Colonel Avraham Adan was reluctant to storm the Egyptian positions with their minefields and well-laid defences but it was vital for the campaign that this should be done as soon as possible. Dayan assumed operational command and ordered the brigade to attack.

He had expected France and Britain to follow their ultimatum of the 30th with the actual bombing of Egyptian airfields on the 31st when his troops would advance quickly to the Canal. Ben-Gurion, however, wanted all Israeli troops withdrawn from the Sinai, because the British and French air strikes planned for the morning of the 31st had not taken place, and the Prime Minister, unclear as to the reasons for this delay, feared that his allies were reneging on their commitment.

For the Egyptians, the battle for Abu Ageila was the key to the entire campaign in the Sinai. It was essential that forward positions were held to delay and impede Israeli forces while Egyptian armour prepared for a counterattack. They planned to unleash two major task forces each consisting of an armoured brigade of T-34 tanks and SU-100 self-propelled guns supported by an infantry brigade. One to move on the central route to reinforce Abu Ageila and the other to the take on the paratroopers at Mitla. When the British / French ultimatum was received in Cairo, however, all such plans were put on hold.

The rest of Sharon's 202nd, minus some tanks that had broken down or got stuck, had moved swiftly to attack Al-Kuntilla, having wheeled round to approach from the setting sun, and then Themed at dawn out of the rising sun which blinded the Sudanese defenders until the Israelis were close. According to the Israeli Haaretz online journal, Benny Broida, a member of the main force racing across the desert remembered that during the trek from Al-Kuntilla to the Mitla Pass a great many Egyptian soldiers were killed. 'A lot of [Egyptian] soldiers were always showing up along the side of the road with their hands up and shouting "Water! Water!" Broida said, and 'Whoever showed up got a bullet. The guys didn't leave a single one alive. Until the next camp we reached, until Nakhl, we didn't take one prisoner alive.'[8] He described one incident that he had witnessed at Themed,

'There were a few prisoners, inside a barbed wire fence. Suddenly a MiG-19 approached and fired at us. One of the shells hit one of the prisoners and tore him to shreds. The prisoners began to go wild and the guys shot them and killed them all, about ten people. On another occasion there were around thirty Egyptian workers with shovels, who were levelling the road. They were told to sit on the side of the hill while two men with machine guns watched over them. When the Egyptians heard people speaking Hebrew, they started to riot, they didn't know that a war had started. The Israeli guards opened fire and killed them all. Another version of this incident that was the subject of an investigation by the Israeli and Egyptian governments in 1995 who heard evidence that 'Paratroopers found two large tents with civilian Egyptian workers and took them captive. Two days later, they moved out toward Ras Sudar and killed their prisoners. There were exactly 49…We tied their hands and made them go down to the quarry. They were startled, broken and shattered [there was no explicit instruction]. Only a fool can ask his commander for permission to do [that].'[9]

Then, after the expiry of the ultimatum when French and British bombers attacked Egyptian airfields destroying much of the Egyptian Air Force on the tarmac, a second, more threatening front had opened up. Nasser feared that now his entire army in the Sinai might be cut off by a European expeditionary force occupying the Canal area. Against the advice of several individuals, including his Minister of War Amer, he ordered a general withdrawal from the Sinai. By early morning of 2 November the relative inactivity within the Abu Ageila complex caused a tank company from the Israeli 37th Brigade to investigate and occupy Umm Qatef. Unfortunately, Israeli forces further west mistook them for Egyptian armour and opened fire on them destroying eight tanks and forcing four others to retreat. The battle had concluded with Israelis killing each other in a tank battle in broad daylight while an undetermined number of Egyptians were dying from thirst in the desert.

Elsewhere the three French destroyers, *Kersaint. Bouvet,* and *Surcouf* were patrolling off the coast of Israel to protect the sea approaches to Haifa and Tel Aviv while thirty-six French Mystères and 36 F-84 Thunderstreaks flew to Israel where they were readied for immediate deployment. Two British destroyers HMS *Daring* and HMS *Defender* led the British battle fleet out of Maltese harbours. Incredibly, only when Stockwell had arrived in Malta on his way to Cyprus on 26 October was he made aware that he was just one part of the bigger plan that had been agreed at Sèvres. Owing to the fiction that the British and French would be going in to separate the two warring factions of Israel and Egypt, prior to this time there had been two planning staffs, one preparing operations against Egypt and the other against Israel. As a consequence, some naval commanders were under the impression that when they went into action it would actually be against Israel. Dayan later lamented that 'only the British are capable of complicating things to such a degree.'[10] Furthermore, again because of Eden's need to distance himself from any accusation of collusion, troops could not be embarked until the ultimatum had expired which put the earliest date for a landing in Egypt as 6 November.

The naval task force would perform its traditional roles in military expeditions, to bring the invasion force safely to the enemy shore, soften up defences prior to the landing, transport the landing force onto the beaches, and provide cover for the troops while they established a secure beachhead. Royal Marine commandos, together with army paratroopers, would form the initial assault force which would have eighteen tank and troop landing vessels. Troopships with larger combat organisations were to follow some hours behind. Altogether, with escorts and auxiliary vessels, the assault force numbered over a hundred ships. The twenty-five radar-equipped Sea Venoms embarked in HMS *Eagle* and HMS *Albion* had night and all-weather capability, giving the Royal Navy the ability to mount around-the-clock air operations. The French carriers operated thirty-six F4U Corsair fighter-bombers and ten TBM Avenger antisubmarine aircraft. HMS *Theseus* was also equipped with a helicopter antisubmarine squadron.

The Israeli action forced the U.S. administration to make a decision which of the two crises they would now focus their main attention on. The situation in Hungary appeared to be moving to a more measured transition towards an easing of Soviet control and gradual recognition of legitimate concerns. In the Middle East, however, things seemed to be getting worse with the prospect of a showdown between the U.S. and its allies, France and Britain. Dulles knew that Britain and France were somehow behind the Israeli attack but was not sure how. He was not helped by the absence of the British ambassador who was enjoying a leisurely crossing of the Atlantic by sea having been deliberately instructed by Foreign Secretary Lloyd not to make the journey by aircraft. It was crude, obvious and exceedingly annoying for Dulles but it was very effective as a ruse to avoid him asking awkward questions.

The U.S. was not entirely unhappy to see what the Israelis were doing and saw clear benefits for U.S. foreign policy if the Egyptians took a beating and were sufficiently cowed to accept U.S terms for a future arms deal, but Eisenhower's main concern was that a situation might arise where a lack of U.S. engagement might see an opportunist Soviet Union become directly involved and thus increase its influence in the region. An emergency NSC meeting was called on the afternoon of 29 October to discuss the likelihood of Soviet involvement and the prospect of a wider war if that happened. In a direct reflection of how the Soviets had reacted to the possibility of U.S. intervention in Hungary, Eisenhower thought it unlikely and invited the meeting to 'look at the map…geography makes [Soviet] intervention in Egypt difficult if not impossible.'[11] Dulles sent an ambiguous message to both Britain and France to say that the U.S. would 'defend the victims of aggression.'[12] In this context, the Sixth Fleet was sent to Crete to prepare for the evacuation of civilians from Alexandria and Haifa.[13]

Chapter Seven

30 OCTOBER

'I want to say this on the question of foreknowledge, and to it quite bluntly to the House, that there was not foreknowledge that Israel would attack Egypt; there was not.'
Sir Anthony Eden to the House of Commons 20 December 1956[1]

Hungary

The worst fears of the Hungarian government, eager to avoid anything that might provoke the retreating Soviets, were realised on 30 October when an unruly mob of armed insurgents laid siege to the headquarters of the Budapest City Communist Party in Köztársaság Square. Prior to this, Soviet tanks and columns of troops had nervously continued to make their withdrawal through streets lined with people who showed their approval by jeering and cheering in equal measure. The radio had broadcast a stern warning that Soviet forces would respond with force if there were any incidents of hostility aimed at the departing troops. Had these people known that the Soviet forces were withdrawing only from Budapest and not from the country entirely they may have been rather more demonstrative but that was the deal that the Kremlin had struck with the Hungarian government.

Moscow was still not sure what to do. At least one group in the Politburo felt that Soviet strength in Eastern Europe was overextended and that therefore some sort of compromise might have to be made with Nagy and his followers. Zhukov was open to the idea of withdrawing from the country completely in the face of widespread anti-Soviet sentiments thinking that it was the only pathway to a long-term solution and, remarkably, he found few willing to openly disagree with that view. Khruschev had been in a meeting with a delegation of Chinese officials to get the view of his communist ally Mao Zedong which essentially was that the Soviets should seek a negotiated settlement. Official Soviet newspapers gave Nagy a good press on that day lauding his efforts and the Central Committee of the Communist party issued a statement in which it said, 'the Soviet government is prepared to enter into the appropriate negotiations with the government of the Hungarian People's Republic...on the question of the presence of Soviet troops on the territory of Hungary'.[2]

Michael Korda had been an undergraduate at Magdalen College, Oxford, when he heard about the Hungarian uprising and had arranged with friends to go to that country and take with them as much medical supplies as they could pack into his 'stiffly sprung and noisy' Volkswagen car. He reached Budapest on 30 October and handed over the medicines to Professor Hajnal at the Second Medical Clinic and then took time to survey the city with its 'huge, ornate public buildings.' He walked into a nightmare scenario of 'blackened and burned-out tanks and artillery pieces... litter of death and destruction...scattered all over the streets and pavements,' There were many bodies, including women, still lying where they had fallen, sprinkled with lime, some covered with small bouquets of flowers. Many streets were blocked by improvised barricades of trams and buses, interlaced with torn, twisted tram rails and ornamental fencing from the parks. The streets were littered with broken glass, debris, rubble, and spent cartridge cases. Some of the tanks were still burning, filling the air with dense diesel fumes and the smell of charred human bodies.[3]

Armed gangs still roamed the streets, many of them made up of criminals, that had been unwisely released form the city's prisons and given free access to guns, who used the revolt as a cover for criminal looting and theft. They were also not averse to seeking revenge on the police who had put them in prison and others against whom they bore grudges. Nevertheless, the number of violent incidents was diminishing in general until one of the very worst of the whole revolution erupted in Köztársaság Square which was stormed by armed groups from the poorest areas of the city that now included many criminals and members of fascist organisations eager to exploit the absence of Soviet tanks to further their subversive ambitions and crucially a Hungarian tank crew that had crossed over to the rebels. Inside the Party headquarters work staff were trying to restore some order and get back to work. A party of about fifty, mostly young, freshly recruited, security force personnel had been drafted in at the beginning of the troubles and were still there having been reinforced by a few older hands from the hated ÁVH secret police section. A number of Soviet soldiers who had been on duty outside left at around 09.30hrs as part of the overall Soviet withdrawal plan. About half a dozen rebels tried to enter the building unaware of the security forces inside and were quickly ushered out. It was then that they recognised the uniforms of the notorious ÁVH and opened fire on them as they fled the building. The crowd of rebels now surged towards the entrance and, at first, called for the security forces to lay down their guns and come out but the ÁVH knew what that might mean and opened fire on them. The rebels took cover and a fierce gun battle ensued.

Workers inside the building called for help and five tanks of the Hungarian 33rd Tank Regiment were sent. When they arrived, they saw a tank with Hungarian markings firing on the building. Thinking that this tank was firing on rebels inside the building they started firing also on the ÁVH in the building. The Paris-Match photographer Jean-Pierre Pedrazzini, stepped out from behind a tank to take a picture and instead took a bullet to the stomach, an injury from which he died a few days later. The tanks were doing a huge amount of damage to the font of the building and, bravely, the Budapest Party's boss, the plump and normally cheerful, Imre Mező came out under a white flag to plead for a ceasefire. He was also shot and died of his wounds.[4] The rebels now stormed the building. ÁVH men were dragged out into the square and beaten to death or shot. John Sadovy, a reporter from *Life* magazine wrote '[in three years of war] nothing I saw could compare with the horror of this.'[5] One ÁVH officer, László Elek, barely out of his teens, who came out was hung upside down from a tree and photographed. Colonel Papp was strung up by his feet with cable wire, soaked in petrol and his face and torso were burned. The level of barbarity seen in Republic Square horrified both the government and the overwhelming majority of the opposition forces. Even Dudás' *Magyar Függetlenség* condemned those who 'took delight in the devastation and destruction'.[6]

At noon, as a gesture of goodwill to placate the population, Nagy ordered that Cardinal József Mindszenty, the Prince Primate of Hungary, be released from his house arrest in the castle of Felsopeteney. On 8 February 1949, he had been sentenced to life imprisonment by Rákosi's new Hungarian People's Republic for treason and espionage but had remained a symbolic leader of the people for his opposition to communism. Mindszenty was only one of about 8,000 political prisoners that were released throughout the country at the same time. Further earth-shattering reforms were announced hours later when Nagy abolished the one-party system of government and introduced 'democratic co-operation' between parties in a move that he knew would enrage the Kremlin. It is not clear how he thought he was going to get away with it. Perhaps, as Mikoyan had predicted, he was simply carried away with the emotional intensity of the moment and lost his political footing. He was certainly on slippery ground.

Mikoyan and Suslov had returned to Budapest with clear instructions to lull the Nagy government into a false sense of security. They brought with them a copy of a conciliatory article which would appear in *Pravda* the next day. The Pravda Declaration seemed to indicate that Moscow was ready to accept many of the principles of the Revolution admitting that there had been 'many mistakes and hailed the uprising in Hungary as a "just and progressive movement"'. It went on to give what appeared to be an assurance that one of the main arguments of the revolution had been conceded when it said, 'the stationing of troops of one member state of the Warsaw Pact on the territory of another state shall be by agreement of all the member states and only with the consent of the state on the territory of which, and on the demand of which, these troops are to be stationed'. When Nagy tried to widen the discussion by suggesting that non-communists be brought into the government, he was, however, met with a grim silence.[7]

He was not only losing any residual credibility he might have with the Kremlin but was also facing ever more demands for reform from his own colleagues. One delegation called for free elections within three months. Again the stress of all that he had endured over the past week caught up with him and he again threatened to resign, When this failed to have the desired result and brought only muted approval of such a move, Nagy was led away 'red-eyed, deflated and practically in tears'.[8] Pressure increased from Radio Free Kossuth which now told the people that from now on they would hear the truth and no more lies.

At the Kilián Barracks about a hundred people came to a meeting called by the Temporary Revolutionary Council for Public Safety and hosted by Maléter. The debate was over the role of insurgent groups alongside or within the army and police. The revolution had been won, they believed, but there was a real danger that reactionary elements would not accept that and would try to restore the old regime taking advantage of any delay in the departure of Soviet troops. Maléter wanted to arrest József Dudás, whose group of insurgents occupied the Foreign Ministry and whom he considered to be out of control, while Király, pushed for amalgamation of the civil and military insurgents within the National Guards so as to establish the legitimacy of the Nagy government and the state. The only solution was for the immediate creation of a unified force under a united leadership. It is worth noting here that the people who took up arms against the Soviet and Hungarian armed forces saw themselves as revolutionaries but the government, using communist parlance, called them counterrevolutionaries since they acted against the government which saw itself as the enduring embodiment of the original 1917 revolution that brought the communists to power in the first place.

Official Soviet newspapers gave Nagy a good press on that day and lauded his efforts. The mood changed, however, after Mikoyan, shaken by the violence at Communist Party headquarters in Budapest, reported to the Kremlin that far from improving, the situation in Hungary was deteriorating. Khruschev saw danger for himself if Soviet forces withdrew from Hungary and the situation did not stabilise from within. His rivals in the Kremlin would act against him swiftly if they suddenly decided that he had lost control in Hungary and the Western Powers were given a significant propaganda victory. Any perceived Soviet weakness in the eyes of the West was the one thing the Politburo would not countenance.

Khruschev decided to canvas authoritative opinion from outside his own Soviet circle and turned to the other great communist power. Right at the start of the demonstrations, the iron gates of the Chinese Embassy in Gorky Avenue had been locked, and staff lost all direct contact with Hungarians. Employees at the embassy were not permitted the leave the building and Ambassador Hao ordered all of the scholarship students studying in Budapest to move into the embassy.

Khruschev had a meeting with a delegation of Chinese officials, led by Liu Shao-chi, Vice-Chairman of the Chinese Communist Party's Central Committee, to get the view of his communist ally Mao Zedong which essentially was that the Soviets should seek a negotiated settlement but that troops must stay in Hungary.

Patience was required, he said, so that the revolutionaries (what Mao called counterrevolutionaries) should be allowed time to reveal their true nature, and only then should the government move against them.[9] Confidence in the ability or willingness of the Hungarian army to break up the remaining rebel strongholds such as at the Corvin Cinema was rapidly diminishing. Right from the start, Serov had been telling Moscow just how unreliable the Hungarian security forces were and it beggars belief that Khruschev had based his earlier decision on the assumption that Hungarian forces could be expected to take control of the situation. The lull in fighting was not guaranteed to last and when it started up again it was hard to know which side the Hungarian army would be on. This prompted a significant shift of opinion in the Kremlin and when it was suggested that Marshal Ivan Konyev, Commander-in-Chief of all Warsaw Pact countries should go to Budapest himself to assess the situation 'on the ground', there were no dissenting voices.

Despite the debate going on in the Kremlin, as Soviet troops were withdrawing from Budapest, plans were already underway for more to arrive as news of the Köztársaság Square engagement had reached Moscow. Given that there was still no clear successor to Stalin firmly in control of the Politburo it is likely that the military, with the covert support of the more militant Politburo members, secretly made the decision to send more troops as a precaution to safeguard the security of troops already in the country. This was not necessarily the start of a major deployment but troops who had been heading out of the country through the border town of Csaroda had turned and were taking a circular route that brought them onto another road leading back towards Budapest.

More than a thousand men of the 114th Parachute Regiment of the 31st Air Mobile Guard Division with full armoured support flew from Lvov to Veszprém. They were followed later in the day by members of the 381st Parachute Regiment. When Nagy called in Andropov and demanded to know what was going on he was referred to Mikoyan who assured him that there were no plans to bring in any new formations 'on the assumption' that the Hungarian government was 'dealing with the situation.'[10] At the same time Mikoyan suggested to Moscow that they hold off on sending any further troops but continue to concentrate them on Soviet soil in readiness. As a result roads all along the Romanian-Hungarian border and all through Slovakia were full of Soviet heavy armoured units waiting to cross over. The few Hungarian aircraft able to operate were trying to fly reconnaissance over the border areas but were shot down or driven off by Soviet fighters. Railway stations in Záhony, Kisvárda and Nyíregyháza were completely taken over by the Soviets so that armour could be entrained and advanced quickly.

Unaware of the seismic shift of Kremlin opinions, the British Ambassador William Hayter reported to London that he was confident the Soviets were genuinely looking for a compromise, but Bohlen had noticed that Soviet leaders had suddenly become 'noticeably more glum', and warned Washington that Nagy was on a knife-edge and if he lost control, the Soviets would change tack in an instant. The CIA evaluation also advised that the Soviets would resort to force of arms rather than see Hungary slide further out of their control.

In Moscow, Molotov was telling everyone on the diplomatic circuit that Britain and France were behind the Israeli advance into the Sinai, a charge that Hayter was quick to deny. Khruschev claimed that British and French diplomats had suggested that Moscow might like to go easy on their governments over Suez and they would take a similar line over Hungary. Whether or not that was the truth it seems certain that Moscow had rather more leverage over Suez than either of the others had over the situation in Hungary apart from generally holding Moscow to account which, given the mess Britain and France were getting into, was becoming more difficult by the hour. The Soviet propaganda machine went into overdrive over Suez to voice its anti-imperialist principles and divert attention away from its own imperialist adventure in Hungary.

For its part, the Eisenhower Administration failed to understand how the splits within the Soviet leadership had left an opening for them to intervene. Right from the start, despite calls from Nagy for diplomatic help, Eisenhower made no effort to support the Hungarian cause fearing that the Soviet leadership would react with force against the insurgency and he did not want to make any move that might precipitate that. Had he realised that for the first week of the crisis this was not the case then he might have been more proactive in supporting the revolution. As it was his inaction emboldened those in the Kremlin who favoured a strong line on intervention and allowed them to set the agenda for continued strict Soviet control of its satellites in Eastern Europe for a further three decades.

Suez

In the absence of a direct diplomatic link to London, a frustrated Dulles had requested a U.N. Security Council meeting in which he called for a debate on resolution S/3710. Britain and France were able to delay the start until 16:00hrs New York time to give their governments a chance to prepare and issue the ultimatum to Israel and Egypt as part of the Sèvres plan which they did at 11:00hrs. It was handed directly to the ambassador at the Egyptian embassy and the chargé d'affaires at the Israeli Embassy in London.

Eden called a Cabinet meeting then went to the House of Commons and read out what one U.S. official called 'the most brutal ultimatum in history'. On the one hand, it called upon Egypt to surrender the Canal and a very large part of its territory and on the other hand, Israel was allowed to keep the territory which it has occupied in the Sinai Peninsula. This Anglo-French ultimatum to Egypt and Israel was timed at noon and called on the combatants to cease fighting and withdraw their military forces to a distance of ten miles from the Canal within twelve hours. In reality Israeli troops were nowhere near the Canal, all the action was taking place much further east. It made clear to everyone that Britain was on the side of the Israelis and was preparing to go to war without the parliamentary consent or even knowledge. Opposition to Eden and Lloyd within the British Parliament was growing but he still had considerable support from the right-wing of the Conservative Party and a marginal approval rating with the public. A number of prominent members of the government threatened to resign in protest, however. The Labour opposition called the British action 'an act of disastrous folly' with Eden having 'broken every pillar of British foreign policy' and trade unions even threatened to strike in protest.[11] It was becoming ever more difficult to maintain the fiction that the Israelis had acted alone.

Moscow reacted violently to the news of the Israeli attack and the Anglo-French ultimatum. Molotov accused Ambassador Bohlen of U.S. collusion in the Israeli attack. *Pravda* called it premeditated aggression against Egypt and held London, Paris, and Jerusalem fully responsible for the "dangerous consequences which may result from [their] aggressive actions." Directing its message to the non-aligned countries, it went on to say that '[The attack was conceived] with the object of crushing the national-liberation movement of the Arab peoples [and was intended] to restore the colonial system throughout the Middle East and North Africa.'[12] Soviet reaction throughout the Suez crisis, however, was profoundly limited by the position taken by the U.S. which, in reality, was the only great power able to influence the outcome of the conflict in the Middle East. Moscow was not prepared to move until it could be quite certain of Washington's attitude toward both the Hungarian and Suez crises. The Soviet leaders knew only too well that without Washington's support the British and French efforts in Egypt were doomed to an early and decisive failure and only when it became clear that the U.S. would not take any practical steps to support the Hungarians did Khrushchev commit the Soviet Union to a military occupation of the country. When it came down to exactly what the Soviets could do in practice, however, it was left to Zhukov to spell it out. 'Are we supposed to send our armies through Turkey, Iran and then into Syria and Iraq and on into Israel and so eventually attack the British and French forces?' he asked of those who clamoured for action to help Egypt.[13]

It is well known that Eden was ill and that his health deteriorated after taking office in 1955. It is therefore worth looking at what relationship there might have been between his health, which went into serious decline after 6 October, and his subsequent decision to use force against Nasser. One of the contributing factors to Eden's health issues was the time difference between Cairo, London and Washington. Eden wanted to make himself available to respond to developments almost on a round-the-clock basis which robbed him of much-needed sleep.

On 21 August he had recorded in his diary 'Felt rather wretched after a poor night. Awoke 3.30 am onwards with pain. Had to take pethidine in the end.' On 7 September he admitted to feeling 'quite exhausted' after two difficult days in the House of Commons and he spent the weekend of 5-8 October in hospital having, in his own words, 'suddenly felt freezing cold and began to shake uncontrollably' with a temperature of 106^0F.[14] Afterwards, his personal physician, Sir Horace Evans, wrote a note for Eden to carry on any foreign trip, 'his health during the past year has been maintained with extensive vitamin therapy – sodium amytal gr 3 and seconal enseal gr 1.5 every night and often a tablet of Drinamyl every morning...The general condition was one of extreme over-strain with general physical nerve exhaustion.'[15] His medication was what later became known as 'purple hearts' an illegal stimulant that produced a feeling of energy and confidence by the release of noradrenaline into the blood stream and would go on to gain a certain popularity as a 'recreational drug' during the 'swinging sixties' in Britain. This drug did not create energy, it merely used it up and caused insomnia, restlessness, anxiety, irritability, over-stimulation and overconfidence. Some of these side-effects were noticeable in Eden by July 1956 but there is no evidence that he had developed any drug dependence.

Had Eden taken advice at that time to retire temporarily from his leadership role to recuperate, it is almost certain that the Suez crisis would have developed differently. Robert Carr, Eden's Parliamentary Private Secretary said, 'I find it difficult to accept the judgement that Anthony's health did not have a decisive influence at least on the conduct of his policy...I find it very hard to believe that he would have made such obvious miscalculations in [the execution of his policy] both in the political and the military spheres.'[16] It was well attested by a number of doctors that 'the Suez Canal debacle ... was significantly contributed to by the disastrous and tragic consequences of [Eden's] bile duct injury'. His reputation as a 'cool head' in a crisis had been well earned from his deliberate and careful contribution to Chamberlain's appeasement strategy in 1938 to the stability he offered to Churchill's decision-making during the Second World War but his performance over Suez can hardly be seen in the same light. Professor David Dutton, speaking on BBC Radio 4 in 1998 said 'it is difficult to understand why Eden believed that he would get away with the Franco/Israeli plan and conceal it from the United States, unless you believe that his judgement was not what it was at its peak.' Dutton concluded that Eden was probably seriously ill by the beginning of October, weak and tired and desperately in need of a rest and probably on the verge of a nervous breakdown. We cannot know the exact dosage of amphetamines Eden was taking in October, but it could have affected his judgement and decisions, making him more changeable and unpredictable from one day to another, depending on whether he was under greater influence of their stimulant or their sedative actions.

This also begs the question as to why calmer heads in the British government had not intervened more decisively to try and force a change of strategy. The answer is probably that few knew more than the barest outlines of what was going on. Rumour and counter-rumour would have been rife in such a crisis. By the time the full extent of Eden's plan was emerging, few would have wanted to resign or stand up and make protest. The traditional position was to support the nation during conflict and the popular mood was one of enthusiastic support for action against the demonised Nasser.

In Tel Aviv, nerves were jangling. A British official in the Tel Aviv Embassy got a call from the Deputy Head of the Israeli Foreign Office asking what had happened to the ultimatum. With Canberra bombers warming up on the runways in Malta, obviously, Tel Aviv had not received a copy. At this point, tragedy risked turning into farce. Having received the ultimatum, the Israeli embassy in London had to translate it into Hebrew before it could be coded. Once this was done and the coded message sent to Jerusalem, it had to be decoded and taken by road through dense fog to Tel Aviv. Just in time the reply came back to London accepting the ultimatum.

Meanwhile, two and a half hours before the ultimatum expired, the French destroyer *Kersaint* fired on an Egyptian frigate, *Ibrahim al-Awwal*, which was trying, unsuccessfully, to shell the Haifa oil refinery. When the Egyptian ship tried to flee it was chased by two Israeli destroyers and several French Mystères jets. It was eventually boarded and towed into Haifa, where it was declared a prize of war and recommissioned in the Israeli navy.[17] The French were already seen to be engaging on the side of the Israelis hours before the ultimatum expired.

The Egyptian Government was asked to agree to Anglo-French forces moving temporarily into the key positions of Port Said, Ismailia, and Suez. Failure to accept the ultimatum would entail the intervention of British and French forces 'in whatever strength may be necessary to secure compliance.'[18] Egypt lost whichever way it turned. On the one hand, the ultimatum called upon Egypt to surrender the Canal and a very large part of its territory and on the other hand, Israel is allowed to keep the territory which it had occupied in the Sinai Peninsula.

Eisenhower's administration was surprised and disappointed with this call having been deceived so egregiously by its allies. The President was livid and called it a double-cross. When he urged Eden to show restraint, the British Prime Minister disingenuously replied by insisting that his main concern was to prevent Israel from attacking Jordan and he had sent a message to Ben-Gurion to that effect. He went on to say that the British government felt itself under no obligation to come to the aid of Egypt who had 'to a very large extent brought this [Israeli] attack on herself by insisting that the state of war persists, by defying the Security Council and by declaring her intention to marshal the Arab States for the destruction of Israel.' Eisenhower told Dulles 'we should let [Britain] stew in their own juice for a while.'[19]

In Cairo, news of the ultimatum was received with 'astonishment bordering on disbelief'.[20] The British embassy was making a bonfire of documents when the Ambassador was called in to see Nasser who could not believe that this was a serious ultimatum and took it for a bluff. Britain, he thought, would never risk alienating itself from the Arab world by conniving so openly with Israel. He firmly rejected the ultimatum. In blacked-out Tel Aviv and Jerusalem, the people were taking precautions against an enemy attack in a somewhat desultory fashion but the government was starting to get nervous about its forces in Sinai who would face massive aerial bombardment the next day unless Britain stepped up to the plate and sent in its bombers to crush the Egyptian Air Force as had been agreed at Sèvres. Britain, however, had got cold feet while it waited for an answer to its ultimatum. The British Canberras were stood down for twelve hours during which time Dayan called the British 'bastards' who could not keep to an agreement but assured Ben-Gurion, who wanted to pull Sharon's force back from Mitla that on the contrary they should be reinforced and allowed to go all the way to Suez. This might not be so easy, though. His Central Task Force under Colonel Yehudah Wallach were still held up around Abu Ageila where they met stiff resistance.

The force at the Mitla Pass had been specifically ordered not to enter the Pass which Sharon believed to be undefended. Had they moved in on 30 October they would indeed have found it free of Egyptian forces but overnight, the Egyptian command had deployed the 5th and 6th Infantry Battalions of the 2nd Egyptian Infantry Brigade to Jebel Heitan while other units had occupied the area around the Parker Memorial despite coming under Israeli air arrack. Upon getting intelligence about the Israeli forces at Mitla, the Egyptians were unable to see the logic of them being out in the open and 'occupying an empty position'. They decided that it was some sort of crude diversionary tactic to draw attention from a probable main attack elsewhere, but they were not about to take any chances.

The Israeli purpose was simply to create a pretext for the British and French to issue their ultimatum but Sharon and Eitan, ignorant of the political subterfuge, challenged the logic of their troops trying to defend a position in the open desert vulnerable to Egyptian air attack. Sharon's next move was described by Professor Ian S. Lustick as a willingness to sacrifice the lives of his soldiers for personal glory. To many of his men, however, Sharon was an heroic figure, One young sergeant of the Nahal Brigade remembers 'a fabled commander leading a convoy of paratroopers, always going forward, [as he] stood at the Paran Pass waving each vehicle through.'[21] Seriously under-armed Sharon's 3,000 men would be badly mauled if they had to face an Egyptian armoured brigade and there were no reinforcements within 100 miles. Rehavam Ze'evi, the chief of the Southern Command, equally unaware that they were mere pawns in the great game, agreed to Sharon sending up a reconnaissance patrol to assess the situation at Mitla but warned Sharon, 'just don't get involved in a battle.'[22] Sharon's idea of a reconnaissance unit was a full combat team of two infantry companies with half-tracks, three tanks and a troop of heavy mortars under the command of the future Israeli Chief of Staff, Mordechai Gur.

Overnight, the Egyptian infantry had positioned themselves on the defiles of the Mitla Pass occupying rifle pits dug along the tops of ridges and caves cut into the steep walls on either side. These forces had been harassed by Israeli jets as they moved up so their position should have been known to Sharon. Elsewhere the 1st and 2nd Armoured Brigade with 200 T-34 tanks and SU-100 self-propelled guns were sent up to defend the main central route through Sinai and be in position to move to either Mitla or to intercept Israeli reinforcements if they appeared. An infantry brigade was sent to Bir Rod Salim.

As the Israeli reconnaissance patrol entered the pass they came under heavy fire. Their fuel truck went up in flames and the ammunition truck was hit also. Supporting heavy mortars were knocked out of action along with their half-tracks, a tank, a jeep, and an ambulance. Gur's force took cover where they could but became split up and found communication difficult. For seven hours they were under fire from the Egyptian AMX-13 tanks with Vampires and MiGs strafing their positions. They got some relief when Israeli jets intervened but were unable to extricate themselves. They desperately needed reinforcements to lay down covering fire so that they could scale the steep sides and trap Egyptians against the north wall. Lieutenant-Colonel Aharon Davidi managed to extricate himself and a small unit from the pass and find a position from which he could see into the battle area. He called for a volunteer to drive an open jeep through the pass so that the Egyptian firing positions could be pinpointed. Kan Dror stepped forward and was told to drive fast so that all the Egyptian guns would open up at the same time and expose themselves. It was clearly a suicide mission.

As night fell the Israeli forces broke out of their trap and, in hand-to-hand fighting, drove the Egyptians, much less effective than during daylight, out of their positions inflicting heavy casualties on their erstwhile tormentors. Notwithstanding the dire circumstances they had found themselves in, at the end of the day, the Israelis had taken the pass at a cost of 38 killed, and 120 wounded. On the other side, around 200 Egyptian soldiers were killed. Dayan and Sharon bitterly disputed responsibility for the catastrophe. Sending forces into action, forces that had been trained to use initiative and make decisions on the spot, without giving them the sort of information they needed to do that effectively was a high price to pay for the skulduggery hatched up at Sèvres.

A diplomatic storm that had been brewing for days suddenly blew up into a hurricane. British, French and Israeli diplomats were working overtime both within their own countries and on the wider international stage to assert that there was no collusion but that was not going to be sustainable. The British House of Commons forced an admission out of the Foreign Secretary that Britain had 'never claimed that we have acted in agreement with the United States' although they had been 'in close touch with [their] government throughout this controversy.'[23] This would certainly have come as news to Dulles. It was 'quite wrong to state that Israel was incited to this action by Her Majesty's Government', Selwyn Lloyd declared in the House of Commons, 'there was no prior agreement between us about it.' which was technically correct since it had been the French who instigated it but was misleading at best.[24] The Israeli attack in Sinai might be explained by security concerns and the ultimatum might just pass off as a reaction to the Israeli action. The bombing of Egyptian airfields was only just credible as a last-minute operation but when the invasion force turned up off the coast of Egypt nobody would doubt that it was at the sharp end of many weeks or months of preparation. By that time, Eden, more so than Mollet whose relationship with the U.S. was less critical, was probably hoping that Nasser would be long gone, the Suez Canal back under international management and the world's attention moved on to some other crisis elsewhere.

Eden wrote to Eisenhower saying that 'we would not wish to support or even condone the action of Israel.' The President felt that Britain and

France were presenting him with a *fait accompli* and expected that he would have no choice but play along but he would not do that. 'I've just never seen great powers make such a complete mess and botch of things,' Eisenhower said. Serious discussions now took place in Washington about how to respond. A furious Eisenhower saw that Britain would be likely to lose access to the Suez Canal for its shipping, especially its oil tankers, when its whole escapade blew up in its face as it must surely do. He ordered that U.S. fleet tankers should be put on standby to assist with the extra tonnage that Britain would need if it had to bring oil from the Middle East by Cape Horn and from Venezuela. This help would be paid for in sterling which would put a squeeze of Britain's balance of payments and cause much economic pain in the country. The President's response, nevertheless, was rather calmer than that of the State Department who were 'whipping themselves into an anti-British frenzy'.[25] It was hard to say at this point which side the U.S. would take.

Eisenhower now came under sustained attack from his presidential opponent, Adlai Stevenson. 'What happened to Eisenhower's earlier assertion that the Suez crisis was over?,' he asked. The questions mounted up. If the President acted against Israel, his Jewish vote in at least four states would disappear but how were they going to be stopped? What would Britain and France do and how would the Soviet Union respond? Would the U.S. be dragged into a shooting war on the eve of an election? That seemed to be a distinct possibility with prevarication seemingly not an option and time running out to prevent a catastrophe.

At 16:00 New York time, the U.S. tried to distance itself from Britain and France and shore up its prestige in the Arab world by bringing to the U.N. resolution S/3710 which stated;

> Noting that the armed forces of Israel have penetrated deeply into Egyptian territory in violation of' the armistice agreement between Egypt and Israel, expressing its grave concern at this violation of the armistice agreement,
> 1. Calls upon Israel immediately to withdraw its armed forces behind the established armistice lines;
> 2. Calls upon all Members
>   a. to refrain from the use of force or threat of force in the area in any manner inconsistent with the Purposes of the United Nations;
>   b. to assist the United Nations in ensuring the integrity of the armistice agreements;
>   c. to refrain from giving any military, economic or financial assistance to Israel so long as it has not complied with this resolution;

Inevitably, Britain and France did not support it. It was the first time that Britain had used its U.N. veto and it was the first time that Britain and the U.S. had been on opposite sides of a U.N. vote. Something that the U.S. Ambassador in London, Winthrop Adrich, called a 'tragic thing.'[26] This resolution was followed by another presented by the Soviet Union, S/3713 which differed from S/3710 in two respects. It called on 'all the parties concerned immediately to cease fire' and omitted clause 2(c). This again was vetoed by Britain and France.

The U.S. State Department sent out urgent calls to 'use every diplomatic and intelligence source' to find out what, if any, agreement existed between Britain, France and Israel covering the recent moves. Dulles called it 'a great tragedy' affecting U.S. relations with France and England neutralising any opportunities which had so recently been presented in Eastern Europe. Eisenhower instructed his U.N. ambassador to block Anglo-French military action with every means at his disposal and he sent an urgent personal message to Eden and Mollet urging them to refrain from employing armed force. Privately, he was furious not only with his intelligence agencies who had failed to warn him that Britain, France and Israel had cooked up their invasion plans without him getting wind of them but also with Eden for what he saw as a devastating betrayal of friendship right at a critical moment of his re-election campaign.

Eden had failed catastrophically to strike quickly and decisively against Nasser which had really been the only strategy that had any chance of success. In reality it had never been an option at all given the complexities and lack of preparedness, but he now failed completely to accept that his position was becoming untenable because world opinion had been given time to regiment against Britain and France and other powers were circling to take advantage of his stubborn refusal to reconsider it. The rage against Nasser that had so blinded Eden's judgement and his inability to cast off the 'great power' syndrome were taking him into a diplomatic cul de sac at the end of which lay a military disaster from which Britain would never recover.

The U.S. Sixth Fleet was doing its bit also by trying to slow down the progress of the Anglo-French invasion fleet. Dulles was determined to make it clear that the U.S. fleet was close by and poised to intervene if ordered to do so. The U.S. had, since its Declaration of Independence, claimed a fundamental maritime right when at war to stop and search any ship, belligerent or neutral. It may have been a stretch to apply it now but clearly the presence of the Sixth Fleet in the vicinity was a grave concern for the task force. The British ships sailing under blackout at night were suddenly and frequently illuminated by the powerful searchlights of U.S. aircraft flying from carriers of the Sixth Fleet that was sailing on a parallel course and generally getting in the way. The U.S. submarine *Hardhead* was detected by a British destroyer and forced to surface. It was not clear to the British commander whose side the Americans were actually on. He wasn't the only one to ask that question. Admiral Burke signalled to Admiral Charles Randall Brown, commander of the Sixth Fleet to 'prepare for imminent hostilities.' Brown infuriated the British task force commander, Vice-Admiral Richmond, by sailing the USS *Coral Sea* right through the middle of the task force. Somewhat puzzled by his orders, Richmond asked Burke whose side he was supposed to be on. Burke ignored the question and told him to 'take no guff from anybody'.[27] Brown was forced to issue a statement categorically denying reports that 'units of the Sixth Fleet were deliberately manoeuvred in any fashion to embarrass British and French units'.[28]

Meanwhile in Malta the British 6th Battalion began loading their Centurion tanks on landing ships that had already received the 40th and 42nd Commandos with their tracked amphibians. At the same time, Eisenhower got a message from Nasser asking for military support against a British-French invasion. Ambassador Raymond Hare in Cairo was instructed to reply that it was not possible for the U.S. to intervene against its allies. Nasser knew this well enough but he still took the refusal badly and had to settle for having sent a gentle hint to the U.S. that if they could not step up then others might.

The Israeli attack had also impacted negotiations that had been going on for some weeks over an IMF loan that Tel Aviv had requested. It had been due for discussion on 31 October, but the day before, the Acting Managing Director of the IMF, Merle Cochran, pulled the Israeli request from the agenda while it waited to see what effects the Israeli action was having on its economy. This inflationary pressure on Israel due to its military build-up would, however, in reality be much less than the IMF feared because much of it was financed by France and at this stage, the extent of Franco-Israeli collusion in the attack was not widely known.[29] France, who was facing a $700 million deficit in its balance of payments due to the war in Algeria, had previously waved its own begging bowl. On 17 October it had asked for a standby arrangement for $130 million which was quickly approved.

Britain's relations with the IMF, however, would be of a wholly different character. Sterling had come under immediate selling pressure in the wake of the nationalization of the Canal on 26 July. The sale of the Trinidad Oil Company to an American firm had netted $177 million for the government but more was required to protect the pound and maintain its parity with the U.S. dollar. Macmillan looked to the U.S. to either temporarily waive the interest due on the $3.75 billion of British debt from the lend-lease credits advanced during the Second World War, or they could provide new loans through the Export-Import Bank. Failing that a loan from the IMF would be needed but that would be a last resort, it was the U.S. that held the key. A meeting with Dulles and Eisenhower at the end of September seemed to reassure Macmillan that U.S. financial support would be forthcoming although no explicit promises had been made. With this in mind the British government continued selling off its dollar reserves to maintain the $2.80 exchange rate with the U.S. dollar but after the Israeli attack of 29 October, an attack of a different kind was launched on sterling which started to drain its reserves at an alarming rate. Now a loan from the IMF seemed much less certain since the IMF's Articles of Agreement prohibited it lending finance against the sort of 'large and unsustained' outflow of capital which Britain now faced.

Eden's commitment to oppose Nasser in circumstances where victory was highly uncertain had shifted market sentiment against sterling despite Britain's strong trading position and balance of payment surpluses. There followed what was an almost pure speculative attack on a stable currency against a backdrop of reasonably sound economic policies. Chancellor of the Exchequer, Macmillan could have chosen to devalue the pound or allowed it to float and find a new level but the Governor of the Bank of England declared that 'we should regard a further devaluation of sterling [after the devaluation of 1949] as a disaster [that would lead to currency instability and severe inflation] and consequently to be fought with every weapon at our disposal.'[30] All through October, the Bank of England continued to sell off its dollar reserves.

Eisenhower was absolutely not willing to intervene against either Britain or France militarily over the Suez crisis but now that Britain was essentially at the mercy of the U.S. financially it would open up other possibilities for aggressive actions to force Britain to radically change its policy in Egypt.

Chapter Eight

31 OCTOBER

It is the beginning of the collapse of the Soviet Empire [and] the idea is out that we can be dragged along at the heels of Britain and France in policies that are obsolete. This is a declaration of independence for the first time that they cannot count on us.
　　　　　　　　　　John Foster Dulles to Vice President Richard Nixon[1]

Hungary
On the night of 30/31 October, Khruschev could not sleep claiming that Hungary was 'like a nail in my head.' He was racked with indecision knowing that his rivals for power in the Politburo would not hesitate for one second to pounce if he made a false move. The late hours of Tuesday and early hours of Wednesday were spent in talks with Liu Shao-chi in Lenin's old dacha at Volynoskoye but they could not find a definitive solution to the problem of Hungary. By early light he was already back in his office and what he found quickly convinced him of what he had to do. The first thing he saw was a gloomy report from Mikoyan with a plea to send Konyev to Budapest without delay. Serov poured fuel on the fire with his colourful and lurid accounts of atrocities against the forces of law and order. Reports from Poland spoke of 300,000 people in an pro-Hungary rally in Warsaw. There were marches in Romania in support of the Hungarian rebels. A KGB report from Czechoslovakia told of student demonstrations, inspired by events in Hungary, and 'a growing hostility and mistrust of the Soviet Union'.[2] Even inside the Soviet Union itself, at the Moscow State University, there were the first murmurings of unrest.

At a reception in Moscow on the previous evening, U.S. Ambassador Bohlen had taken Molotov aside for a private conversation and had made remarks that seemed to convince Molotov that the U.S. would definitely not interfere in Hungary.[3] This may have precipitated what happened next. Khrushchev called up a session of the Council of Ministers. His first delivery to the assembled leaders at around 10:00hrs included that rarity in a Politburo debate: an admission that he had been wrong the day before to agree to a withdrawal of troops from Hungary. 'If we withdrew from Hungary,' he said 'it would encourage the American, English, and French imperialists. They would attribute it to our weakness and would swing into attack...Besides Egypt, we would give them Hungary as well.'[4]

It signalled a debate that swung between 'crushing the mutiny' or 'getting out of Hungary altogether.' Khruschev later claimed that they 'changed [their] minds back and forth'.[5] He was not slow to realise that his whole political future was in the balance. Not the least of Soviet worries was if the U.S. intervened in Egypt to help their allies to unseat Nasser at the same time as the Soviets were being hounded out of Hungary it would be a critical blow to Soviet prestige and make them look weak at a time when they were desperate to extend their influence in many parts of the world. If the capitalists took the view that the Soviets were 'weak or stupid' many feared that they would end up camping on the Soviet border. When the interventionist views of Zhukov and Molotov started to hold sway, there was really no other choice for him. There was no government worthy of the name in Budapest with which they could negotiate, he said. This initiated a discussion of who to install in place of Nagy who was now seen as someone who had either abandoned his communist principles or had simply lost control of events. Two runners led the field: Kádár, whom most of the Soviet Supreme Council 'could not stomach' and Ferenc Münnich, a long-standing KGB agent and a man who could be relied upon to do Moscow's bidding absolutely. Both remained options with the final decision held over. Rákosi offered his services but Khruschev, ever the peasant and ever ready with an earthy riposte, told him that he could go back to Budapest if he wanted but if he did the people would 'string him up.'[6]

It was dawning on the Soviet leaders that unity within the Hungarian Government was largely absent which inevitably made it easier for Moscow to exploit the divisions and allowed them to develop a strong interventionist strategy to confront the rebellion. It had been a shock for them, however, to realise quite how ineffective their forces had been up to this point. They would not make the mistake of underestimating the strength of resistance again and their next move would be made with overwhelming superior forces and heavy weaponry to put an end to the insurrection quickly and decisively. Soldiers from the Asian regions, far to the east of Moscow would be brought in. Men who had no concept of the situation into which they were being drawn and who, unlike the Soviet troops that had been stationed in Hungary and who failed to act with sufficient ruthlessness, could be relied upon to act without qualms, obey orders to the letter and crush the rebels with no quarter given.

Konyev was called in for his assessment of how long it would take to crush the revolution given all necessary resources. He thought about three days. There and then the decision was made. The Soviets would return to Budapest and impose their will ruthlessly, efficiently and without mercy but first Khruschev would have to embark on a lightning tour of his allies to explain his decision. His first stop was Moscow airport where he was just in time to see Liu Shao-chi before he boarded his flight home. The Chinese delegate was pleased to say that Moa had come to the same conclusion during the night and whilst not wishing to influence the Soviet decision Liu Shao-chi was authorised to fully endorsed it if asked for his approval.

The Chinese had actually published a statement to that effect but had clouded the issue by including a criticism of Soviet 'great-power chauvinism,' which 'seriously harms the solidarity and common affairs of socialist countries.' Whilst he had little choice but support the Soviet decision since he was not yet strong enough for open confrontation with Moscow, Mao was taking advantage of the situation to extend his influence in the largest possible measure over the European countries in the Soviet orbit. This was interpreted in the Hungarian press as "China stands by us." Articles containing this interpretation appeared in *Népszava* (People's Word) on 2 November which said, 'An important Chinese Government statement on the correctness of the Hungarian and Polish people's demands', and in *Új Magyarország* (New Hungary) which said 'China views the Soviet armed forces' intervention in the Hungarian revolution as imperialist aggression'.[7]

Keen observers wondered why Soviet units were moving west out of the city towards Austria rather than heading home to the Soviet Union. Nevertheless, the U.S. delegation cabled Washington to say that "In a dramatic overnight change, it became virtually certain in Budapest this morning that this Hungarian Revolution is a fact of history,'[8] This may well have been wishful thinking or another dismal example of failed U.S. intelligence because Soviet tanks were lining up on the Hungarian border and the Hungarian government was in disarray. Mikoyan and Suslov certainly knew what was coming and, with no further role to play inside the country, took their leave as they had come, driven to the airport in an armoured car convoy. Nagy had been invigorated after his meeting with Mikoyan earlier in the day. 'The tanks are leaving,' he told Kopácsi, 'we will have elections in which all democratic parties will take part.' Mikoyan was in tears as he embraced Nagy saying, 'save what can be saved.'[9]

While RFE continued to encourage the insurgents to keep fighting and disregard anything that Nagy said about anything, the Prime Minister took to the airwaves to give his side of the argument. In an effort to take some of the sting out of accusations against him he denied that it was he who had signed the request for Soviet troops in the first place. Referring to himself as a champion of Hungarian sovereignty, freedom and independence, he told his audience that he would take Hungary out of the Warsaw Treaty and pleaded for the people to have patience with him to meet their other aspirations. Crucially, however, he said nothing about how the criminal acts perpetrated by both sides of the conflict over previous days, and indeed of the previous decade, would be addressed. It was a significant demand of the revolution that ÁVH torturers and murderers be brought to justice but Nagy knew just how impossible that was and how it would mire the country in recriminations for years if he started down that road. It was not unlike the dilemma faced by the victorious allies after the Second World War when dealing with Nazi war criminals. There had to be a line drawn at some point and Nagy wanted it drawn right at the start. However pragmatic his approach to this issue he was never going to be popular for pursuing it.

Now that the revolutionaries had power through possession of weapons and new status as a result of Nagy's acceptance of their validity, they were determined to hold the government to account. There would be no backing down from their commitment to reform. Even government soldiers who had fought for the revolution were berated for earlier acts of suppression against the people. One of the most belligerent critics of the government was Dudás, riding on a wave of celebrity in the western press for his flamboyant persona which lent itself perfectly to the glamorous spectacle of revolution in contrasted to the grim reality. He came into Nagy's office surrounded by armed thugs but had little to offer seeming only to be revelling in being there at all. His claims to represent all the armed groups and demands to be given control of law and order in the city were, naturally, ignored. By now Nagy was almost at the end of his tether and couldn't get Dudás out of his office quick enough which inevitably earned a scathing attack on him in Dudás' daily rag. In the streets of Budapest there was a mood of celebration which was destined to be very short-lived.

It is a further sign of how poorly U.S. intelligence was assessing the Hungarian Uprising when the CIA Director Allen Dulles reported to Eisenhower that he believed the Soviets were sticking to their word and pulling out and he had never been one to take the word of the Kremlin at face value. The President was less willing to accept Moscow's assurances, however. He had a long history of working with the Soviets all through the war when he had seen Soviet soldiers fighting first alongside the Nazis and then, by force of Hitler's treachery, in a desperate existential struggle against them. He was not prepared to bet on which way they would go this time.[10]

Suez

Neither was Eisenhower at all sure what was happening in Egypt. He was anxious to reassure Nasser that the U.S. had no foreknowledge of the Israeli attack and wanted the Egyptians to do everything in their power to 'localise the fighting and end the conflict.'[11] Secretary Dulles thought about getting the U.S. Sixth Fleet to obstruct the Anglo-French armada that was moving south but there were a number of ways that could play out and none of them were particularly desirable. The presence of the U.S. ships, *Chilton*, *Thuban* and *Fort Snelling*, evacuating over 1,800 civilians of twenty-nine different nationalities through Alexandria Harbour, however, would give the British pause for thought when it came to bombing it.

As night fell on 31 October, Nasser believed that the widespread condemnation of Israel would force it to withdraw from Sinai and deter Britain and France from going through with their attack. He planned to use the night to re-deploy his ground forces and prime his air force to drive the Israelis back but never got the time. The Anglo-French air offensive began at dusk, forty-eight hours after the Israeli drop at Mitla. Two hundred English Electric Canberras, de Haviland Venoms and Vickers Valiants with forty American-built Republic F-84F Thunderstreaks of the French Air Force operating out of Malta and Cyrus as well as from the British aircraft carriers *Albion*, *Bulwark* and *Eagle* took off and headed for Egyptian airfields in the Nile Delta and in the Canal Zone at Kabrit and Abu Sueir. The bombers would crater the runways and leave the aircraft stranded on the ground after which jet fighters would follow behind to destroy them with strafing and rocket attacks.

Seven Canberras from Cyprus and eight Valiants from Malta were en route to bomb Ilyushin Il-28 Beagles at Cairo West airport but while the bombers were only ten minutes from their target, however, Eden suddenly got word that over a thousand U.S. nationals were being evacuated along a road that was perilously close to the airport. Unable to recall the bombers, he was at least able to get Keightley to divert aircraft from that target and strike at Al-Maza airfield instead where MiG-15, Meteor, C-46, C-47, and Il-14 aircraft were stationed.[12] Unfortunately, given only minutes notice of the change of target and the city of Cairo under a blackout, the bombers failed to accurately establish new attack coordinates and hit the nearby Cairo International Airport instead. While damage to runways was extensive, many Egyptian aircraft avoided destruction. Under cover of darkness, twenty Ilyushins and twenty MIGs, flown by Russians and Czech pilots had been flown to Syrian and Saudi Arabian airfields escorted by a further twenty Egyptian MIGs. Another fourteen Ilyushins escaped to Luxor in the far south, thirteen of which would be destroyed by French F84 Thunderstreak fighters fitted with long-range fuel tanks operating out of Lydda in Israel four days later. The next morning, low-level daylight raids were launched from aircraft carriers and bases in Cyprus. Royal Navy Sea Hawks and Sea Venoms strafed airfields around Cairo at dawn while R.A.F. Hunters and Venoms did the same to the Canal airfields with no Egyptian aircraft in sight. In all, 260 Egyptian aircraft would be destroyed during the first thirty-six hours mostly by ground attack aircraft using machine guns and rockets but high-level bombing against small military targets had been particularly disappointing. Air attacks continued on Egyptian military installations, rail and road traffic in an effort to break the morale of the defenders and possibly bring Nasser down without having to execute the landings.

When Eisenhower saw the U-2 reconnaissance photographs of the bombed airfield he asked, 'What does Anthony [Eden] think he is doing? Why is he doing this to me?'[13] That night a total of four airfields were bombed and a further nine were hit at dawn. Nothing in the ultimatum had hinted at actual bombing and the fear now was that this significant escalation would inflame Arab opinion across the whole region and risk a wider war. Nasser, watching from the rooftop of his house, was now in no doubt that the ultimatum had been serious. At midnight, in a coordinated attack, French and Israeli warships pounded the Egyptian army base at Rafah at the southern end of the Gaza Strip. At around the time of the bombing, Eisenhower assured the American people in a speech that he had no foreknowledge of the action and condemned it as an error saying it was not 'a wise or proper instrument for the settlement of international disputes.'

Nasser ordered an immediate withdrawal of forces from Sinai. Believing the Egyptian forces to be close to collapse there, Beaufre and French political leaders urged immediate action. Beaufre had been working on Plan Omlette (later Simplex) which called for three simultaneous air assaults on key facilities in Port Said. The British 16th Paratroop Brigade would make a battalion sized drop on Gamil Airfield to the west of Port Said while Royal Marines, travelling by helicopter, would occupy bridges spanning Junction Canal at Raswa, after which additional Canal Zone drops would secure Anglo-French control of Suez.[14] French parachutists, also in battalion strength, would land south of the city and capture the two key bridges over the Junction Canal and on the east side of the Canal to secure the town of Port Fuad. Further operations included an additional airdrop at El Qantara and Ismailia but Stockwell was reluctant to give the order to start Omlette until he had intelligence about the strength of Egyptian forces in the drop zone. Keightley thought the plan entailed considerable risk and rejected this and a flurry of other French initiatives such as a request for immediate airborne raids or using warships to ferry marines to Egypt more quickly. Beaufre then came up with Operation Telescope which called for airborne drops on 5 November followed by landings on the following day. This new plan Telescope was accepted by Stockwell but he still refused to implement it. Eden was still trying to delay the attack hoping perhaps that the bombing campaign would bring Nasser down without the need for landings.

On 31 October, Eisenhower made a brief speech in which he tried to balance U.S. commitment to its allies with assurances to non-aligned nations, which he hoped to protect from communist influence, that the U.S. did not condone their actions. This speech was the first time that a U.S. President had made the case for a uniquely American mission to take responsibility for maintaining law and order in the region independently of other powers.[15] A few months later, Eisenhower echoing his 31 October speech, would go on to say that it was U.S. policy to 'assist any nation or group of nations in the general area of the Middle East with economic or military aid that may be threatened by any form of Communist aggression.'

Chapter Nine

1 NOVEMBER

'My conviction was that the Western world had got into a lot of difficulties by selecting the wrong issues about which to be tough. To choose a situation in which Nasser had legal and sovereign rights and in which world opinion was on his side was not, in my opinion, a good one on which to make a stand.'

President Dwight D. Eisenhower

Hungary
Anastas Mikoyan arrived back in Moscow from Budapest late on the evening of 31 October to be told that all his efforts over the past week had been in vain and that a decision had been made for a full invasion of Hungary. It was, he said, a terrible misjudgement that would plunge the world into a new more dangerous phase of the cold war but the hardliners in the Politburo had never had much time for Mikoyan and his mealy-mouthed philosophies. He would become marginalised from now on and maybe Khruschev, if he was not careful, would see his status and reputation dented too which would not be a particularly unwelcome development in the eyes of Molotov and Kaganovich. In the early hours, Mikoyan phoned Khruschev and woke him from his sleep to argue his case for restraint but Khruschev trying to catch up on lost sleep before his planned diplomatic initiative was in no mood to listen and cut him off.

Konyev flew into Szolnok to take personal charge of Operation Whirlwind, as the invasion was called. He called a meeting of his senior officers and conducted an investigation, in his inimitably ferocious fashion, into what had gone wrong in the first Budapest intervention. Whatever mistakes had been made would not be repeated. Laschenko told him that the Soviet forces had found themselves in wholly unusual circumstances. They had not been trained for street fighting. Air strikes, he said, would not have been effective since there were no big centres of resistance only relatively small pockets widely scattered and air attack would have caused much collateral damage to occupied buildings outside the combat zone. Konyev assured Laschenko that this time they would act without mercy.

The city's defences were believed to consist of around 50,000 men controlling fifty anti-aircraft batteries and about 100 tanks. Konyev had boasted to his political masters that three days would be enough to deal with that, but Laschenko said that he still did not have sufficient forces to mop up all the resistance in such a short time. Konyev authorised reinforcements to be brought up. Laschenko then went back to Tököl to make detailed plans. The 2nd Mechanised Guard Division would take the Danube bridges, secure the Parliament building, the Ministry of Defence and occupy the north-east and central areas of the city. The 33rd Mechanised Guard Division would take the telephone exchange, the Corvin Cinema stronghold, the Csepel Steel Works and occupy the south-east areas securing the munitions factory and army barracks in the sector. Special forces, each one supported by ten tanks and 150 paratroops along with KGB officers were primed to capture the main rebel leaders and members of the government. Meanwhile, the families of more than 600 Soviet officials who lived in Hungary were hurriedly evacuated at first by road and rail to Czechoslovakia but the last ones to leave were flown out.

At around the same time the formidable Soviet 31st Tank Division was mobilised and moved up to Beregovo on the Hungarian border and the 35th Mechanised Guards Division was loaded up onto railway wagons at Reni in the Soviet Union and Gelati in Romania and made ready to move in the direction of Timisoara and Békéscsaba while the 1,000-strong 108th Parachute Guards Regiment boarded trains in Kaunus in Lithuania. Roads all along the Romanian-Hungarian border and all through Slovakia were full of Soviet heavy armoured units waiting to cross over. On the other side, the historian and researcher Alexandr Kirov claims that 3,000 soldiers of the Hungarian Veszprém garrison went over to the rebels.

In Budapest the morning streets were eerily quiet. Long queues had formed outside bakeries and a few flower sellers were back out. Workers drifted back to the factories. The strikes were petering out without actually formally ending. Only the drone of the occasional aircraft impinged on the quietude. Nagy was woken on the morning of 1 November with startling reports of large number of Soviet troops at Miskolc and moving south across the Tisza river crossing on two hastily erected pontoon bridges. Ferihegy airport was under Soviet occupation and the only one left under Hungarian control was at Budaörs where about 100 Mig fighters were stationed and two passenger aircraft were on standby to get him out of the country if need be. Király, who had been appointed Budapest City Commander, told him candidly that there was no possibility of organising an effective defence of the capital if the Soviets attacked in force. Maléter told Nagy that he expected the Soviets to exact revenge for their humiliation and would do it regardless of the cost in public opinion in the rest of the world. Hungary would be a lesson to other Soviet satellites about the cost of revolt.

With impressive irony, the Soviet government issued a statement on this day condemning aggression in Egypt and appealing to the U.N. Security Council to take immediate action to stop it. *Pravda* then came out carrying a declaration promising greater equality in relations between the U.S.S.R. and its East European satellites saying 'the Soviet Government is prepared to enter into the appropriate negotiations with the government of the Hungarian People's Republic and other members of the Warsaw Treaty on the question of the presence of Soviet troops on the territory of Hungary.' Nagy took this as a positive sign and somehow continued to view the situation optimistically. He refused to believe that a full attack was being mounted. After all he had a deal with Moscow that Hungary would be given time to reach an acceptable solution to the troubles. After living in the Soviet Union for so many years and having to deal with them at the highest level when he had returned to Budapest it beggars belief that he still trusted them to keep their word even when his calls to the Kremlin were not put through to any of the leaders. Khruschev was not there. He was on his way to Brest on the Polish border. Eventually Nagy called in Ambassador Andropov who claimed that he had no information about Soviet troop movements but he would make inquiries.

Nagy placed a news blackout on Soviet troop movements knowing full well what panic that would cause on the streets and urged Maléter to do all he could to use his reputation to calm the armed groups and prevent them from reacting to rumours that were bound to circulate. Everything had to be done to try and get the striking workers back into the factories, especially the most militant group at Csepel. The Soviets must not be given any excuse around which they could fabricate a justification for intervention. People were out on the streets clearing away the rubble and trying to get back to some sort of normality. Western journalists were drifting away from Budapest. As Sefton Delmer reported 'This is not news anymore.' There were much more interesting things happening in Egypt.

Nagy spoke to the people in Kossuth Square in the early afternoon. He reiterated his assertion that it had not been he who had requested the Soviet forces come in on 24 October and called again for their complete withdrawal for Hungary. Always feeling himself to be a true man of the people, he afterwards mingled with the crowd and spoke to many trying to reassure them. Michael Korda was there and saw a 'short, plump man, with the graceful walk wearing a neat bourgeois suit and highly polished shoes, and his eyes bulging slightly behind his pince-nez, his face aglow with the applause that had greeted [his speech]'.[1]

Khruschev arrived in Brest and met the Polish leader Gomułka to explain why he was ordering Soviet forces to go back into Hungary and crush the rebellion once and for all. This can't have been comfortable news for Gomułka who had, to some extent, quietly encouraged Nagy in his opposition to Kremlin rule. Poland was the country that was most likely to be destabilised by events in Hungary and it was vital for Khruschev that it should remain calm. Gomułka privately expressed his opposition to Soviet intervention in Hungary but was wise enough to refrain from criticism beyond the Polish parliament. Khruschev settled for that and moved on to Sofia, Prague and Bucharest where he got a more reassuring response. Finally he was joined by Malenkov and they moved on to Yugoslavia where they would hold talks with Marshal Tito. Tito was a worry for the Soviets. His third-path concept of communism was providing other communist states with an ideological sanction for disobedience, and it was threatening a spill-over effect 'contaminating' the Hungarian people and energising the revolt. Tito's relations with Khrushchev had been tense during the previous weeks and whilst Tito was keen to maintain good relations with other Soviet Bloc members, he was equally determined to demonstrate a level of independence and not get pulled back into the Soviet sphere of influence.

Khruschev and Malenkov had got to Yugoslavia by flying through a tremendous thunderstorm in the dark over mountains in a small, twin-engine Ilyushin 14 which had left them a bit weak in the knees and lacking composure. After landing at Pula they had to make a sea trip in a small motor launch over rough seas again in darkness before they arrived at Tito's holiday home on the island of Brioni. For two of the most powerful men in the world at the time it was a particularly uncomfortable way to travel. Fortunately, Tito was the perfect host and raised no objections to Soviet plans for Hungary, even adding his weight to Kádár's candidacy to replace Nagy. For some time it had been a worry in Moscow that Tito's brand of communism was 'infecting' Hungarian intellectuals and encouraging their own ambitions to take a step away from Soviet control. Andropov and Gerő had repeatedly complained about it. Khruschev took this opportunity to urge Tito to send arms to miners in Miskolc who had remained loyal to the Hungarian government during the previous days and to 'try some political action' against Nagy.[2] Tito had shown some sympathy for Nagy on his own Hungarian 'different road to socialism' but much of this had dissipated when things appeared to be going too far too quickly and might have a deleterious effect on his own leadership of Yugoslavia.

Whilst Khruschev was on Brioni, Tito received a telegram from the U.S. State Department. There has been speculation that it was sent to that place at that time because it was intended for Khruschev's eyes also but there is no evidence to support the idea that U.S. Intelligence knew that the Soviet leaders were meeting Tito at that time. The telegram read 'The Government of the United States does not look with favour upon governments unfriendly to the Soviet Union on the borders of the Soviet Union'. It was another clear message that the U.S. was not about to interfere in Hungary.[3]

When Dulles made his daily report to the NSC he called the Hungarian revolution 'a miracle' and one that 'belied all our past views that a popular revolt in the face of modern weapons was an utter impossibility'. He did, however, point out that the rebels lacked a guiding authority. Eisenhower was, as usual, unnerved by Dulles' gung-ho approach. He thought him too optimistic about developments. 'I've had a lot more experience with these fellows', he said 'and you can't count on their doing the rational thing. They are not rational.'[4]

Andropov came back to face the Hungarian Council of Ministers with reassurances that any Soviet troop movements were simply part of a normal operation to ensure that the departing troops were not harassed as they withdrew. He had rather more difficulty explaining why all but one of the Hungarian airports had been surrounded by tanks and occupied by airborne troops. There was more than the usual coolness in Andropov's attitude to Nagy and this, coupled with a noticeable lack of diplomatic courtesy, caused Nagy some discomfort. He made a formal complaint that Andropov would convey to Moscow where it would be ignored but Nagy's threat to pull Hungary out of the Warsaw Pact, despite not having the faintest idea how that might be accomplished, gave the Ambassador rather more pause for thought. Nagy followed this up with a call to the U.N. General Secretary, who already had his hands full with Suez, requesting that the General Assembly put Hungary on its agenda.

Kádár had given only tacit support to Nagy during the day, especially in front of Andropov, and in the early evening, he stepped into a Mercedes car with curtained windows along with Münnich and was driven to the Kerepsi cemetery where they changed into a Soviet Zis limousine which took them to the Soviet Embassy. Andropov told them quite frankly that the Soviets were preparing for a full invasion and Nagy's time would soon be over. Kádár's simple choice was to work with Moscow or go the way of Nagy. With Münnich eagerly waiting in the wings to step in if he refused, Kádár agreed to go to Moscow and fall in with the Soviet plans. A pre-recorded message went out on the radio to announce that, along with Münnich and other leading politicians Kádár had formed a new political party, the Hungarian Socialist Workers Party. 'We cannot remain silent,' he said, 'while our country is driven into the yoke of counter-revolution.' He went on to say that his new party had 'appealed to the Soviet troop command in the interest of our people...to help crush the dark forces of reaction and counter-revolution...and create law and peace.'[5] Later that night Kádár and Münnich went to Tököl Airport where the Soviet Special Corps was stationed. There they were met by Serov and all three left the next morning for Moscow.

Suez

On 1 November the Egyptians sank the 5,000-ton *Akka* and the 1,390-ton *Edgar Bonnet* loaded with cement at Ismalia. The frigate *Abu Kir* was another that went down just north of Suez. These were just three of the many blockships with which the Egyptians closed the Suez Canal to traffic. From now on oil tankers from the Middle East oilfields would have to make the long trip around the Cape of Good Hope but that was not the only impact the war had on oil supplies. The Syrian army had blown up three major pumping stations on the Iraq petroleum line to Tripoli. The inevitable result was a hefty increase in the price of oil on world markets.

The British-French part of the invasion plans was running into predictable difficulties. Right from the start, the French commanders had been exasperated by having to play second fiddle to the British whose idea it hadn't even been in the first place. They were no better pleased now as they came under pressure from the French government to get a move on but found themselves unable to have any influence with Keigthley, whose disdain for them was barely concealed. Having arrived late to the party, the British had taken over the planning and operation. Musketeer was essentially their idea that the French had been obliged to go along with. Intensely frustrated by up to seven revisions of the plan in a dozen weeks, Beaufre now saw the landings at Port Said instead of Alexandria as a huge mistake. The first twelve miles of the road from there to Cairo was an open invitation to saboteurs and interdiction. The plan could, however, be ameliorated by a preliminary assault on El Qantara to cut off Egyptian forces at Ismalia but when he suggested it, Keighley brushed it aside. The French were becoming increasingly frustrated by Britain's apparent delay and were deeply concerned that the delays were putting the whole operation in peril. The British military planners, furthermore, were still some way from finalising the details of the landings. The French were not keen to have their paratroops dropped two days before the Royal Navy turned up with its covering guns and landing force. Keightley had still not been put fully in the picture about the interconnectedness of operations Kadesh, Musketeer and Telescope. According to the public ultimatum, Britain was going in to separate the two combatants, Israel and Egypt and it was still not clear to the task force commanders who their enemy was. Admiral of the Fleet, Lord Mountbatten, wrote to Eden about his 'great unhappiness' at the prospect of military action and begged him to call off the attack on Port Said which would only bring 'misery and worldwide repercussions'. In the U.S. Admiral Burke told Dulles that the British were doomed to failure because they had been given too little time to prepare. He urged Dulles to give more support otherwise the British would be facing a disaster but Dulles would not be moved. He wondered whether Burke's ships might disrupt the British fleet but he had no idea of what might happen if two fleets started interfering with each other's passage. Burke enlightened him and the idea was dropped.

There was little in the rest of Keightley and Stockwell's plan to reassure Beaufre either. Committed to the concept of 'overwhelming force' carried over from the Second World War, the British had amassed a large force of men and machines which were to be transported from bases in Malta and Cyprus over the course of five or six days during which international opposition would be given time to escalate. Fear of failure and overestimation of Egyptian military prowess battled French prudence. In the end a compromise was reached in which paratroops would be dropped at Port Said and Port Fuad, with weapons flown in by helicopter, to test Egyptian defences. This would take place on 5 November, one day before the amphibious assault was to take place.

The British contingent in the invasion fleet was now a floating indictment of the state of the British military preparedness ten years after the end of the Second World War. Many of the ships were in a poor state having been in dock and unused for years. Hasty maintenance was barely enough to keep them afloat. All three carriers were still using hydraulic catapults one of which on the most modern one, HMS *Eagle*, broke down just before the assault began. Its second one also broke down one day after the invasion force had landed. The fleet was forced to move at the speed of its slowest ships which was around ten knots. Crews had been drawn from wherever they could be found. Two of the aircraft carriers, HMS *Theseus* and HMS *Ocean* which were unable to support aerial operations and henceforth non-operational, were refitted to play three roles simultaneously, troop carrier, hospital and helicopter carrier in what Rear-Admiral Sayer called a combination of roles that 'tended to prejudice the efficient conduct of some of them'.[6]

Arab countries rallied to support Egypt but Nasser was eager to ensure that the war did not spread across the region. He was having some success in gaining U.S. support which, in the long run, would be a significant diplomatic coup for him and was preferable to seeing his country come under the Soviet umbrella. He managed to persuade Jordan and Syria to hold off their Operation Beisan, a joint attack on Israel and was able also to prevent any further dislocation of oil supplies through Syria which he thought would only prejudice relations with the U.S.

In New York, Dulles was getting ready to address the U.N. General Assembly. Preparing for his speech, he had mulled over the 'tragedy' of having to choose between supporting the outdated colonialism of the U.S. allies which would allow the Soviet Union to win an easy propaganda victory in Africa or break with Britain and France and threaten the unity of N.AT.O. An afternoon NSC meeting discussed the contents of a resolution Dulles was bringing to the Assembly later in the day. There was a determination not to be seen as 'tied to British and French colonial policies' at a time when they should be focussing on the 'long-hoped-for victory over Soviet colonialism in Eastern Europe'. Britain and France, however, were long-standing allies and countries whom the U.S. would rely on in time of war against their true enemy, the Soviet Union.[7] Dulles prepared a statement to be read ahead of the debate in which he said, 'As a provisional measure, the United States is suspending the shipment of goods of a military character and Governmental programs to the countries of the area of hostilities which in the judgment of this Government might prolong the hostilities.'[8]

The wording of the resolution was important to prevent the Soviet Union bringing one of its own that would be significantly more hostile to Britain and France. Resolution 997 ES-1 called for 'all parties now involved in hostilities in the area to agree to an immediate cease-fire and, as part thereof, halt the movement of military forces and arms into the area' and 'Urges the parties to the armistice agreements promptly to withdraw all forces behind the armistice lines, to desist from raids across the armistice lines into neighbouring territory, and to observe scrupulously the provisions of the armistice agreements'. Addressing the Assembly, Dulles began 'I doubt that any delegate ever spoke from this forum with as heavy a heart as I have brought here tonight... the United States finds itself unable to agree with three nations with whom it has ties, deep friendship, admiration and respect, and two of whom constitute our oldest, most trusted and reliable allies.' ES-1 was a blunt rejection of the British and French position which he later said was 'in many ways the hardest decision [he] had ever taken.'[9] The British Ambassador to the U.N., Sir Pierson Dixon, revered as the diplomat's diplomat, found it disappointing that 'the apparent reluctance of the Americans to harass the Russians on Hungary contrasted oddly with the alacrity with which they were pursuing their two closest allies in the Assembly in the Middle East'.[10]

The French tried to stall debate on the resolution by claiming that Soviet forces had moved into Syria in readiness for military intervention in the Middle East threatening a serious escalation and a risk of all-out war. Dulles doubted that the intelligence was reliable given the many difficulties the Soviets would have in order to mount a military operation from Syrian bases. His conclusion was that a false scare had been cooked up probably by the British who wanted to give the French ammunition to block the resolution and stall for time in order to progress their own invasion plans. He also allowed for the fact that the rumour might have been started by the Soviets themselves to distract from their planned invasion of Hungary which was next up on the General Assembly agenda after ES-1 had come to the floor and passed with a 64-5 majority, the most decisive vote in the history of the U.N. up to that date. At a stroke it stripped Britain, France and Israel of U.N. legal and moral authority for their actions but they responded by saying that they intended to continue with their 'police action' to 'separate the combatants and stabilise the position' and would only stop when that had been achieved. All the pressure for U.N. action on the Hungary issue was coming from the Nagy government.

Chapter Ten

2 NOVEMBER

'It was a mockery [for the British and French] to come in with bombs falling all over Egypt [and denounce the Soviets] for perhaps doing something that is not quite as bad.'[1]

John Foster Dulles

Hungary
Friday 2 November was All Souls' Day in Hungary, the day people remembered the dead. Church bells rang throughout the city, people lit candles and black flags hung everywhere. Despite that, the atmosphere in Budapest on that morning as icy rain was driven in on a bitterly cold wind, was still upbeat. Vaguely aware that they were not yet out of the wood, the people hoped that signs of life returning to normal were not illusory. With public transport operating where conditions allowed, shops opening, strikes over and the children back at school they dared to hope that rumours now circulating freely of Soviet troop movements were false but news that Austria had closed its border with Hungary was forcing them to look beyond their false optimism and face reality. Government officials who supported the Nagy line were thinking hard about whether to leave or stay with the people even though they knew what fate awaited them if the Soviets came back in force.

And coming back they were. The 12th Transport Battalion, the 15th Signals battalion and the 13th Independent Engineering Company were already at Debrecen. The 20th Independent Mechanised Battalion was at Szolnok, the 11th Independent Transport Battalion at Püspökladány and the 27th Independent Transport Battalion was at Cegléd. By the end of the day the 8th Mechanised Army and the 38th Field Army were readied for deployment. To all intents and purposes, by 2 November, Hungary had been re-invaded.

Nagy arrived at his office and asked Andropov to come in and see him. With blatant disrespect and lack of decorum the Ambassador arrived unshaven with his tie undone and looking exhausted which was highly unusual for a man who was usually very careful about his appearance.² Nagy slapped down on the desk in front of Andropov report after report of Soviet troop movements but if he expected a clear response he would be sadly disappointed. Nothing more than routine manoeuvres, said Andropov, who then drew Nagy into a discussion about how Soviet troop withdrawals would be organised. Both sides would send a delegation to talks on the matter he suggested. Nagy knew full well that he was being played for a fool but had nothing in his armoury with which to counter it. The Kremlin would not take his calls, nothing he said was taken seriously by Andropov and the U.N. was paying him scant attention. He saw no alternative but to play along with Andropov and hope that he could somehow mediate and prevent a catastrophe for his country. He warned Kopácsi to make doubly certain that there were no provocations that could give the Soviets any excuse to break off talks. What he feared most was another armed struggle against what this time would be an immeasurably stronger Soviet force that would inevitably lead to massive loss of life. The almost comical figure of Dudás entered the fray again when members of his group under the command of Tibor Sziefert attempted to take over the Hungarian Foreign Ministry by force but were thwarted by swift action by Király who sent a crack team to break up the attack. More security forces went to Dudás' home and brought him in for questioning. He was released after several hours and rumours spread that on the next day his men robbed the National Bank.

Soon after this encounter, Nagy became aware that both Kádár and Münnich could not be found. What he might have suspected but could not know for sure was that both men were in Moscow and getting ready for talks with Molotov and Suslov. The level of Soviet obscurantism was such that neither of the two Hungarians actually knew exactly what they had been brought to Moscow for. They were both, in fact, attending job interviews for the post of Hungarian Prime Minister. Kádár introduced sophisticated argument to justify what had occasionally seemed like an anti-Soviet position during the early days of the insurrection. If the Soviet Union tried to hold onto Hungary by force, he had said only a couple of days previously, it will 'harm the socialist countries'.³ Münnich, however, who knew the Kremlin as well as any outsider, had no time for such niceties and said that Hungary was in a state of chaos implying that it required blunt force to bring it back to order and that the socialist system 'can be maintained only with the support of the Soviet Union'. His line was clearly more to the Kremlin's liking but on a personal level, he was disliked by Khruschev, who was actually still on his way back from Yugoslavia. Although in his seventieth year, Münnich was not above thinking that he still had enough support amongst his friends in the Kremlin to play one last major role in the drama.

At the U.N., a second urgent request from Budapest for the Council to take up the question of Hungary was met with Soviet delegate Arkady Sobolev's blunt denial that Soviet troops were moving into Hungary and demanded that discussion of the issue be dropped to which the Council acceded and postponed all official debate on Hungary until at least 5 November. The Soviet news agencies again called for the U.N. to deal with the 'treacherous attack on Egypt' and highlighted the industrial strikes all over Hungary even though most of the strikers had now returned to work. Hundreds of aircraft were heading east from Austrian airfields filled not with food and medicines as had been claimed but with fascist troops, said *Izvestia*. The same organ followed up on the next day with a headline of 'Fraternal Cooperation and Mutual Aid according to Leninist Principles' with which it covered the Soviet line on both Suez and Hungary. It claimed that Western attempts to put Hungary on the U.N. agenda was nothing more than a smokescreen to distract attention from what was happening in Egypt. It gave details of the many changes made in the Hungarian Cabinet mentioning the ousting of Münnich in particular but pointedly stating that Kádár was still a member of the government. That seemed to highlight Kádár's legitimacy as a successor to Nagy and put paid to any hope Münnich might have had about getting the top job.

In the U.S. a circular was sent round to all its major embassies. Secretary of State, Dulles, wrote that it appeared as if Hungary was becoming a test case for the extent to which the Soviet Union would accept greater independence for its satellites. It was likely, he thought, that the Soviets would continue to avoid a major battle with the Hungarian government and instead would mark time until they came to terms with the hopelessness of their position and restored communist control from within the country. The fact that Nagy had repudiated the Warsaw Pact agreement, declared neutrality, appealed to the U.N. and openly accused the Soviet Union of invading his country would seem to have been ample evidence to anyone that this would not be the case.

Eisenhower, who was already annoyed that the Hungarian crisis had blown up while he was in the last days of campaigning for re-election, was finding the situation in Suez much more difficult to ignore and was forcing Hungary even further down his agenda.

Upon entering an NSC meeting on 1 November, he said that 'he did not wish the Council to take up the situation in the Soviet satellites. Instead, he wished to concentrate on the Middle East.[4] Intelligence had reported on the Soviet military movements towards the Hungarian border showing clear evidence that they meant business. Peer De Silva had U.S. agents who were in close contact with employees of the Hungarian State Railway system, and they were reporting that Soviet officials on the Soviet-Hungarian frontier were issuing "detailed and voluminous" requests for flatcars and boxcars, to be assembled on the Soviet side of the border...rolling stock for eleven armoured or infantry divisions from the Ukraine and points east to be moved into Hungary at the earliest possible moment'.[5] It was, perhaps, another reason for Eisenhower's reticence to get more involved. He had no military options available to him to counter the Soviet build-up and probably did not want to advertise how impotent the U.S. was in Eastern Europe. Whatever he did, the U.S. would look weak, so he chose to do nothing on the ground. The Suez crisis, however, was an area in which the U.S. had a distinctly stronger hand to play and it was here, where the world's attention was now focussing, that he had the best chance of demonstrating U.S. power.

Suez
Egypt accepted the ceasefire early on 2 November and pulled all of its forces out of Sinai. Nasser sent warm words of appreciation to Washington telling Eisenhower that he realised that the U.S. had played no part in the invasion of Sinai or the bombing of Egyptian airfields. Syria broke off diplomatic relations with Britain and France and further committed its forces to support Egypt. The International Petroleum Company's pipeline was cut and there was wholesale looting and burning of British property in Bahrain. Eden was backed into a corner by the U.N. decision and the abandonment of him by the U.S. Mollet chose to respond by speeding up the landings but there was a limit to that. The main British landing force was still three days sailing away and ships of the U.S. Sixth Fleet were sitting in the middle of a British carrier zone, refusing to budge.

Anglo-U.S. relations were growing ever colder. Dulles accused Britain of pestering the U.S. to be more vocal in its condemnation of the Soviets in Hungary at the same time as British bombers were pounding Egyptian airfields. The British retorted by saying that the apparent reluctance of the Americans to harass the Russians on Hungary contrasted oddly with the alacrity with which they were opposing their allies in the Assembly on the Middle East. Sir Pierson Dixon, lamented that 'abnormal relations now exist between [Britain] and the Americans...as a result of our differences over the Middle East.'[6]

Fear of causing huge civilian casualties had now become a significant factor in the air assault on Egypt. Strategic objectives were abandoned for political not military reasons. Fear of enraging other Arab nations endangering Britain's oil supplies meant that Egyptian oil storage tanks were no longer targeted. Radio Cairo that was a mainstay of Egyptian morale could not be hit although its destruction had been a central aim of the plans. Two million leaflets had been printed as part of a psychological offensive but aircraft were never allocated to their distribution for fear of unnecessary losses.

Chapter 11

3 NOVEMBER

'It is said that when a man is fatally sick, he frequently experiences a day of euphoria a little before his death, when the functioning of his organs seems almost normal, giving him the illusion that recovery is possible.'[1]

Hungary
Michael Korda awoke on 3 November to 'a day of amazing beauty, a clear cold sky [reminding him] what a beautiful city Budapest is. The flower sellers in the streets were joined by vendors of roasted chestnuts, with the smell that marks every autumn and winter day in central Europe. Bars and espresso coffee shops were open; the pastry shops were open for the first time; the streets were full of strolling people, very few of whom were armed.'[2]

On the afternoon of 3 November an attempt was made to reorganise the Pétőfi Circle into a wider socialist and non-socialist coalition. They planned to publish newspapers and magazines in which they would publish their manifesto, but their efforts were dogged continuously by the essentially individualistic character of its membership that tended to prevent it achieving any sort of cohesive nature or common ambition. According to what had been agreed on 2 November, Maléter led a delegation of Hungarian military in the Parliament building to discuss the details of the withdrawal of Soviet forces from the country. Malinin, in full ceremonial military costume with medals led the Soviet team that included Shcherabanin and Stepanov. The Soviets laid out plans which included a full-scale military parade as they left. However, it would take some time to make all arrangements and, in the meantime, the Hungarian garrisons must cease denying the Russians food and fuel. Because the winter was setting in, he said, the evacuation of Soviet troops could not possibly be completed before 15 January because the Soviet forces in Hungary were not prepared for a winter movement and the Hungarians would have to be patient. The Hungarians agreed that during that time all Hungarian armoured units would be confined to barracks. The meeting adjourned in the early afternoon and the Hungarians were invited to continue discussion later that evening at Tököl. Despite repeated warnings, Maléter refused to take this an ominous development. 'We've discussed delicate problems,' he said ignoring laughter from his audience, 'as well as formalities such as the military music and speeches that would accompany the Soviet withdrawal'.[3] Nagy then went on the radio to reassure the public that the Soviets had agreed to leave. Király was certainly not fooled. 'There are [Soviet] troop movements everywhere,' he told Kopácsi, 'ten divisions and five heavy-armoured columns were converging on Budapest.' When Kopácsi asked if Nagy had been told, Király mordantly replied that his political master 'believes in miracles.'[4]

The Revolutionary Council for Public Safety held its inaugural meeting at the Kilián Barracks to elect officers of the National Guard Supreme Command selected from the different units. Király was confirmed as leader with Kopácsi as his deputy and an announcement to that effect went out on Free Kossuth radio during the afternoon. In it workers were urged to continue returning to the factories and called on insurgents to give up their weapons or face arrest. The meeting went on to demand that Király be made Minister of Defence but he refused to consider it calling it a 'crime' to make such a proposal.[5] The many tasks facing the new Command were itemised, and plans made for implementation of the necessary changes but there was never going to be enough time to even get started on that before the next phase of the revolution took over.

Rumours of a U.N. delegation arriving at the airport had been started when remarks by a Cuban delegate at the U.N. were misinterpreted. The false story was carried by several western radio networks and journalists rushed to witness their arrival at Budapest airport but they waited in vain. When other journalists drove through the quiet streets of Budapest carrying flags of their diverse nations, people came into the street to cheer them thinking they were from the U.N.

In the Kremlin the Soviet leadership without Serov, Konyev and Zhukov, who were tied up planning the invasion, were making their final choice and it was Kádár clearly out in front now although he had, on the previous day, warned the Soviet leaders that 'the use of military force will be destructive and lead to bloodshed' and would 'erode the authority of the socialist countries', causing 'the morale of the communists [in Hungary] to be reduced to zero'.[6] The Soviets, having set the wheels (and tank tracks) in motion, now looked at how they would deal with Nagy. The Yugoslavs came up with the idea that they would somehow inveigle him into their Budapest Embassy after the tanks had rolled in and persuade him to make a broadcast in support of Kádár. The Soviets took that on board as one of the possible solutions but would not commit themselves at this point.

Maléter arrived for the second round of talks at Tököl just before 22:00hrs along with Major-General Istvan Kovács, Chief of Staff, Colonel Szűcs, Chief of Operations and Ferenc Erdei. They were given an honour guard on arrival and talks went well for a couple of hours during which Maléter was able to call Király and report on developments. Malinin was being 'exquisitely polite' while discussing the wording of the final communique but then, just before midnight, a dozen Soviet soldiers burst into the room pointing their guns at the Hungarian delegation.[7] Serov followed and calmly informed them that he was placing them under arrest effectively decapitating the Hungarian military command. To round off the coup, Mecséri, was arrested by Soviet special forces during the night also. Malaschenko questioned Maléter about Hungarian forces defending the city but got no response. Maléter did say, however, that during the previous few days he had been visited by military attachés of both Britain and the U.S. with whom he pleaded for their governments to make some sort of statement of moral support.

Suez

It was at this time that Washington's approach to the Hungarian crisis was most affected by events in Egypt. For the Soviets, they were glad to see the world's attention diverted from eastern Europe but they chose to exercise caution until such time as they might profitably take a more belligerent position.[8] It was all the more important for them to settle the Hungarian issue quickly and decisively and they gambled that the U.S. would be sufficiently wary also. Bringing the Hungarian problem to a resolution by extreme violence was certainly a gamble risking condemnation in the U.N. but if it lasted for only a day or so it could be contained. Therefore, for them, all means would be justified to get Hungary off the agenda as quickly as possible and that was bad news for the population of Budapest.

At the same time, they did not want to get embroiled in the Suez conflict, certainly until Hungary had been tamed. The possibility of giving any sort of military aid to Egypt seemed remote given the logistical problems but there was plenty that could be done in the political arena. In the meantime, their military advisers and technicians had been removed to the Sudan and the Soviet Ilyushin-28 bombers had been got out of the way to Syria to eliminate the risk of Egyptians using them to bomb Israeli cities. Nasser was not best pleased by these moves which he saw as desertion by his erstwhile allies. Mustapha Amin, one of Nasser's advisors, made contact with the CIA to say that with Nasser so disillusioned by the lack of support from the Soviets the U.S. should make the most of their current position. Right now, they said, the U.S. could strike a favourable deal with Egypt but the window for that would remain open for only a few days and would slam shut if Egypt suffered defeat on the battlefield.

In the House of Commons, Prime Minister Eden was forced to defend his government against a vote of no confidence. He won fairly comfortably 320-253 and rounded off by telling the house that Britain was not at war but simply 'in a state of armed conflict.' Britain and France then responded to the U.N. resolution of 2 November by saying that they maintained the view that the police action must be carried through urgently for the following reasons; to stop the hostilities which were threatening the Suez Canal; to prevent a resumption of these hostilities and to pave the way for a definitive settlement of the Arab-Israeli war which threatened the legitimate interests of so many countries. They would most willingly stop military action as soon as the following conditions could be satisfied. Both the Egyptian and the Israeli Governments should agree to accept a U.N. force to keep the peace and the U.N. should decide to constitute and maintain such a force until an Arab-Israeli peace settlement could be reached and until satisfactory arrangements had been agreed in regard to the Suez Canal. Both agreements to be guaranteed by the U.N. Until the U.N. force can be constituted, however, both combatants should agree to accept forthwith limited detachments of Anglo-French troops to be stationed between them. Eden then made a broadcast over the radio claiming 'all my life I have been a man of peace, working for peace, striving for peace, negotiating for peace,' and giving an assurance that 'once British and French forces have occupied key positions on the Canal, the British Government will ensure that the Israeli forces will withdraw from Egyptian territory.'[9]

For several months, Eden had been waging a war against the British Broadcasting Corporation (BBC) to restrict its criticism of the government. In August he had called the chairman of the BBC, Lord Cadogan, who agreed that the BBC should do nothing to give the impression of government disunity at a time of crisis but BBC employees did not agree. In the last week of October, as the Suez crisis was reaching its crescendo, the government tried to 'shock the corporation into collective obedience' with a threat to cut the overseas services budget by one fifth. A foreign office liaison officer was installed at Bush House, the headquarters of the overseas services, 'to advise the BBC on the content and direction of their overseas programmes' and 'feed current events programmes with news filtered by the intelligence and propaganda divisions.' So afraid that public opinion would derail their operations, the government told BBC executives to prepare for 'the revival of wartime measures including censorship.'[10] Harman Grisewood, the assistant to Lord Cadogan, later maintained that if the Board had decided to side with Eden most of the senior people in the BBC would have resigned.

Eventually it was decided that Hugh Gaitskeill, the Labour leader of the British opposition in Parliament would be allowed to respond to Eden's speech. He called the previous few days 'by far the worst week, for the world and for our country, since 1939'. In attacking Egypt, he told the listeners, Britain had taken the law into its own hands and was acting in defiance of world opinion. Following Gaitskill's words a large anti-war rally was held in Trafalgar Square and the crowd marched on to Downing Street where a full Cabinet session was under way.

The U.S. Sixth Fleet, now just northwest of Cairo, was brought to maximum readiness but the British and French invasion fleets were sailing east from Malta and heading right for them. It would be a tense time as the ships passed each other. Meanwhile the allied bombing fleet had changed its targets from airfields to Egyptian army barracks and coastal defences but the task force was still three days away. International pressure for a ceasefire was becoming intense especially from the U.S. where economic moves were threatening Sterling. The British Cabinet resisted however and sent urgent calls for task force commanders to get a move on but the only thing they could bring forward was the paratroop drops and that would leave them without support from naval guns and having to hold their ground for twenty-four hours until infantry and armour could be landed. British resolve may to some extent have been galvanised by a signal sent from the American Deputy Director of Intelligence who told the CIA representative in London: 'Tell your friends to comply with the goddamn ceasefire or go ahead with the goddam invasion! Either way, we will back them up if they do it fast. What we cannot stand is their goddam hesitation!' When the CIA officer in London told the JIC, he pointed out that he was 'not speaking without instructions'.[11]

On the morning of 3 November in Washington, Dulles awoke with crippling stomach pains and uncontrollable shivers. Unable to walk, and with the spiral staircase in his Georgetown home making any attempt to carry him to an ambulance on a stretcher impossible, Dulles instead bumped himself down the stairs on his behind, giving out instructions to an aide about what work needed to be dealt with while he was incapacitated. He was admitted to the Walter Reed Army Medical Center, where he immediately underwent a five-hour operation. It was discovered that the problem was a recurrence of a condition he had previously suffered from. A cancerous growth was found to have burst through his large intestine. The cancer was removed along with the damaged portion of his intestine. Attempts were immediately made to reassure the nation and the world that Dulles was still fit to be in post. The U.S. administration's line painted Dulles in heroic terms and suggested he had been laid low by the vigour with which he had pursued the anti-Communist crusade. Dulles's illness, indeed, incapacitated him right at the point that the Suez Crisis was reaching its climax but he continued to keep in touch with the critical situations in Hungary and particularly Suez. During the next ten days he would frequently meet with the President and with the State Department staff in the hospital, and, at one point, even had a meeting there with Selwyn Lloyd. At that meeting, albeit some days after the ceasefire had been agreed, Dulles asked Lloyd 'Why did you stop? Why did you not go through with it and get Nasser down?' which was easy for him to say after the event.[12]

Meanwhile, Task Force commanders were coming under severe pressure from their political masters whose nerves were rapidly being shredded as it was becoming ever clearer that Nasser was not about to fall. With no possibility of the troopships arriving earlier than scheduled on 6 November, the only option was to expedite the deployment of airborne forces but Operation Omlette and the occupation of Port Said was based on the premise of minimal Egyptian resistance which could certainly not be taken for granted. Airfield congestion was also a factor in limiting the number of transport aircraft available. A crash meeting of Defence Chiefs and the Defence Ministry was held at which it was decided to step up the bombing of Port Said. When the new British Minister of Defence, Anthony Head, and General Templer flew to Cyprus to meet Keightley and Barjot it became clear to them that the priority now was to take control of the Canal Zone.

Chapter Twelve

4 NOVEMBER

'The place of every Hungarian communist today is on the barricades'.
Radio Rajk[1]

Hungary
Just after midnight, Király woke Nagy with news that Soviet troops were making reconnaissance sorties in strength against the outer defensive ring of Budapest. 'It is now certain', he said 'that the Soviet Union has launched a war against us.'[2] He urged Nagy to go on the radio and order Hungarian forces to open fire. Nagy bridled at having the military dictate to him over what he saw as essentially a political decision and refused to agree. Király called him back a little later to say that Soviet tanks were moving into the city and gunfire was heard from the outskirts. Nagy again refused to act fearing that a military response would result in an all-out attack by the Soviets with no hope of resisting them and lead to massive loss of life in the city. He had called in Andropov who felt the full weight of Nagy's invective for his treachery but the seasoned diplomat continued to play his deceitful hand well by making calls to Moscow ostensibly to clarify the situation but, of course, in reality simply to play for time and delay any attempt by Nagy to authorise an official order to fight. Knowing that all was now lost, at 05:20hrs Nagy did, however, agree with his Cabinet colleagues to make a grim 35-second radio broadcast in which he said,

> 'This is Imre Nagy speaking. Today at daybreak Soviet forces started an attack against our capital, obviously with the intention to overthrow the legal Hungarian democratic government. Our troops are still fighting; the Government is still in its place. I notify the people of our country and the entire world of this fact.'[3]

This was followed by the playing of the Hungarian national anthem. When Király called again to say that Soviet tanks were moving towards the parliament buildings and he somewhat sarcastically offered to count them as they went past his window, Nagy told him that he did not want to receive any more reports. Nagy then went immediately afterwards to the Yugoslav embassy with Zoltán Szántó and eleven other party leaders and intellectuals with their families.

It seems odd that Nagy should have believed that he would be safe in the Embassy of another communist country rather than going to the U.S. embassy as Archbishop Mindszenty did. On the day before Khruschev had met Tito on Brioni, Szántó, afraid of possible violence against Hungarian government members by the anti-communist insurgents, had already spoken to the Yugoslav ambassador to Hungary, Dalibor Soldatic, about the possible need for political asylum. Soldatic contacted Tito and got tentative approval to take him in at some unspecified date in the future. It is not clear whether it was assumed at this time that Szántó also included other members of the Hungarian government.

Tito told Khruschev about this exchange and the Soviet leader apparently raised no objection possibly hoping that it might be a convenient way of keeping leading Hungarian politicians quiet as the tanks rolled in. It would also prevent them from fleeing the country and causing a stir as a putative government in exile. Tito took this as an agreement. He had been sufficiently supportive of the Soviet invasion plan that Khrushchev evidently assumed that, even if Nagy sought asylum in the Yugoslav embassy, he would be straightway turned over to the Soviet authorities. In a telegram he sent to Soviet Ambassador Firiubin he instructed him to tell Edvard Kardelj, Deputy Head of the Yugoslav Government, that since the Hungarian security organs had virtually ceased to exist, 'it would be expedient to deliver Nagy and his group to our troops'.[4]

At around 05:30hrs Nagy with an entourage of some forty-one of his staff took up the offer. Later, explaining to Khrushchev why he had granted asylum to Nagy so quickly, Tito cited the sheer 'speed of events' and 'absence of detailed information' and the fact that Khruschev had not raised any objections at Brioni.[5] That may not then have been a problem but it became one later when it was clear that Tito was not willing to hand over Nagy and his group of refugees to the Soviets.

Operation Whirlwind began at 06:00hrs Moscow time with broadcast of the codeword Grom (Thunder). Konyev issued Order No. 1 in which he described the Hungarian revolt as an attempt to 'liquidate the people's democratic system...and restore the old land-owning-capitalist order.' 'The rebirth of fascism,' he said, 'poses a direct treat [and] Soviet troops have started carrying out their allied obligations... The duty of Soviet troops is to extend fraternal aid to the Hungarian people [and prevent] the rebirth of fascism.'[6] Soviet troops and tanks made straight for the industrial centres and working-class districts to crush the revolution.

In the absence of political leadership, Király gave the order to resist the attack but he was countermanded by Janza. Király questioned his authority as only an ex-member of the government. The commander of the National Guard told Király that he wanted to offer a truce in return for amnesty but Király still thought that the Nagy government was in place and that only they could negotiate a ceasefire. His aim was to hold the Hungarian forces together to give Nagy some leverage in negotiations with the Soviets.

At around the time of Nagy's broadcast Kádár, still in Moscow at this time, put out a pre-recorded statement on a different radio station proclaiming the formation of a new Hungarian Revolutionary Worker-Peasant government. 'Acting in the interests of our people, our working class and our country,' he began, claiming to be in Szolnok in Hungary, 'we requested the Soviet army command to help the nation in smashing the dark reactionary forces and restoring order and calm in the country,'[7]

It was a statement obviously authorised by the Kremlin but Kádár was still not secure and did not have unanimous support there. Molotov and Kaganovich had no confidence in him but Khruschev put all his weight behind the appointment. There were bitter words exchanged showing once again that Stalin's heir would not yet carry the authority of his predecessor. In Washington, political deafness reached new levels. The U.S. Legation was instructed to receive Hungarian ministers for talks but they should not be allowed to stay overnight and could not expect sanctuary.

On 3 November, the U.S. had brought a resolution before the U.N. Security Council calling for an immediate withdrawal of all Soviet forces from Hungary but effectively killed debate by abstaining when Britain called for more time to debate it and then voting against reopening discussions on the following day. By the time the General Assembly met to discuss the issue, the fighting was almost over. It somewhat belatedly passed a Canadian resolution calling for an emergency international U.N. force to secure and supervise cessation of hostilities but the British abstained on the grounds that the resolution went too far in some respects and not far enough in others. By the time it was put on record, later that day, that the overwhelming majority of the members of the United Nations were appalled by the Soviet action the revolution was dead, if not yet quite buried.

Radio Free Kossuth broadcast its final desperate message at just after 08.00hrs, 'all writers, scientists ... and academics in the world. We appeal for help to all intellectuals in all countries. Our time is limited. You all know the facts. There is no need to review them. Help the Hungarian people. Help, Help, Help!'[8] The station then abruptly went off the air. The occupants of the Parliament building sent out a delegation under a white flag and Soviet officers duly entered the building demanding a written confirmation of surrender. The short, wiry Minister of State, István Bibó, who had been appointed just the previous day was the last to leave the building and before he left wrote,

> Only [I] remain in the Parliament building as the only representative of the only existing legal Hungarian government. Under these circumstances, I make the following declaration:
> Hungary does not wish to pursue an anti-Soviet Policy. On the contrary, Hungary's full intent is to live in the community of free Eastern European nations which want to organise themselves on the principles of liberty, justice and freedom from exploitation. Before the entire world, I also reject the slanderous accusation that the glorious Hungarian Revolution has been despoiled by fascist or anti-semitic excess. The entire Hungarian nation, without class or denominational differences, participated in the struggle. It was moving and marvellous to see the humane, wise and discretionary behaviour of the insurgents, and how they were able to limit their outrage only towards the oppressive foreign army and the local executioner-commandos. The recently-formed Hungarian government had the ability to put an end to the incidents of street justice that repeatedly occurred during the past days, as it would have been able to halt the emergence of the unarmed arch-conservative political elements. The claim that a large foreign army had to be called or recalled into the country to accomplish these objectives is both frivolous and cynical. On the contrary, the very presence of this army is the major cause of the current tensions and disturbances.
> I admonish the Hungarian people to not consider the occupying army or their puppet government as legal authority, and to utilise against them every means of passive resistance except those that would endanger the essential supplies and public utilities of Budapest. I cannot issue an order for armed resistance: I have been in the government for only one day and am not informed about the military situation. It would thus be irresponsible of me to risk the priceless blood of Hungarian youth. The Hungarian people have already sacrificed enough of their blood to show the world their devotion to freedom and truth. Now it is up to the world

powers to demonstrate the force of principles embodied in the United Nations Charter and the strength of the world's freedom-loving peoples. I appeal to the major powers and the United Nations to make a wise and courageous decision to protect the freedom of our subjugated Nation.'[9]

Where orders to resist the Soviets were received by Hungarian forces they came far too late to be acted upon. In reality, the Hungarian army had ceased to exist as an efficient fighting force. Time after time, Hungarian army units stayed in their barracks and gave up their arms but as the Soviets advanced towards the centre of the city, they began to meet resistance around well-defended areas such as the telephone exchange, Corvin Cinema, the Kilián Barracks and the Keltei Railway Station. Konyev, however, was not mounting a police operation he was waging war and ordered up another two tank regiments, two infantry divisions and two heavy trench mortar units. Tactics were altogether more brutal. Groups of more than 500 rebels holding positions the Soviets found hard to penetrate were attacked by flame-throwers and massed artillery. Any building suspected of harbouring rebels was systematically bombarded and reduced to rubble.

At the Corvin Cinema which was by far the best defended of all rebel positions there was ranged a formidable number of anti-tank weapons and bazookas and all the surrounding streets had been sown with landmines. During the lull the defenders had been able to replenish their stocks of ammunition. The position was manned by 1,000 fighters, led by Laszlo Ivan Kovács and Gergely Pongrácz, who had been in action since the first days of the uprising and were significantly more adept at street fighting than the invading Soviet forces but they could not hold off against the full weight of Soviet artillery bombardment and fighter aircraft that strafed the area indiscriminately. When the building went up in flames they were forced to abandon it but many continued to offer resistance for days afterwards.

Michel Korda awoke to the sound of artillery that had opened up on the barracks at Budaõrsi Avenue. In the streets, people were beginning to appear in small groups, heavily armed and grim-faced. They were building barricades on the broad Kossuth Lajos Utca that led down to the Parliament buildings. A truck pulled up full of picks and spades with which the rebels began prising up the big hexagonal cobblestones. Bottles of brandy were handed round to fortify morale. Korda describes his experience as the artillery got closer.

'There's a split second of intense quiet, together with the feeling of being in a vacuum, unable to take a breath; then there's the huge sound of the explosion, momentarily deafening you, making the ground tremble beneath your feet, shattering glass in windows all around you, followed by a swiftly rising plume of smoke and debris that fills your eyes, your nose, and your mouth with foul-smelling grit and the acrid stench of high explosive. Then, finally, comes the spine-tingling clickety-clack of bits of red-hot shrapnel, shattered stone, and odd pieces of plumbing landing. But all this takes place in a fraction of a second.'[10]

Shrapnel came flashing past glowing bright red, slivers that could take your eye out or slice off your ear to great chunks that would cut a person in two. As the shelling intensified, buildings seemed to explode from within and water mains were ruptured sending plumes of water into the air. Newer tank units that had not been in the city during the weeks before carried armour-piercing shells designed for tank-to-tank combat and it was these that penetrated deep into even the most solidly-built structures before exploding that wreaked such havoc and brought many buildings down. There were accounts of shells ploughing through the thick outer wall, leaving a neat hole not more than six inches in diameter, keep going through the thinner and less solid inner walls, and finally blowing up deep inside the building. People who had been in their room when a shell passed through remembered hearing only a deafening crack and a whistle, followed by a dull explosion deeper in the building that shook everything. Survival in a city under bombardment is largely a question of luck. By late afternoon the firing had died down. Tanks were now able to proceed down the wider streets in formation to offer protection to each other. Barricades were blasted away and infantry cleared the streets as they advanced. Soviet tanks fired indiscriminately into buildings even where there was no evidence of sniper fire or resistance of any sort.

By nightfall 300 rebels were dead and hundreds more made captive. The Soviet 128th self-propelled gun regiment moved through Moszkva Square district dislodging the rebels house by house and capturing their leader János Szabó. For propaganda purposes, it was claimed that during these operations the Soviets received assistance from units of the Hungarian army but that referred probably to only a small number of units since so few were left intact. In the countryside, the 38th Field Army with headquarters at Székesfehérvár under General I. A. Tokanyuk had secured the Austrian and Yugoslav borders and all Hungarian lands west of the Danube. In the east, control was established by General Babadjanyan's 8th Mechanised Army based at Dedrecen. In the factory districts of Csepel, Újpest and Pestszenterzsébet, there was strong resistance and almost constant fighting. The Soviets found it harder to break resistance there and some groups in Ujpest and Kobanya would hold out for another week. Local factory workers held on tenaciously with anti-tank guns and other pieces of artillery, machine guns and grenades in the face of repeated attacks by Soviet armour. Soviet troops were constantly harassed when moving about the city. The rebel tactics of hit-and-run urban guerrilla warfare refined over previous days was causing many Soviet casualties. The Soviets responded by pounding the rebel strongholds and the surrounding areas ferociously destroying whole blocks of flats even firing on a queue of women and children outside a baker shop and destroying a Red Cross ambulance killing all on board. The rebels, however, were certain to run out of ammunition before the Soviets and it was only a matter of time before the end came. The Csepel resistance refused all calls to surrender, however, but as resistance was put down elsewhere, more and more Soviet armour was brought in. Csepel workers for those seven days slept eight hours, fought for eight hours and spent the other eight hours working in the factories producing arms and ammunition. The Csepel armoured car made its appearance, a three-wheel mechanised wheelbarrow with a machine-gun in the bucket propped up with sandbags. Outside the capital, Dunapentele lasted until 9 November led by its Workers' Council. In Pecs, the Workers' Council chose to carry out guerrilla warfare in the nearby hills with some miners fighting the Russians for several weeks in this way.[11] In the Pentagon, Assistant Secretary of Defence Gordon Gray felt that the U.S. approach centred on a strategy of 'don't antagonise the U.S.S.R.' needed revision but the general view held that no military assistance could be given without risking 'a full-scale nuclear war'.[12] Suggestions that the U.S. Strategic Air Force should make 'demonstrative movements' and that all military leave should be cancelled were discussed and rejected.

Eisenhower settled for sending a note to Bulganin in which he said,

> 'I have noted with profound distress the reports which have reached me today from Hungary...I urge in the name of humanity and in the cause of peace that the Soviet Union take action to withdraw Soviet forces from Hungary immediately and to permit the Hungarian people to enjoy and exercise the human rights and fundamental freedoms affirmed for all peoples in the United Nations Charter.'[13]

It achieved little. There days later Bulganin replied.

'Answering your letter dated November 4, I feel urged to state that the problem of the withdrawal of Soviet troops from Hungary touched therein comes completely and entirely under the competence of the Hungarian and Soviet governments...I assume that in the meantime you probably could get acquainted with the program of the Revolutionary Workers' and Peasants' Government of Hungary which has been outlined by the Government in an appeal to the Hungarian people...Certainly you will have noted that this program gives complete information on any questions that may interest you.'[14]

Suez

While the Soviets' military was pounding Budapest to rubble, their diplomats were also at full stretch demonising the Anglo-French blockade of shipping lanes in the Mediterranean and Red Seas and trying to force the issue by attempting to send six warships through the Dardanelles. Communist China weighed in with a threat to start sending military aid to Egypt if the situation was not resolved soon. Iraq, Syria and Jordan came to full military readiness. The U.N. agreed by 57-0 with 19 abstentions to set up an emergency command force under Major-General E. L. M. 'Tommy' Burns of the Canadian Army.

Israeli Foreign Office officials wanted direct and immediate talks with Egypt and until that happened Israeli forces would stay exactly where they were claiming complete victory. Israel, they said, was ready to defend itself if attacked by other Arab states. Egypt made overtures to the U.S. about sending ships of their Sixth Fleet to Cairo furthering the prospect of the U.S. forging stronger ties with Egypt after the war was over.

In the early Musketeer plans, the paratroops were scheduled to drop just after the shore landings so that they could benefit from the naval bombardment and have the support of artillery and tanks but the latest revised plan had them going in a full twenty-four hours before any ships would arrive and they would have to achieve their goals unaided.

The latest plan was the implementation of Operation Telescope which had French and British forces attacking Port Fuad and Port Said on the east and west sides of the Canal, and then advancing south to Qantara. To avoid civilian casualties, the naval bombardment preceding the landing was to be abandoned. The British would then seize Abu Sueir and Elgamil airfields, while the French continued south to occupy Ismailia and Suez. The British 3rd Parachute Battalion, led by Lieutenant Colonel Paul Crook, was to land 668 men with seven jeeps, four trailers, six anti-tank guns and 176 containers on Gamil airfield, 3 miles west of Port Said at 07:15hrs local time. Fifteen minutes later, the French 2nd Colonial Parachute Regiment would drop on Port

Fuad, a residential suburb of Port Said on the east bank of the Canal and secure the two Raswa bridges. In the afternoon the British were reinforced by a second drop. They would then be well placed to launch a double-pronged attack on Cairo if that was required. The timing of the various phases of the attack worried the French commanders who were coming under huge pressure from Paris to get a move on and get French boots on Egyptian soil but the main battle fleet would not arrive before 6 November.

Chapter Thirteen

5 NOVEMBER

'If this war is not stopped, it contains the danger of turning into a third world war.'
Marshal Bulganin's Messages to President Eisenhower on 5 November 1956[1]

Hungary

The revolution was essentially crushed on 4 November but there were still a number of direct armed confrontations between the Soviets and the revolutionaries for up to a week afterwards. The rebels still held out some hope that as long as they resisted, there was a chance that the U.S. might come to their aid or at least international pressure would force the Soviets to negotiate. It was a forlorn hope. On 5 November, the Russians began an all-out attack on rebel positions but failed to break resistance at Csespel Island, the Corvin Cinema, Széna Square in Buda and Tűzoltó Street in Pest. The industrial city of Dunaújváros held out until 6 November when most, but not all, armed resistance outside of the capital was quashed.

Whether it had anything to do with Nagy's asylum or not is disputed but on 5 November, at 15:30hrs a Soviet tank fired on the Yugoslav embassy. The building frame was damaged, all the windows were shattered, and the cultural attaché Milenko Milovanov was killed by gunfire. The Soviets claimed that they had not known it was the Yugoslav Embassy building but the Yugoslav Foreign Minister, Koca Popovic, accused the Soviet authorities of having deliberately opened fire knowing perfectly well that it was and that Imre Nagy and his supporters were inside. The Yugoslav government later presented a claim of $84,446 to Hungary for the death of Milovanov.

Now that Nagy's presence in the Embassy was a fait accompli and well covered in the world's major newspapers, Tito faced a dilemma.

He rejected Soviet calls to hand Nagy over and so the Soviets accused Yugoslavia of interfering in the internal affairs of other countries and harbouring the organizer of the counter-revolution and threatened reprisals if they continued to be uncooperative. If they did that, however, it would look as if Yugoslavia was meekly giving in to Soviet bullying and Tito's pride would not condone that. Furthermore, he took the concept of political asylum seriously. He valued Yugoslavia's reputation as a responsible, sovereign state, and was convinced that Yugoslavia should honour the principles of international law as befits such a state. It was also a useful way of reminding Khrushchev that Soviet-Yugoslav relations were not something to be trifled with. Tito was adept at realpolitik. He saw that his protection of Nagy was a practical way of taking the heat out of the Hungarian situation which would enhance his reputation as a statesman on the world's stage, something that might be useful if the Soviets ever tried to impose their political will on Yugoslavia.

Suez

Thirty minutes after sunrise on 5 November, thirteen weeks after the British decision to react to Nasser's nationalisation of the Canal, the 3rd Battalion of the British 16th Independent Parachute Brigade Group, the "Red Devils" with more than 600 men boarded Handley Page Hastings of 70, 99 and 511 Squadrons and Vickers Valetta of 84 Squadron transports on Cyprus. The drop zone was Gamil airfield, located on a narrow strip of water-flanked land three miles west of Port Said. Acting in concert with British forces, 480 paratroopers of the French 2nd Colonial Parachute Regiment (2ème RPC), together with some combat engineers of the Guards Independent Parachute Company were dropped on the south side of two bridges spanning the Raswa Channel below Port Said and in a second zone south of Said's twin city of Port Fuad. Throughout the day they would be supported by ground-attack aircraft to clear the drop zones and give air support where needed. They secured the main Raswa road-and-railroad bridge, Port Said's only land link to the south so that Port Said was cut off completely from Egyptian reinforcements.

The French, with their objectives attained, sent a patrol motoring six miles southward preparatory to the next day's expected drive toward Qantara and Suez. Stockwell and Beaufre, as usual, could not agree on the next move. Stockwell stuck to his methodical approach which lacked both imagination and initiative but reduced risk while Beaufre was an opportunist who was ever willing to alter his plans to suit the circumstances. He suggested a rapid drive to take control of the Canal Zone. Stockwell seemed to agree but hesitated when in the late afternoon, the Port Said military commander Brigadier Salaheddin Moguy called for negotiations. Brigadier M. A. H. Butler, Colonel Pierre Chateau-Jobert, and General Jacques Massu, the three allied commanders on the ground offered terms and gave Moguy four hours to respond during which time there would be a cease-fire. Moguy refused the terms and the cease-fire expired at 22:30hrs. Egyptian defenders had not capitulated and were still in place. Despite French forces holding Port Faud and key areas of Port Said, there would be no swift tactical breakthrough. It was clear that if the Allies wanted to occupy Port Said, there was no alternative to an all-out assault on the following day. The glaring weakness of the plan, which was recognised at the planning stages was and always had been the time lag between the beginning of the bombing and the airborne assault.

The Soviet Union saw the Suez crisis as an opportunity to extend its influence in the Middle East by threat rather than by action. It had a number of options open to it. A British Foreign Office report saw the potential for Soviet intervention in support of Egypt as,

- Clandestine introduction of token volunteer force
- Overt introduction of volunteers by ship
- Clandestine submarine action (disguised as Egyptian) against Anglo-French naval forces
- Introduction of Soviet naval vessels into Egyptian ports
- Introduction of fighters and bombers into Syria

Any direct action against Anglo-French forces, however, would be seen as an attack on N.AT.O. and as such would have the gravest consequences. Amid swirling rumours of large-scale deployment of Soviet forces on the Turkish border, the U.S. Chief of Naval Operations (CNO) estimated that the Soviets,

- Would not attack British or French mainland
- Would probably not employ large forces in the eastern Mediterranean
- Might make clandestine submarine action against Anglo-French naval forces
- Will continue to send material aid to Egypt
- Will probably send volunteer force to help Egypt.
- Could bring into play its Black Sea fleet of warships and air components based in the western Soviet Union

Moscow was very adept at 'talk much and do little' sabre-rattling diplomacy and made no decisive move until after 4 November when the U.N. General Assembly had authorised the setting up of an emergency force to supervise cessation of hostilities in Egypt.[2] It seems as if during the days immediately after the Israeli invasion of Sinai, the Soviet government was unwilling to commit itself in any way to the active defence of Cairo but having achieved its initial objectives in Hungary and having ascertained U.S. determination to halt the war against Nasser, they now chose to act boldly. Having subdued Budapest after a day of brutal bombardment, the Soviets felt empowered to flex their muscles, diplomatically this time. In letters to Eden, Mollet, and Ben-Gurion, that had been drafted by Khruschev himself, Bulganin condemned the collusion between Britain, France and Israel as both unjustified violence against Egypt and a threat to world peace and freedom It was a bold attempt to wider the rift that had opened up within the Western Alliance and to reap as much benefit as possible out of a situation where the eventual political defeat of the aggressors could be easily foreseen.

In a letter to Eisenhower, Bulganin wrote

> 'I approach you on behalf of the Soviet Government... The situation in Egypt calls for immediate and resolute action on the part of the United Nations... At this menacing hour when the loftiest moral principles and the foundations and aims of the U.N. are being put to the test, the Soviet Government approaches the U.S. Government with a proposal of close cooperation in order to put an end to aggression and stop further bloodshed... The Soviet Government calls upon the U.S. Government to join their forces in the United Nations for the adoption of decisive measures to put an end to the aggression...'

In his reply, Eisenhower called it 'an obvious attempt to divert world attention from the Hungarian tragedy' and went on to say that the suggestion that 'the United States should join with the Soviet Union in a bipartite employment of their military forces to stop the fighting in Egypt', was unthinkable and that 'the introduction of new forces under these circumstances would violate the U.N. Charter'. 'It is clear', he went on to say, 'that the first and most important step that should be taken to ensure world peace and security is for the Soviet Union to observe the U.N. resolution to cease its military repression of the Hungarian people and withdraw its troops. Only then would it be seemly for the Soviet Union to suggest further steps that can be taken toward world peace.[3]

He had been less than pleased to have the Soviets say that 'The Soviet Union and the United States [as] the two great powers which possess all modern types of arms including the atomic and hydrogen weapons'. He was worried that the Soviets 'scared and furious' after seeing their position and their policy failing so badly in [Hungary], might be ready to take on any wild adventure'. He wasn't going to take any 'guff' from anybody and told his aides that 'if those fellows start something...we will hit them with everything in the bucket.'[4] Intelligence assessments, however, said that Soviet Union would 'almost certainly not' attack metropolitan areas of the French or British mainlands or undertake large scale military deployments in the Eastern Mediterranean.[5]

Ben-Gurion received a strongly worded and unmistakably threatening message saying that the very existence of Israel as a state 'had been placed in jeopardy'. With exquisite irony, Bulganin wrote, 'all peace-loving mankind indignantly brands the criminal actions of the aggressors who have attacked the territorial integrity, sovereignty, and independence of the Egyptian State. Disregarding this, the Government of Israel, acting as a tool of foreign imperialist powers, continues the foolhardy adventure, challenging all the peoples of the East who are struggling against colonialism for their freedom and independence.'[6] To Britain and France, the tone was marginally less abrupt but clear nevertheless, 'We are fully determined to crush the aggressors and restore peace in the Middle East through the use of force.' While Israel was threatened with outright annihilation, the messages to the United Kingdom and France contained a veiled threat to use 'rocket techniques' in case of their non-compliance with U.N. resolutions demanding an immediate cease-fire and withdrawal of foreign troops from Egypt. Moscow radio reported appeals by Egyptians for help through volunteers, arms, or by any other means from all those who still respected human dignity and law in international relations. The U.N. Secretary-General circulated his proposals for an international police force.

The Soviet's note was far from an empty and meaningless gesture. Together with Bulganin's suggestion that Soviet and U.S. warships cooperate to bring hostilities to an end were skilful diplomatic devices which aimed to improve their international influence without taking any appreciable risks. Any suggestion of even the merest rift between the Western Allies and a hint of U.S.-Soviet collusion as a result of the note would be a huge step towards achieving Khrushchev's ambition of moving towards a world where only two superpowers, the Soviet Union and the U.S. held sway. Even if nothing came of it, the Soviets could present themselves to those nations in Asia and Africa emerging from imperial domination as a champion of their cause.

Whatever the Western Powers' concept of the Soviet nuclear capability at this time, it was in fact nowhere near being sufficiently great to challenge U.S. power. The Soviet T-1 (M101) was a single-stage, liquid-fuelled tactical attack missile with an 800lb nuclear warhead and a range of 450 miles and its bigger brother the T-2 (M103) was two-stage, liquid-fuelled missile with 700lb nuclear warhead and a range of 1,100 miles.[7] Neither of these was being produced in any significant quantity.

All recipients of Bulganin's notes appeared to be highly surprised and alarmed at the severity of the wording. Bluff or no bluff, for a few hours in the late afternoon and evening of 5 November, nobody outside the Kremlin could be positive as to the true nature of Soviet intentions. Would they be mad enough to risk the annihilation of mankind to bring about the humiliation of the British and French and drive a wedge into the N.AT.O. Alliance? It was certainly a skilful diplomatic move by the Soviets who exhibited their customary flair in such situations. U.S. acceptance of the Soviet offer would signify a huge success by setting Washington against its two European allies. It would also give the Soviets a leading role in Middle Eastern politics alongside the U.S. and accelerating Khruschev's agenda of dividing the Middle East and perhaps even the entire world into Soviet and U.S. spheres of influence. If the ploy failed, however, the Soviets would gain important benefits by showing Washington to have aided and abetted Anglo-French-Israeli aggression against Egypt and could profitably be contrasted with Moscow's willingness to render Cairo all-out military support.

Within a few hours, Washington left no doubt of its intention to retaliate in the event of a nuclear attack against its British and French allies as Eisenhower ordered the immediate alert of the air defence command and dispatched more American aircraft carriers into European waters. Nasser was singularly unimpressed by Moscow's action, however. He would later claim that during the eight days it took the Soviets to make up their mind how to react to the Israeli invasion, Egypt had 'not the slightest intimation of support from any foreign state, even the Soviet Union. We relied on God and ourselves. . . . Had it not been for our firm stand during those nine days, our whole country would have now been dominated by imperialism'.[8] The Soviet threat had its desired effect in London and was taken advantage of in Washington. Eisenhower had made it clear to Britain that if the U.S. made a public stand against the Soviet notes, Eden would have to abandon the Egyptian policy upon which the British Prime Minister had staked his political reputation and career.

Chapter Fourteen

6 NOVEMBER

'the development of modern communications, though intrinsically of great value, is inclined to produce a number of last-minute queries and instructions from London which cannot fail to upset the Command on the spot'
      Naval Task Force Commander off Port Said on 6 November 1956

Hungary
The Moscow-installed puppet government of János Kádár was not able to assume office and remained in Szolnok for a few days, eventually arriving in Budapest in a Soviet tank. Even then, Soviets kept the members of the Kádár cabinet practically under house arrest, fearing that Kádár might be assassinated. General Grebenik, the Soviet commandant of the city of Budapest, imposed martial law on 6 November, and Soviet military courts ordered subsequently an unknown number of executions. Széna Square fell and János Szábo was captured trying to escape to Austria. Dudás's headquarters were overrun on the same day.

Suez
Contrary to what was taking place in Egypt, a top priority signal was sent to Eden. It was read out in the House of Commons at 16.50 on 5 November by the Earl of Home during a debate that was not going well for the government. It read, 'Governor and military commander, Port Said, now discussing surrender terms with Brigadier Butler. Ceasefire ordered.'[1] The House erupted with loud cheering. A reply went out, 'Our most sincere congratulations to you all...you should now cease all air bombing unless you receive special authority.'[2]

Musketeer's amphibious phase began the next day on 6 November. The main naval Task Force took up positions five miles offshore and the passage into Port Said was swept for contact and magnetic mines. Bombing runs against the landing beaches were followed at dawn by naval gunfire which caused considerable damage to the Egyptian gun emplacements and to the town of Port Said. Then, at first light the Royal Marines of 42 Commando stormed the beaches, using landing craft of Second World War vintage followed by tanks of the 6th Royal Tank Regiment. The French, meanwhile, landed unopposed on the other side of the Canal's eastern breakwater. An hour after these initial landings the first helicopter-borne assault landing in history, took off from the British carriers *Theseus* and *Ocean*. In just over an hour, 22 Westland Mark 2s helicopters, each carrying five green-bereted men of the No 45 Commando of the Royal Marines put ashore 415 marines and 23 tons of stores. After 90 minutes, helicopters began bringing back casualties long before the landing was completed, A later U.S. assessment of the operation said, 'All this...demonstrated as nothing else could have done the full and startling potentialities of the combination of carriers, helicopters, and parachutists.'[3] By noon they had linked up with the French paratroops. 45 Commando came in an hour after 40 Commando in order to clean up the port area and there was fighting in the streets of Port Said. The drop proved to be successful thanks to effective support provided throughout the day by naval aircraft directed by air contact teams dropped with the paratroopers. Seahawks and Corsairs were constantly on call with never less than twelve aircraft patrolling above the British troops, plus six Corsairs for the French. French paratroopers, well-trained veterans of colonial wars blasted their way northward with little regard for civilian casualties. All the attackers then dug in to await reinforcements.

It was election day in the United States. The Joint Chiefs convened and made plans 'to improve readiness for a general war,' and requested that the President return immediately to the White House and convene what amounted to a council of war. When his re-election was confirmed, Eisenhower told the American people that he would continue to work 'for peace in the world' at the very moment that he was preparing for war.[4]

A U.S. Task Force consisting of *Forrestal, F. D.R., Des Moines*, Destroyer Squadron 26 (DESRON 26) and Destroyer Division 322 (DESDIV 322) sailed from home ports to operate in the Eastern Atlantic as a stand-by force. Submarines were deployed 'to reconnaissance patrols in the North Atlantic for surveillance of Soviet Naval Forces.' With orders to 'maintain readiness to execute emergency war plans'.[5] Reports had

Iraqi, Syrian, and possibly Saudi Arabian, forces massing on the Israeli-Jordan border. The next day, a British Canberra was shot down over Syria and the suspicion was that the assailant had been a MiG piloted by a 'volunteer'. Communist China announced that it had 28,000 'volunteers ready to go to Egypt. The U.S. Commander of Middle East Forces was instructed that 'In event that contact attacks, counterattack using every available means to destroy... but no publicity be given to the state of readiness'. Hours later all U.S. fleets were put on wartime alert. The Sixth Fleet shifted to an operating area southwest of Crete 'in order [to] improve readiness posture for general emergency.'[6]

Eisenhower now employed financial warfare in three particular ways to force Britain and then France to withdraw from the Suez Canal. Firstly it blocked the IMF loan to Britain. Secondly, it prevented the U.S. Export-Import Bank from extending $600 million in credit to Britain and thirdly it threatened to dump America's holdings of pound-sterling bonds which would have catastrophically increased the amount of British currency in circulation with deflationary consequences for the pound. Britain would no longer have the purchasing power or the foreign reserves to cover the cost of its food and energy imports. The U.S. action froze Britain's ability to borrow and forced it back onto its negative cash flow, effectively bankrupting it and threatened British ability to trade internationally.[7]

When the British saw the U.N. resolution and the U.S. Treasury Secretary told Macmillan, 'You will not get a dime from the U.S. Government until you have gotten out of Suez' the British Chancellor of the Exchequer threw up his arms and saw the inevitability of halting the offensive. The essential problem for Britain was oil. It could no longer buy oil from the Arab nations and so its only recourse was to buy oil from the U.S., but they would insist on payment in dollars and Britain did not have sufficient dollar reserves to do that. It would have to ask for credit and the U.S. would only agree if the advance south of Port Said was halted. Macmillan now panicked and reversed his previous position. It was clear to him now that he had calamitously misread Eisenhower's position which caused him to temporarily discard his cloak of unflappability to reveal a highly-strung, temperamental side to his character. It is said that when he felt fearful of exposing this trait in public he would feign exhaustion, retire to bed and immerse himself in a Jane Austin novel until his calm had been restored.[8] What his personal feelings were during the Suez crisis is unclear since he destroyed his diaries for the period.

The main Franco-British force was seventy-five miles from the Canal when the British Cabinet met on the evening of 6 November to vote on continuation of the war. Eden wanted to continue so that Britain had control of the whole Canal, but Macmillan grossly exaggerated the extent of the already perilous financial crisis threatening to resign unless there was a ceasefire. Eden failed to carry the room and was forced to accede to the wishes of the Cabinet setting the end of British military operations at midnight that night. Nutting recorded that it had been the political and economic pressures that were building up almost hourly upon the British and French Governments, the closing of the Canal and stoppage of Middle East oil shipments, the run on the pound, the fury of the Americans and the hostility of the Commonwealth that underlay the decision. The French thought the Canal Zone was within grasp and were furious.

In addition, the Israelis had accepted a ceasefire, so the pretext for British intervention had now gone.[9] The U.S. Sixth Fleet was breathing down the neck of the Suez Task Force showing the world that the U.S. was not condoning the invasion. Eden tried to cloak his humiliation in diplomatic terms. He wrote to Bulganin and said "the essential aim of the action taken by the British and French Governments was to stop the fighting between Israel and Egypt and to separate the combatants' and added, 'This aim has now been virtually achieved.' His French allies were less than pleased. Mollet wanted a few more days to consolidate their position along the canal before halting but Eden was adamant.

Eisenhower sent a telegram (3285) to Eden and Mollet at 14:29 Washington time saying how 'delighted' he was that a cease-fire had been agreed 'without condition so as not to give Egypt with Soviet backing an opportunity to quibble or start negotiations'. In Paris, Pineau opposed the ceasefire but found himself holding a minority opinion and eventually gave way.

Not least amongst the pressures on the invading countries was an invitation from Nasser for the U.S. Sixth Fleet to enter Port Said and land marines. The Soviets were taken aback by the new cosiness between the U.S. and Egypt and were not about to let it scupper their own plans. They upped the stakes by recruiting 'volunteers' to go to Egypt to fight against the invasion forces and sent six warships through the Dardanelles into the Aegean. While the actual fighting in Egypt had passed its peak, the international standoff between the two superpowers was only just ramping up.

AFTERMATH

'Western historians consider Hungary 1956 to be the most significant historical event in the second half of the 20th century.'[1]

Hungary

The Soviets had not been at all happy with Tito's shielding of Nagy in the Yugoslav Embassy in Budapest and decided to get him out. Kadar's government was instructed to give assurances of safety for Nagy and his aides if they left the embassy. On 22 November, a bus was driven up to the Yugoslav embassy, supposedly to transport Nagy and the other officials with their families to their apartments but while the Hungarians were climbing into the bus, a Soviet military official also entered the bus, despite the Yugoslavs' vehement protests. To make sure that the Hungarians were taken to their homes, the diplomat Milan Georgievic and military attaché Milan Drosa were ordered to accompany the group. The bus proceeded just around the corner from the Embassy, and then the Soviet lieutenant colonel forced Georgievic and Drosa to get off. The bus took the Nagy group first to the Soviet military headquarters in Budapest, and then continued on to Romania where the group was imprisoned. Tito was left humiliated and furious. By this time, the fighting had mostly ended, the Hungarian resistance had essentially been destroyed, and Kádár was entering the next phase of his strategy to neutralize dissent for the long term.[2]

Eventually Nagy was secretly brought back to Budapest, where he was made to stand trial. This time there was no theatrical show, only a quiet and unpublicized murder. His final words as he told his Hungarian executioners on 16 June 1958 were,

> My only consolation in this situation is that, sooner or later, the Hungarian people and the international working class will acquit me of these heavy accusations, the weight of which I have to carry now, as a consequence of which I have to give my life, but the responsibility for which I have to take. I feel that the time will come when, in a calmer

atmosphere, with clearer vision, with a better knowledge of the facts, justice can be administered in my case too. I feel I am the victim of a grave mistake, the mistake of the court. I do not ask for pardon.[3]

After 4 November, the Temporary Executive Committee of the Hungarian Socialist Workers' Party gave the all-clear to start shooting any who continued to resist Soviet control. After the Soviet invasion strikes and demonstrations had broken out all around the country. A women's demonstration in Budapest on 4 December was followed by a similar event two days later in Székesfehérvár. On 7 December militia opened fire on demonstrators in Tatabánya. One of the bloodiest mass shootings was carried out by the militia in the northeastern mining town of Salgótarján, in which at least 50 people were killed. Demonstrators, who included workers from the glass and steel factories, miners and other sympathisers, were protesting against the arrests early that morning, by Soviet troops, of miners Lajos Gál and Lajos Viczián of the Miners Trust Workers' Council. The town square had been sealed off to trap the protestors. Mihály Horányi described what happened next,

> 'Behind some of the windows, militiamen were standing or moving around, submachineguns hanging from their arms. They were about 100–150 metres away. I saw them moving quickly to set up a light machine-gun behind one of the windows ... and then I realised what was going to happen. I turned and started running to warn everybody away, but I was too late. I heard a dull thud behind my back. And with a horribly loud noise, the shooting began. I threw myself onto the sidewalk. ...
>
> Many of the injured were in shock, or on the verge of madness. It was a horrible sight to see all the women who were killed, some of them pregnant, with their shopping bags spilled around them. Two Roma children, about ten years old (they were siblings), who earned some money as street musicians, were killed in each other's arms.'

This mass murder was only one of a series of bloody reprisals.[4]

Suez
The ceasefire agreement had halted the Suez invasion armada seventy miles short of its target but it was far from the end of the crisis. On 7 November the Soviet Union began recruiting 'Soviet citizen volunteers who wish to take part in the struggle of the Egyptian people for their independence' and it was reported that six Soviet warships were heading out of the Black Sea through the Dardanelles.[5] Western

intelligence took this to mean that the Soviets were no longer content to view the situation from the sidelines and were intent on exploiting it in whatever way they could. Bohlen reported from Moscow that the Soviet preparations 'appeared to be genuine'.[6]

They had some 2,000 jet fighters and about 500 jet bombers located in areas close to the Black Sea with their heavy bombers able to cover the entire Mediterranean area. Intelligence reports noted unidentified jet aircraft overflying Turkey while the U.S. Sixth Fleet made contact with several "possibly hostile" submarines in the Mediterranean. Soviet frogmen were reported to be in Alexandria harbour. On 6 November a British Canberra PR7 was shot down over Syria at 45,000 feet by a Syrian Gloster Meteor. Four Soviet jet aircraft were reported to be at the airfield at Aleppo, Syria.

While the U.S. State Department thought the Soviets would 'probably not' make a direct attack on British of French mainland, small-scale attacks by air or submarine against their forces in the Middle East was thought a distinct possibility. Eden wanted to know if the N.AT.O. agreements extended to cover forces in the Middle East. Eisenhower had no intention of going easy on his errant allies but neither did he want to show weakness against the Soviet threat. His reply to Eden was that 'the Government of the United States will respect its obligations under N.AT.O. arrangements.' Which cannot have calmed the Prime Minister's nerves. It was only after both Britain and France had agreed the ceasefire that Eisenhower clarified the U.S. position by saying 'if Soviets should intervene directly against British and French troops, N.AT.O. obligations would come into play'.[7]

The U.S. responded by putting a naval task force on standby and deploying submarines to make 'reconnaissance patrols in the North Atlantic for surveillance of Soviet Naval Forces.'. Messages to commanders of all vessels ended with 'maintain readiness to execute emergency war plans'.[8] Commanders were also instructed that 'In event that contact attacks, counterattack using every available means to destroy.'[9] The Sixth Fleet shifted to an operating area southwest of Crete "in order [to] improve readiness posture for general emergency.[10]

On 10 November Khrushchev threatened to send trained Soviet "volunteers" to join the Egyptian armed forces unless what they termed the 'aggressors' withdrew from Egyptian lands. In Moscow, U.S. Ambassador Bohlen thought it more likely that aid would not be directed to Egypt but to Syria, and possibly Jordan and Iraq with Israel as the principal target. The State Department began an urgent reappraisal of the Middle East situation with a view to both increasing U. S. prestige and working towards a more permanent settlement of the Arab-Israeli problem. Time would show, however, that as far as the Middle east was concerned, it was somewhat naïve of them to 'take hope from the fact that sometimes, in an atmosphere of crisis and basic change, it is possible to achieve solution of problems which otherwise would not be feasible'.

Nasser was more popular than ever with his people. Egypt had raised its international profile and was now basking in the support of other Arab nations and was taking centre stage at the U.N. The U.S. election had returned Eisenhower to the White House and he was now much freer to act. Douglas Hurd, who would later become a British Foreign Secretary wrote that 'no rhetoric about a special relationship influenced...the chilly American calculation of [their own] interests... too often [the British] clothe the Anglo-U.S. relationship in a warm, fuzzy haze [but] its basis is the real usefulness of one country to the other. If that usefulness dries up, no amount of speech-making will prevent the relationship from withering.'[11]

Eden still hoped to retrieve some benefit from his adventure and proposed a British-French-U.S. summit meeting to bring pressure to bear on Nasser and restore Britain's reputation as a U.S. ally but, although Eisenhower was willing, the State Department strongly advised against it. After due consideration, Eisenhower decided to let the British 'stew in their own oil' for a while. His objective now was to curb Soviet power in the Middle East but he need not have worried in the short term. Heavy-handed Soviet propaganda and attempts to influence Egyptian politics soon saw Egyptian-Soviet relations cooled.

Any suggestion that Suez would lead to long-term damage of British-U.S. relations, however, was quickly dispelled later when Eden's successor, Macmillan and Eisenhower patched things up. 'Those British,' Eisenhower would say, 'they are still my right arm.'[12] While the British and the U.S. were kissing and making up, the French turned towards the construction of a pan-European power which could exert leverage over America. There should be a European policy distinct from the American, a view that had been greatly influenced by Suez. The French became even more distrustful of Britain, which they believed would always serve American interests rather than those of Europe. In Britain, Suez ended the illusion which 1940 engendered, that the fate of the country lay entirely in her own hands. There was a loss of national self-confidence.

Eden had been concerned with the weakening of international order, which was threatened by Nasser, just as, in the 1930s, he had been concerned with the weakening of international order through the action of Mussolini and Hitler and Eden was the first to realise that the great threat to international order was not so much from the communist powers, who were weak and cautious and highly risk-averse, but from radical third world dictators who were much less risk-averse. When Eden died in 1977, his obituary in the Times said: 'He was the last Prime Minister to believe Britain was a great power, and the first to confront a crisis which proved she was not.'[13]

Israeli troops stayed in Sinai and the Gaza Strip; their complete withdrawal would be announced by Dag Hammarskjöld on 8 March 1957. During the intervening months, they mapped and photographed every part of the Sinai and hid caches of food and water in anticipation of future wars.

The events of October-November 1956 revealed the limited power both the U.S. and the Soviet Union had in their rival's sphere of influence. While the Soviets had been forced to abandon Egypt in its hour of greatest need, in Hungary the U.S. had been left with little choice but to sit back and see Hungary's attempt to break away from Moscow's grasp crushed by Soviet tanks. Both superpowers had deemed it wiser to maintain the status quo rather than risk a complete breakdown in the existing power balance. Neither was prepared to risk a major war over an area it had little prospect of controlling. The crushing of the Hungarian uprising encouraged the Soviets to believe in the effectiveness of military power as a means of controlling eastern Europe but forfeited its appeal to emerging nations. On the western side, the bitter divisions over Suez were largely repaired following Eden's resignation in January 1957, and by the emergence of a good working relationship between Eisenhower and Macmillan.

Appendix 1

THE SEVRES PROTOCOL

There is no preamble as in most international treaties because there was no time to compose one.

The results of the conversations which took place at Sevres from 22 to 24 October the representatives of the Governments of the United Kingdom, the State of Israel are the following:
1. The Israeli forces launch in the evening of 29 October 1956 a large scale Egyptian forces with the aim of reaching the Canal Zone the following day.
2. On being apprised of these events, the British and French Governments 30 October 1956 respectively and simultaneously make two appeals Government and the Israeli Government on the following lines:
   A. To the Egyptian government
      a. halt all acts of war.
      b. withdraw all its troops ten miles from the Canal.
      c. accept temporary occupation of key positions on the Canal by the forces to guarantee freedom of passage through the Canal by vessels until a final settlement. *(This demand was inserted in order to ensure that Egypt could not possibly accept the appeal.)*
   B. To the Israeli government
      a. halt all acts of war.
      b. withdraw all its troops ten miles to the east of the Canal.

In addition, the Israeli Government will be notified that the French and British have demanded of the Egyptian Government to accept temporary occupation along the Canal by Anglo-French forces.

It is agreed that if one of the Governments refused, or did not give its consent, hours the Anglo-French forces would intervene with the means necessary to demands are accepted.

   C. The representatives of the three Governments agree that the Israeli not be required to meet the conditions in the appeal addressed to it, in Egyptian Government does not accept those in the appeal addressed to it

3. In the event that the Egyptian Government should fail to agree within the to the conditions of the appeal addressed to it, the Anglo-French forces will operations against the Egyptian forces in the early hours of the morning
4. The Israeli Government will send forces to occupy the western shore of and the group of islands Tiran and Sanafir to ensure freedom of navigation Aqaba.
5. Israel undertakes not to attack Jordan during the period of operations against Egypt. But in the event that during the same period Jordan should attack Israel, the British Government undertakes not to come to the aid of Jordan. (*Israel. The purpose of this provision was to minimize the risk of a military clash between Israel and Britain on the Jordanian front. In effect, it meant that Britain and Israel were guilty of collusion against Jordan as well as against Egypt*)
6. The arrangements of the present protocol must remain strictly secret.
7. They will enter into force after the agreement of the three Governments.

(signed)
DAVID BEN-GURION
PATRICK DEAN
CHRISTIAN PINEAU

Appendix 2

16-POINT RESOLUTION OF BUDAPEST STUDENTS.

1. We demand the immediate evacuation of all Soviet troops, in conformity with the provisions of the Peace Treaty.
2. We demand the election by secret ballot of all Party members from top to bottom, and of new officers for the lower, middle and upper echelons of the Hungarian Workers Party. These officers shall convene a Party Congress as early as possible in order to elect a Central Committee.
3. A new Government must be constituted under the direction of Imre Nagy; all criminal leaders of the Stalin-Rákosi era must be immediately dismissed.
4. We demand public enquiry into the criminal activities of Mihály Farkas and his accomplices. Mátyás Rákosi, who is the person most responsible for crimes of the recent past as well as for our country's ruin, must be returned to Hungary for trial before a people's tribunal.
5. We demand general elections by universal, secret ballot are held throughout the country to elect a new National Assembly, with all political parties participating. We demand that the right of workers to strike be recognised.
6. We demand revision and re-adjustment of Hungarian-Soviet and Hungarian-Yugoslav relations in the fields of politics, economics and cultural affairs, on a basis of complete political and economic equality, and of non-interference in the internal affairs of one by the other.
7. We demand the complete reorganisation of Hungary's economic life under the direction of specialists. The entire economic system, based on a system of planning, must be re-examined in the light of conditions in Hungary and in the vital interest of the Hungarian people.
8. Our foreign trade agreements and the exact total of reparations that can never be paid must be made public. We demand to be precisely informed of the uranium deposits in our country, on their exploitation

and on the concessions to the Russians in this area. We demand that Hungary have the right to sell her uranium freely at world market prices to obtain hard currency.

9. We demand complete revision of the norms operating in industry and an immediate and radical adjustment of salaries in accordance with the just requirements of workers and intellectuals. We demand a minimum living wage for workers.
10. We demand that the system of distribution be organised on a new basis and that agricultural products be utilised in rational manner. We demand equality of treatment for individual farms.
11. We demand reviews by independent tribunals of all political and economic trials as well as the release and rehabilitation of the innocent. We demand the immediate repatriation of prisoners of war (World War II) and of civilian deportees to the Soviet Union, including prisoners sentenced outside Hungary.
12. We demand complete recognition of freedom of opinion and of expression, of freedom of the press and of radio, as well as the creation of a daily newspaper for the MEFESZ Organisation (Hungarian Federation of University and College Students' Associations).
13. We demand that the statue of Stalin, symbol of Stalinist tyranny and political oppression, be removed as quickly as possible and be replaced by a monument in memory of the martyred freedom fighters of 1848-49.
14. We demand the replacement of emblems foreign to the Hungarian people by the old Hungarian arms of Kossuth. We demand new uniforms for the Army which conform to our national traditions. We demand that March 15 be declared a national holiday and that October 6 be a day of national mourning on which schools will be closed.
15. The students of the Technological University of Budapest declare unanimously their solidarity with the workers and students of Warsaw and Poland in their movement towards national independence.
16. The students of the Technological University of Budapest will organise as rapidly as possible local branches of MEFESZ, and they have decided to convene at Budapest, on Saturday October 27, a Youth Parliament at which all the nation's youth shall be represented by their delegates.

NOTES

Chapter One: The Soviet Occupation of Hungary
1   Lomax, Bill, *The Working Class in the Hungarian Revolution of 1956*, (Columbia University, 1979) p.2
2   Reynolds, David A.J., *The Roots of Communist Hungary in the Allied Occupation*, (The Hungarian Review, 2020) unpaginated
3   ibid
4   ibid
5   Kramer, Mark, *Stalin, Soviet Policy, and the Consolidation of a Communist Bloc in Eastern Europe 1944-1953*, (Amazon web Services, 1993) p.13
6   Schoenfeld, H.F. Arthur, *Soviet Imperialism in Hungary*, (Foreign Affairs, Vol. 26, No. 3, 1948) p.555
7   Reynolds
8   ibid
9   ibid
10 ibid
11 Schoenfeld, p.566
12 Fehér, Ferenc and Heller, Agnes, *Hungary 1956 revisited*, (George Allen & Unwin, 1983) p.26
13 Granville, Johanna, *Cold War International History Project Bulletin, no. 5*, (Woodrow Wilson Center for International Scholars, Washington, DC, 1995)
14 Kopacsi, Sandor, *In the Name of the Working Class*, (Fontana, 1979) p.94
15 Harman, Mike, *The Hungarian Revolution 1956*, (Scorcher Publications, 1984) p.27
16 ibid, p.33
17 ibid, p.34
18 Fehér, p.28
19 ibid, p.27
20 Kopacsi, p.100

21 Granville, Johanna, *Josip Broz Tito's Role in the 1956 'Nagy Affair'* (The Slavonic and East European Review, Vol. 76, No. 4, 1998) p.672
22 Lomax, Bill, *Hungary 1956*, (Allison and Busby, 1976) p.44
23 ibid p.47

Chapter Two: Colonel Nasser and the Suez Canal

1 Hamilton, Eamon, *Sir Anthony Eden and the Suez Crisis of 1956, The Anatomy of a Flawed Personality*, (University of Birmingham, 2015) p.94
2 Pierre, Jean-Marc, *The 1956 Suez Crisis and the United Nations*, (Fordham University, New York, 1992) p.74
3 Selak, Charles B. Jnr, *The Suez Canal Base Agreement of 1954*, (The American Journal of International Law, Vol. 49, No. 4, 1955) p.488
4 Warner, Geoffrey, *The United States and the Suez Crisis*, (International Affairs Vol. 67 No. 2, 1991) p.304
5 Laron, Guy, *Cutting the Gordian Knot: The Post-WWII Egyptian Quest for Arms and the 1955 Czechoslovak Arms Deal*, (Cold War International History Project, Woodrow Wilson International Center for Scholars, 2007) p.24
6 Warner, Geoffrey, *The United States and the Suez Crisis* p.305
7 Hamilton, Eamon, *Sir Anthony Eden and the Suez Crisis of 1956, The Anatomy of a Flawed Personality*, (University of Birmingham, 2015) p.38
8 Warner, The United States and the Suez Crisis, p.306
9 Hamilton, p.69
10 Bogdanor, Vernon, *The Suez Crisis of 1956*, (summarize.tech,) p.3
11 Suez Crisis 1956, Institute of Naval Studies Washington 1974, p.11
12 Fullick, Roy and Powell, Geoffrey, *Suez: The Double War*, (Pen and Sword, 2006) p.27
13 Suez Crisis 1956, Institute of Naval Studies Washington 1974, p.147
14 von Tunzelmann, Alex, *Blood and Sand*, (Simon and Schuster,) p.13
15 Unwin, Peter, *1956 Power Defied*, (Michael Russell, 2006) p.50
16 Hansard 27 July 1956, Suez Canal Company (Expropriation),
17 von Tunzelmann, p.63
18 Unwin, p.51
19 Skardon, C. Philip, *A Lesson for Our Times: How America Kept the Peace in the Hungary-Suez Crisis of 1956*, (Author house) location 17328
20 Unwin, p.62
21 ibid
22 Hamilton, p.71

23 Pearson, p.16
24 ibid, p.36
25 ibid, p.21
26 Turner, Barry, *Suez 1956: The Inside Story of the First Oil War*, (Hodder & Stoughton,) location 3040
27 Bogdanor, p.5
28 Pearson, p.27
29 Bogdanor, p.6
30 Jouko, Petteri, *Strike Hard, Strike Sure - Operation Musketeer, British Military Planning during the Suez Crisis, 1956*, (Taktiikan laitos - Department of Tactics, Helsinki, 2007) p.320
31 Economic Impact of Suez Crisis on Middle East, The Economic Weekly, U.N. Headquarters, (1957)
32 von Tunzelmann, p.60
33 Suez Crisis 1956, Institute of Naval Studies Washington, *1974*, p.13
34 Warner, *The United States and the Suez Crisis*, p.309
35 Unwin, p.86
36 Pearson, p.34
37 ibid, p.31
38 Bogdanor, p.8
39 ibid, p.9
40 Jouko, p.142
41 Turner, location 3130
42 Turner, location 3177
43 Hamilton, p.77
44 ibid, p.74
45 Turner, location 3214
46 Steed, Danny, *British Strategy and Intelligence in the Suez Crisis*, (Springer, 2016) p.106
47 Necky, Patrick L., *Operation Musketeer – the End of Empire: A Study of Organizational Failure in Combined Operations*, (Operation Musketeer – the End of Empire: A Study of Organizational Failure in Combined Operations, 1991)
48 Smolansky, O.M., *Moscow and the Suez Crisis, 1956: A Reappraisal*, (Political Science Quarterly, Vol. 80, No. 4, 1965) p.582
49 ibid, p.584
50 Suez Crisis 1956, Institute of Naval Studies Washington 1974, p.21

51   Fowler, Randall, *Lion's Last Roar, Eagle's First Flight: Eisenhower and the Suez Crisis of 1956*, (Rhetoric and Public Affairs, Vol. 20, No. 1, 2017) p.41
52   Turner, location 3869
53   Unwin, p.93
54   ibid, p.94
55   Turner, location 5203
56   Hamilton, p.58
57   Unwin, p.138
58   Boughton, James M., *Northwest of Suez: The 1956 Crisis and the IMF*, (IMF Staff Papers, Vol. 48, No. 3, 2001) p.428
59   Hill, Jill M., *Suez Crisis 1956*, (Institute of Naval Studies Washington, 1974) p.29
60   Coles, Michael H., *1956: A Successful Naval Operation Compromised by Inept Political Leadership*, (U.S. Naval War College Press, 2006) p.5
61   Warner, Geoffrey, *Collusion' and the Suez Crisis of 1956*, (International Affairs Vol. 55, No. 2 (1979) p.586

Chapter Three: The Sevres Protocol

1   Hamilton, p.94
2   von Tunzelmann, p.74
3   ibid, p.70
4   Jones, Matthew, *Macmillan, Eden, the War in the Mediterranean and Anglo-American Relations*, (Twentieth Century British History, Volume 8, Issue 1, 1997)
5   Louis, William Roger, *Harold Macmillan and the Middle East Crisis of 1958*, (University of Texas, 1996)
6   Pearson, Jonathan, *Sir Anthony Eden and the Suez Crisis, Reluctant Gamble*, (Palgrave, 2003) p.139
7   ibid, p.147
8   von Tunzelmann, Alex, *Blood and Sand*, (Simon and Schuster,) p.58
9   Unwin, p.50
10   Pearson, p.2
11   Warner, The United States and the Suez crisis, p.234
12   ibid
13   Shlaim, Avi, *The Protocol of Sevres, 1956: Anatomy of a War Plot*, (International Affairs Vol. 73, No. 3, Globalization and International Relations, 1997) p.514
14   Warner, The United States and the Suez crisis, p.234

15 von Tunzelmann, p.59
16 Cohen, Michael J., *Suez-Sinai, 1956: The International, Strategic and Military Aspect*, (Israel Studies Forum, Vol. 17, No. 1, 2001) p.72
17 Shlaim, p.519
18 Warner, The United States and the Suez crisis p.236
19 Shlaim, p.521
20 ibid, p.522
21 von Tunzelmann, p.116
22 Shlaim, p.528

Chapter Four: 22-24 October

1   My Revolution – Recollections of the 1956 Revolution – Part II, Friends of Hungary Foundation Hungarian Review Vol VII No. 6, *2016*
2   Landa, Ronald D., *The 1956 Hungarian Revolution; A Fresh Look at the U.S. response*, (National Security Archive, nsarchive.gwu.edu, 2012) p.1
3   ibid, p.71
4   Study Prepared for U.S. Army Intelligence, "Hungary: Resistance Activities and Potentials," January 1956, National Security Archive, unpaginated,
5   ibid
6   Lomax, Bill, *The Working Class in the Hungarian Revolution of 1956*, (Critique No 12, 1979) p.81
7   Mandoki, Anna, *Molotov Cocktails*, (Kindle edition,) p.53
8   ibid, p.56
9   Bass, Warren, *The Suez War 1956*, (Rand Corporation,) p.258
10 Malashenko, Yevgeny, *Soviet Military Intervention in Hungary, 1956*, (Central European University Press, 1998) p.221
11 Kramer, p.181
12 Korponay, Irene, *Escaping Communist Hungary 1956*, (Ryan von Schwedler, Kidle edition,) p.75
13 Sebestyen, Victor, *Twelve Days*, (Phoenix Kindle edition,) location 1965
14 Kopacsi, p.120
15 Jobbágyi, Gábor, *Bloody Thursday, 1956; The Anatomy of the Kossuth Square Massacre*, (Hungarian Review Vol V No1, 2014) unpaginated
16 Mandoki, p.63
17 ibid, p.100
18 Hegedüs, András B., *Ungarische Revolution 1956*, (Walter de Gruyter, 2000) p.122

19   Archard, Louis, *Hungarian Uprising*, (Pen and Sword, 2018) p.70
20   Borhi, László, *Dealing with Dictators*, (Indiana University Press. Kindle Edition,) p.117
21   Lomax, p.70
22   ibid, p.106
23   Sebestyen, location 2225
24   Korponay, p.77
25   Mandoki, p.95
26   Sebestyen, location 2204
27   ibid, location 2286
28   Györkei, Jeno, *Soviet Military Intervention in Hungary 1956*, (Central European University Press, 1999) p.181
29   Dent, Bob, *Locations of a drama. Budapest 1956*, (Európa Könyvkiadó, Budapest, 2006) p.76
30   Malashenko, p.222
31   Lomax, p.71
32   Varga, Zsolt, *Contemporary American Press Coverage of the Outbreak of the 1956 Hungarian Revolution*, (Hungarian Journal of English and American Studies Vol 8, 2002)
33   Borhi, p.108
34   Landa, p.35
35   Chester, Eric Thomas, *Covert Network: Progressives, the International Rescue Committee, and the CIA*, (Routledge, 1995) p.132
36   Landa, p.36
37   Borhi, p.119
38   McCauley, Brian, *Hungary and Suez, 1956: The Limits of Soviet and American Power*, (Journal of Contemporary History, Vol. 16, No. 4, 1981) p.781
39   Györkei, p.31
40   Landa, p.42
41   Swartz, Martin Ben, *A new look at the 1956 Hungarian Revolution: Soviet opportunism, American acquiescence*, (1989,) p.294
42   Granville, Cold War International History Project Bulletin, no. 5, p.68
43   Györkei, p.21
44   Kopacsi, p.148
45   Borhi, p.111
46   Chester, p.131

47 Malashenko, p.239
48 Swartz, p.363
49 Lomax, p.121
50 ibid, p.116
51 Sebestyen, location 2391
52 Archard, p.84
53 Jobbágyi, Gábor, *Provocation? The Outbreak of the Revolution of 1956*, (Hungarian Review isssue 6, 2011)
54 Györkei, p.46
55 Malashenko, p.239
56 ibid, p.232
57 Györkei, p.101
58 ibid, p.20

Chapter Five: 25-28 October

1   Korponay, p.58
2   Sebestyen, location 2633
3   ibid
4   Archard, p.92
5   Fehér, Ferenc and Heller, Agnes, *Hungary 1956 revisited*, (George Allen & Unwin, 1983) p.25
6   Jobbágyi, Gábor, *Bloody Thursday, 1956; The Anatomy of the Kossuth Square Massacre*, (Hungarian Review Vol V No1, 2014)
7   Apor, Peter, *Fabricating Authenticity in Soviet Hungary*, (Anthem Press, 2015) p.72
8   Lomax, p.124
9   Mandoki, p.99
10 Györkei, p.85
11 Mandoki, p.50
12 Sebestyen, location 2450
13 ibid, location 3112
14 McCauley, p.782
15 ibid
16 Sebestyen, location 2555
17 Marcetic, Branco, *U.S. Deliberation During Hungary's 1956 Uprising Offers Lessons on Restraint*, (Current Affairs, 2022)

18　Landa, p.46
19　Sebestyen, location 2953
20　Granville, Cold War International History Project Bulletin, no. 5, p.71
21　ibid, p.73
22　Sebestyen, location 2831
23　Korda, Michael, *Journey to a Revolution*, (Harper Collins e-book,) p.125
24　Sebestyen, location 2789
25　Radnika, Dan, *Hungary 1956: "the proletariat storming heaven"*, (libcom.org, 2011)
26　Györkei, p.65
27　McCauley, p.784
28　Györkei, p.35
29　McCauley, p.782
30　Landa, p.34
31　Korponay, p.95
32　Sebestyen, location 3841
33　Györkei, p.53
34　Sebestyen, location 3254
35　ibid, location 3117
36　ibid, location 3178
37　Landa, p.40
38　McCauley, p.783
39　Boyle, Peter G., *The Hungarian Revolution and the Suez Crisis*, (History, Vol. 90, No. 4, 2005) p.560
40　Swartz, p.294
41　Granville, Johanna, *Josip Broz Tito's Role in the 1956 'Nagy Affair'*, (The Slavonic and East European Review, Vol. 76, No. 4, 1998) p.679
42　Swartz, p.326
43　ibid, p.330
44　Sebestyen, location 3323
45　Malashenko, p.225
46　Sebestyen, location 3364
47　von Tunzelmann, p.124
48　Turner, location 4736
49　Bass, p.5
50　Mantle, Alan, *The Suez Canal 1956: The Crisis, the Invasion & the Aftermath*, (The South African Military History Society, 2008)

Chapter Six: 29 October

1 Swartz, p.290
2 Lomax, p.130
3 Sebestyen, location 3533
4 ibid, location 3742
5 Gawrych, George W., *The Battles for Abu Ageila in the 1956 and 1967 Arab-Israeli Wars*, (Combat Studies Institute,) p.22
6 Cohen, P.75
7 Gawrych, p.30
8 Rapoport, Meron, *Into the Valley of Death*, (Haaretz.com, 2007)
9 Los Angeles Times 16 August 1995,
10 Coles, p.4
11 McCauley, p.785
12 Hill, Jill M., *Suez Crisis 1956*, (Institute of Naval Studies Washington, 1974) p.39
13 Garrett, William B., *The U.S. Navy's Role in the 1956 Suez Crisis*, (Naval War College Review, Vol. 22, No. 7, 1970)

Chapter Seven: 30 October

1 Warner, *Collusion and the Suez Crisis of 1956*, p.229
2 Landa, p.50
3 Korda, p.130
4 Sebestyen, location 3809
5 ibid, location 3837
6 Lomax, p.127
7 Swartz, p.59
8 Sebestyen, location 3914
9 Vámos, Péter, *Chinese Foreign Ministry Documents on Hungary, 1956*, (Wilson Centre, 2008)
10 Györkei, p.73
11 von Tunzelmann, p.244
12 Smolansky, O.M., *Moscow and the Suez Crisis, 1956: A Reappraisal*, (Political Science Quarterly, Vol. 80, No. 4, 1965) p.588
13 von Tunzelmann, p.225
14 Owen, David, *The effect of Prime Minister Anthony Eden's illness on his decision-making during the Suez crisis*, (An International Journal of Medicine, Volume 98, Issue 6, 2005) p.394
15 ibid, p.399
16 Dutton, Anthont D., *Eden: Life and Reputation*, (Hodder Arnold, 1997) p.424

17 Turner, location 4944
18 Hill, p.41
19 von Tunzelmann, p.223
20 Gawrych, p.58
21 The Jewish Chronicle 18 April 2008,
22 von Tunzelmann, p.238
23 ibid, p.230
24 Warner, *Collusion' and the Suez Crisis of 1956*, p.229
25 von Tunzelmann, p.234
26 ibid, p.251
27 The United States Navy: Keeping the Peace, Volume 968 United States. Naval History Division U.S. Government Printing Office, 1968
28 Hill, p.69
29 Boughton, p.432
30 ibid, p.435

Chapter Eight: 31 October

1 von Tunzelmann, p.242
2 Sebestyen, location 4097
3 Landa, p.51
4 Kecskés, Gusztáv, *The Suez Crisis and the 1956 Hungarian Revolution*, (East European Quarterly, volume XXXV, 2001)
5 Boyle, p.557
6 Györkei, p.103
7 Vámos, Péter, *Chinese Foreign Ministry Documents on Hungary, 1956*, (Wilson Centre, 2008)
8 Sebestyen, location 4133
9 Kopacsi, p.179
10 Landa, p.55
11 Hill, p.44
12 Varble, Derek, *The Suez Crisis 1956*, (Osprey e-book,) p.74
13 Turner, location 5083
14 Varble, p.71
15 Fowler, Randall, *Lion's Last Roar, Eagle's First Flight: Eisenhower and the Suez Crisis of 1956*, (Rhetoric and Public Affairs, Vol. 20, No. 1, 2017) p.35

Chapter Nine: 1 November
1   Korda, p.148
2   Granville, *Josip Broz Tito's Role in the 1956 'Nagy Affair'*, p.679
3   Swartz, p.376
4   Landa, p.59
5   Malashenko, p.247
6   Turner, location 5280
7   Warner, p.314
8   Skardon, C. Philip, *A Lesson for Our Times: How America Kept the Peace in the Hungary-Suez Crisis of 1956*, (Author house,) p.1196
9   Hill, p.45
10 Landa, p.61

Chapter Ten: 2 November
1   Landa, p.61
2   Sebestyen, location 4596
3   Györkei, p.81
4   Swartz, p.338
5   ibid, p.340
6   Boyle, p.562

Chapter Eleven: 3 November
1   Sebestyen, location 4775
2   Korda, p.154
3   Kopacsi, p.210
4   Sebestyen, p.4851
5   Györkei, p.98
6   Granville, *Josip Broz Tito's Role in the 1956 'Nagy Affair'*, p.700
7   Kopacsi, p.211
8   McCauley, p.786
9   Turner, location 5477
10 ibid, location 5501
11 Bogdanor, Vernon, *The Suez Crisis of 1956*, (summarize.tech,) p.13
12 ibid, p.14

Chapter Twelve: 4 November

1. Harman, Mike, *The Hungarian Revolution 1956*, (Scorcher Publications, 1984)
2. Györkei, p.106
3. ibid
4. Granville, *Josip Broz Tito's Role in the 1956 'Nagy Affair'*, p.689
5. ibid, p.684
6. Malashenko, p.257
7. Sebestyen, location 5001
8. Archard, p.145
9. For Freedom and Truth, Wikisource
10. Korda, p.167
11. Harman
12. Landa, p.74
13. Message from Dwight D. Eisenhower to Nikolai Bulganin (4 November 1956)
14. Message from Nikolai Bulganin to Dwight D. Eisenhower (7 November 1956)

Chapter Thirteen: 5 November

1. Keesing's Record of World Events (formerly Keesing's Contemporary Archives), Volume X, November, 1956 Soviet Union, United States, United Kingdom, France, Israel, Israeli, Soviet, American
2. Smolansky, p.592
3. Keesing
4. Hill, p.50
5. Warner, *The United States and the Suez Crisis*, p.315
6. Keesing
7. von Tunzelmann, p.345
8. Smolansky, p.597

Chapter Fourteen: 6 November

1. Unwin, p.157
2. ibid, p.158
3. Hill, p.49
4. Lahav, Pnina, *The Suez Crisis of 1956 and its Aftermath*, (Boston University Law Review Vol 95, 2015) p.1343

5   Hill, p.53
6   ibid, p.54
7   Katz, David J., *Waging Financial War*, (Parameters 43, no. 4, 2013) p.78
8   Louis, William Roger, *Harold Macmillan and the Middle East Crisis of 1958*, (University of Texas, 1996) p.212
9   Bogdanor, p.13

Aftermath
1   Jobbágyi,
2   Working Notes from the Session of the CPSU CC Presidium on 27 November 1956 (Re: Protocol No. 60), November 27, 1956, Wilson Center Digital Archive
3   Granville, Johanna, *Cold War International History Project Bulletin, no. 5*
4   Pethő, Tibor, *Quickly and Without Mercy*, (Hungarian Review, 2013)
5   The Suez crisis; A test for the U.S.S.R.'s Middle East Policy CIA Staff Study V-A-56 1957, p.12
6   Hill, p.72
7   U.S. State Department, Memo of Conversation (Alpband, Mlrphy, November S, 1956).
8   U.S. Navy, #070451 CNO to all (November 7, 1956)
9   U.S. Navy, #081642 CINCNELM to COMSIXTHFLT (November 8, 1956)
10 U.S. Navy, #081822 CINCNBLM to SBCSTATE
11 Unwin, p.167
12 Bogdanor, p.14
13 ibid, p.15

SOURCES

Aid, Matthew M., *The Declassified History of American Intelligence Operations in Europe: 1945-2001* (brill.com, 2014)

Alterman, John B., *American Aid to Egypt in the 1950s: From Hope to Hostility* (Middle East Journal Vol. 52, No. 1, 1998)

Apor, Peter, *Fabricating Authenticity in Soviet Hungary* (Anthem Press, 2015)

Archard, Louis, *Hungarian Uprising* (Pen and Sword, 2018)

Bass, Warren, *The Suez War 1956* (Rand Corporation,)

Békés, Csaba, *President Kliment Voroshilov's Telegram to Queen Elizabeth of Great Britain on the Soviet Intervention in Hungary on 4 November 1956* (The Slavonic and East European Review, Vol. 71, No. 1, 1993)

Bogdanor, Vernon, *The Suez Crisis of 1956* (summarize.tech,)

Borhi, László, *Dealing with Dictators* (Indiana University Press. Kindle Edition,)

Boughton, James M., *Northwest of Suez: The 1956 Crisis and the IMF* (IMF Staff Papers, Vol. 48, No. 3, 2001)

Boyle, Peter G., *The Hungarian Revolution and the Suez Crisis* (History, Vol. 90, No. 4, 2005)

Chester, Eric Thomas, *Covert Network: Progressives, the International Rescue Committee, and the CIA* (Routledge, 1995)

Cohen, Michael J., *Suez-Sinai, 1956: The International, Strategic and Military Aspect* (Israel Studies Forum, Vol. 17, No. 1, 2001)

Coles, Michael H., *1956: A Successful Naval Operation Compromised by Inept Political Leadership* (U.S. Naval War College Press, 2006)

Cox, Terry, *Hungary, 1956* (History Ireland, Vol. 14, No. 3 (2006)

Dent, Bob, *Locations of a drama. Budapest 1956* (Európa Könyvkiadó, Budapest, 2006)

Dutton, Anthont D., *Eden: Life and Reputation* (Hodder Arnold, 1997)

Fehér, Ferenc and Heller, Agnes, *Hungary 1956 revisited* (George Allen & Unwin, 1983)

Fowler, Randall, *Lion's Last Roar, Eagle's First Flight: Eisenhower and the Suez Crisis of 1956* (Rhetoric and Public Affairs, Vol. 20, No. 1, 2017)

Fullick, Roy and Powell, Geoffrey, *Suez: The Double War* (Pen and Sword, 2006)

Garrett, William B., *The U.S. Navy's Role in the 1956 Suez Crisis* (Naval War College Review, Vol. 22, No. 7, 1970)

Gawrych, George W., *The Battles for Abu Ageila in the 1956 and 1967 Arab-Israeli Wars* (Combat Studies Institute)

Gibianskii, Leonid, and Naimark, Norman, *The Soviet Union and the Establishment of Communist Regimes in Eastern Europe, 1944-1954; A Documentary Collection* (The National Council for Eurasian and East European Research, 2006)

Granville, Johanna, *Josip Broz Tito's Role in the 1956 'Nagy Affair'* (The Slavonic and East European Review, Vol. 76, No. 4, 1998)

Granville, Johanna, *Caught with Jam on Our Fingers: Radio Free Europe and the Hungarian Revolution of 1956* (Diplomatic History, Vol. 29, No. 5, 2005)

Granville, Johanna, *Cold War International History Project Bulletin, no. 5* (Woodrow Wilson Center for International Scholars, Washington, DC, 1995)

Györkei, Jenő, *Soviet Military Intervention in Hungary 1956* (Central European University Press, 1999)

Hall, Simon, *The World in Revolt* (Faber and Faber, 2016)

Hamilton, Eamon, *Sir Anthony Eden and the Suez Crisis of 1956, The Anatomy of a Flawed Personality* (University of Birmingham, 2015)

Harman, Mike, *The Hungarian Revolution 1956* (Scorcher Publications, 1984)

Hegedüs, András B., *Ungarische Revolution 1956* (Walter de Gruyter, 2000)

Hill, Jill M., *Suez Crisis 1956* (Institute of Naval Studies Washington, 1974)

Jobbágyi, Gábor, *Bloody Thursday, 1956; The Anatomy of the Kossuth Square Massacre* (Hungarian Review Vol V No1, 2014)

Jobbágyi, Gábor, *Provocation? The Outbreak of the Revolution of 1956* (Hungarian Review issue 6, 2011)

Jones, Matthew, *Macmillan, Eden, the War in the Mediterranean and Anglo-American Relations* (Twentieth Century British History, Volume 8, Issue 1, 1997)

Jouko, Petteri, *Strike Hard, Strike Sure – Operation Musketeer, British Military Planning during the Suez Crisis, 1956* (Taktiikan laitos – Department of Tactics, Helsinki, 2007)

Katz, David J., *Waging Financial War*, (Parameters 43, no. 4, 2013)

Kecskés, Gusztáv, *The Suez Crisis and the 1956 Hungarian Revolution* (East European Quarterly, volume XXXV, 2001)

Kopacsi, Sandor, *In the Name of the Working Class* (Fontana, 1979)

Korda, Michael, *Journey to a Revolution* (Harper Collins e-book,)

Korponay, Irene, *Escaping Communist Hungary 1956* (Ryan von Schwedler, Kidle edition,)

Kramer, Mark, *The Soviet Union and the 1956 Crises in Hungary and Poland: Reassessments and New Findings* (Journal of Contemporary History, Vol. 33, No. 2, 1998)

Kramer, Mark, *Stalin, Soviet Policy, and the Consolidation of a Communist Bloc in Eastern Europe 1944-1953* (Amazon web Services, 1993)

Lahav, Pnina, *The Suez Crisis of 1956 and its Aftermath* (Boston University Law Review Vol 95, 2015)

Landa, Ronald D., *The 1956 Hungarian Revolution; A Fresh Look at the U.S. response* (National Security Archive, nsarchive.gwu.edu, 2012)

Laron, Guy, *Cutting the Gordian Knot: The Post-WWII Egyptian Quest for Arms and the 1955 Czechoslovak Arms Deal* (Cold War International History Project, Woodrow Wilson International Center for Scholars, 2007)

Lomax, Bill, *The Working Class in the Hungarian Revolution of 1956* (Critique No 12, 1979)

Lomax, Bill, *Hungary 1956* (Allison and Busby, 1976)

Louis, William Roger, *Harold Macmillan and the Middle East Crisis of 1958* (University of Texas, 1996)

Malashenko, Yevgeny, *Soviet Military Intervention in Hungary, 1956* (Central European University Press, 1998)

Mandoki, Anna, *Molotov Cocktails* (Kindle edition,)

Mantle, Alan, *The Suez Canal 1956: The crisis, the Invasion & the Aftermath* (The South African Military History Society, 2008)

Marcetic, Branco, *U.S. Deliberation During Hungary's 1956 Uprising Offers Lessons on Restraint* (Current Affairs, 2022)

McCauley, Brian, *Hungary and Suez, 1956: The Limits of Soviet and American Power* (Journal of Contemporary History, Vol. 16, No. 4, 1981)

Meray, Tibor, *Thirteen Days that shook the Kremlin* (Thames and Hudson, 1958)

Mohsen, Ashraf Mohsen Mohamed, *Anglo-Egyptian Relations in the Aftermath of the Suez Crisis* (School of Oriental and African Studies, University of London, 1993)

Molnar, Miklos, *Budapest 1956* (George Allen & Unwin, 1971)

Necky, Patrick L., *Operation Musketeer – the End of Empire: A Study of Organizational Failure in Combined Operations* (Operation Musketeer – the End of Empire: A Study of Organizational Failure in Combined Operations, 1991)

Nimer, Benjamin, *Dulles, Suez, and Democratic Diplomacy* (The Western Political Quarterly Vol. 12, No. 3, 1959)

Owen, David, *The effect of Prime Minister Anthony Eden's illness on his decision-making during the Suez crisis* (An International Journal of Medicine, Volume 98, Issue 6, 2005)

Pearson, Jonathan, *Sir Anthony Eden and the Suez Crisis, Relucrtant Gamble* (Palgrave, 2003)

Pethő, Tibor, *Quickly and Without Mercy* (Hungarian Review, 2013)

Pienkos, Donald E., *A Look Back: Poland and the Historic Events of 1956* (The Polish Review, Vol. LI, No. 3-4, 2006)

Pierre, Jean-Marc, *The 1956 Suez Crisis and the United Nations* (Fordham University, New York, 1992)

Radnika, Dan, *Hungary 1956: "the proletariat storming heaven"* (libcom.org, 2011)

Rapoport, Meron, *Into the Valley of Death* (Haaretz.com, 2007)

Reynolds, David A.J., *The Roots of Communist Hungary in the Allied Occupation* (The Hungarian Review, 2020)

Schoenfeld, H.F. Arthur, *Soviet Imperialism in Hungary* (Foreign Affairs, Vol. 26, No. 3, 1948)

Sebestyen, Victor, *Twelve Days* (Phoenix Kindle edition,)

Selak, Charles B. Jnr, *The Suez Canal Base Agreement of 1954* (The American Journal of International Law, Vol. 49, No. 4, 1955)

Sewell, Bevan, *John Foster Dulles, Illness, Masculinity and U.S. Foreign Relations, 1953–1961* (The International History Review 39, 2016)

Shlaim, Avi, *The Protocol of Sevres, 1956: Anatomy of a War Plot* (International Affairs Vol. 73, No. 3, Globalization and International Relations, 1997)

Skardon, C. Philip, *A Lesson for Our Times: How America Kept the Peace in the Hungary-Suez Crisis of 1956* (Author house)

Smolansky, O.M., *Moscow and the Suez Crisis, 1956: A Reappraisal* (Political Science Quarterly, Vol. 80, No. 4, 1965)

Solti, Leo, *Hungary 1956* (Elite Publishing, 2022)

Steed, Danny, *British Strategy and Intelligence in the Suez Crisis* (Springer, 2016)

Swartz, Martin Ben, *A new look at the 1956 Hungarian Revolution: Soviet opportunism, American acquiescence* (1989)

Troen, Ilan, *The Protocol of Sèvres: British/French/Israeli Collusion against Egypt, 1956* (Israel Studies Vol 1 No 2, 1996)

Turner, Barry, *Suez 1956: The Inside Story of the First Oil War* (Hodder & Stoughton)

Unwin, Peter, *1956 Power Defied* (Michael Russell, 2006)

Vámos, Péter, *Chinese Foreign Ministry Documents on Hungary, 1956* (Wilson Centre, 2008)

Varble, Derek, *The Suez Crisis 1956* (Osprey e-book,)

Varga, Zsolt, *Contemporary American Press Coverage of the Outbreak of the 1956 Hungarian Revolution* (Hungarian Journal of English and American Studies Vol 8, 2002)

von Tunzelmann, Alex, *Blood and Sand* (Simon and Schuster, 2016)

Warner, Geoffrey, *'Collusion' and the Suez Crisis of 1956* (International Affairs Vol. 55, No. 2 (1979)

Warner, Geoffrey, *The United States and the Suez Crisis* (International Affairs Vol. 67 No. 2, 1991)

Suez Crisis, 1956 (Institute of Naval Studies, 1974)

Hungary and the Middle East: A Chronology of Events, 19 October — 6 November 1956 (The World Today, Vol. 12, No. 12 Royal Institute of International Affairs, 1956)

Hungary's Post-War Economic Difficulties (The World Today, Vol. 3, No. 8, Royal Institute of International Affairs, 1947)

The 1956 Hungarian Revolution: A Fresh Look at the U.S. Response (U.S. National Security Archive, 2012) *https://nsarchive.gwu.edu/document/22906-1956-hungarian-revolution-fresh-look*

INDEX

Adan, Avraham, 123
Adrich, Winthrop, 141
Amin, Mustapha, 168
Andropov, Yuri, 65, 73, 97, 105, 109, 113, 132, 153, 155–156, 161, 171
Angyal, István, 71, 97
Aviyashar, Ya'acov, 120

Barjot, P.E.M.J., 32, 42–43, 46, 170
Barnes, Spencer N., 71, 79, 107
Beaufre, André, 32–34, 36, 42–43, 46, 149–150, 157, 181
Beer, Israel, 114
Bem, Josef, 67
Ben-Gurion, David, 20, 52–59, 114, 123, 196
Benke, Valéria, 71
Bergus, Donald, 114
Bibó, István, 174
Bohlen, Charles, 46, 97, 108, 117–118, 132, 134, 144, 192
Booth Luce, Claire, 83
Bracken, Brendan, 49,
Brown, Charles Randall, 142
Budaházy, Suzanne, 70, 95
Bulganin, Nikolai, 47, 111, 177, 180, 183–185, 189
Burke, Arleigh, 28, 47, 142, 157
Burns, E.L.M.'Tommy', 178
Butler, M.A.H., 182
Butler, R.A., 53

Cabot Lodge, Henry, 97
Carr, Robert, 135
Challe, Maurice, 49–54, 59
Chateau-Jobert, Pierre, 182
Churchill, Winston, 21–22, 24, 29, 33, 50, 135
Cochran, Merle, 142

Corson, William, 83
Crook, Paul, 178
Csongovai, Per Olaf, 97

Dabasy, János, 63–64, 80
Davidi, Aharon, 138
Davis, Richard, 98
Dayan, Moshe, 44, 54–57, 121–123, 125, 137, 139
Dean, Patrick, 35, 56–58, 196
Dixon, Pierson, 159, 164
Dror, Kan, 139
Drosa, Milan, 190
Dudás, József, 115–116, 129–130, 147, 161, 186
Dulles, Allen, 78, 104, 148
Dulles, John Foster, 18, 20–23, 27, 29, 39–40, 46–48, 56, 77–78, 82–83, 89, 97–98, 107, 111, 114, 118, 125–126, 133, 137–139, 141, 143–144, 148, 155, 157–160, 162–163, 169–170
Dutton, David, 135

Eban, Abba, 114
Eden, Anthony, 14, 21–30, 33–36, 38, 40–45, 47–53, 55–59, 90, 113, 125, 127, 133–137, 139, 141, 143, 148–150, 157, 163, 168–169, 183, 185–186, 189, 192–194
Edgcumbe, Oliver, 5
Eisenhower, Dwight D., 23, 25, 27–30, 40, 48, 50–52, 56, 60, 76–79, 82–84, 89, 97–99, 104, 107–108, 111, 114, 116, 118, 125–126, 133, 137, 139–143, 148–151, 155, 162–163, 177, 180, 183, 185, 187–189, 192–194
Eitan, Raful, 120–121, 138
Elek, László, 129

Erdei, Ferenc, 167
Evans, Horace, 135

Fehér, Ferenc, 93, 105
Ferenc, Szálasi., 1
Fitzmaurice, Gerald, 34
Foster, Andrew, 22–23

Gaitskill, Hugh, 22, 169
Gál, Lajos, 191
Gazier, Albert, 49
Georgievic, Milan, 190
Gerő, Ernő, 9, 12, 65–67, 71, 73–75, 80, 86–87, 92, 94, 97, 102, 107, 109, 155
Glubb, John Foster, 24–25
Goldstein, Ze'ev, 114
Gomułka, Władysław, 12–13, 103, 154
Gosztonyi, Péter, 71
Gray, Gordon, 177
Grisewood, Harman, 169
Gur, Mordechai, 138
Gyurkó, László, 71

Hammarskjöld, Dag, 194
Hare, Raymond, 142
Hayter, William, 132
Head, Anthony, 53, 170
Hegedüs, András, 10, 68, 74–75, 87, 103, 105, 109, 111, 113
Hoover, Herbert Jnr., 25
Horányi, Mihály, 191
Horváth, Miklós, 94
Hurd, Douglas, 193

Jamza, Károly, 106

Kádár, János, 71, 93, 109, 145, 156, 161–162, 166–167, 173, 186, 190
Kardelj, Edvard, 172
Katek, Charlie, 83
Katona, Geza, 84
Kennedy, Stetson, 80–81
Key, William, 5
Khruschev, Nikita, 4, 8–13, 19, 73–75, 77, 87, 89, 92, 109–110, 112, 117, 127, 131–132, 144–146, 151, 153–155, 162, 172–173, 183
Kilmuir, Lord, 35
Király, Béla, 116–117, 130, 153, 161, 166–167, 171–173

Kirkpatrick, Ivone, 35, 39
Konyev, Ivan, 131, 144, 146, 151–152, 166, 172, 175
Kopácsi, Sándor, 11, 67, 72, 81, 92, 94, 116, 147, 161, 166
Korda, Michael, 101, 128, 154, 165, 175
Korponay, Irene, 66, 70, 105
Kós, Péter, 109
Kovács, Béla, 6
Kovács, Miklós, 71
Kovács, László Iván, 96, 175
Kovács, István, 112, 167, 175

Laschenko, Petr, 80, 115, 151–152
Lloyd, Selwyn, 21, 23–24, 45, 48, 50, 52–56, 125, 134, 139, 170

Macmillan, Harold, 23, 25–26, 28–30, 34, 49, 53, 143, 188–189, 193–194
Malashenko, Yevgeny, 64–65, 83, 85, 88, 96
Malenkov, Georgy, 10, 154
Maléter, Pál, 96, 106, 117, 130, 153, 165–167
Malinin, Mikhail, 66, 86, 94, 165, 167
Malinovsky, Rodion, 2
Manningham-Buller, Reginald, 34
Martin, Clifford, 20
Márton, András, 106
Massu, Jacques, 182
Menzies, Robert, 40
Mező, Imre, 129
Mikoyan, Anastas, 12, 64, 74–75, 80, 86–87, 92–93, 102–103, 105–106, 109–111, 129–132, 144, 146–147, 151
Mindszenty, József, 5, 129, 172
Mollet, Guy, 25–26, 45, 58, 139, 141, 163, 183, 189
Molotov, Vyecheslav, 73, 103, 110, 132, 134, 144–145, 151, 161, 173
Montgomery, Bernard, 51
Murphy, Robert, 28

Naguib, Mohamed, 19
Nagy, Imre aka Vladimir Iosifovich, 5, 8–11, 62–69, 73–76, 85–87, 91–94, 97, 102–103, 105, 107–109, 111–113, 115–117, 127–133, 145–147, 152–156, 159–162, 166–167, 171–173, 180–181, 190
Nagy, Ferenc, 6

Nasser, Gamal Abdel, 14–17, 19, 21–31, 33–24, 39–43, 45, 47, 49, 52–54, 58–59, 122, 124, 134, 136–137, 139, 141–143, 145, 148–151, 158, 163, 168, 170, 183, 185, 189, 193
Nomy, Henri, 30
Nutting, Anthony, 22, 25, 50, 53, 189

Paice, Mervyn, 20
Pálos, István, 67
Pedrazzini, Jean-Pierre, 129
Pétőfi, Sandor, 68
Pineau, Christian, 40, 45, 47–48, 54–56, 58, 189, 196
Piros, László, 67
Pongrácz, Gergely, 97

Rajk, László, 11, 66, 93
Rákosi, Mátyás, 2, 4, 8–11, 64, 70, 73–74, 87, 105, 145
Ray, Mike, 83
Rehavam, Ze'evi, 138
Renton, James, 79
Rokossowski, Konstantin, 13
Rountree, William, 114

Sadovy, John, 129
Ságvári, Ágnes, 67
Schäffer, Öcsi, 95
Schoenfeld, Arthur, 7
Serov, Ivan, 66–67, 74, 86, 88, 94, 109–110, 131, 144, 156, 166–167
Shao-chi, Liu, 131, 144, 146
Sharett, Moshe, 44
Sharif, Sami, 114

Sharon, Ariel, 47, 121, 137–139
Shuckburgh, Evelyn, 22–24
Silva, Peer de, 79, 83, 163
Simhoni, Asaf, 121–122
Sobolev, Arkady, 162
Solymosi, János, 72
Stefko, József, 101, 105
Stevenson, Adlai, 77, 140
Stockwell, Hugh, 34, 36, 38, 43, 124, 150, 181–182
Suslov, Mikhail, 10, 64–65, 74–75, 86–88, 102, 109–111, 130, 146, 161
Szabó, György, 101
Szabó, János, 102, 176, 186
Szántó, Zoltán, 172
Szirmai, Ottó, 71
Szűcs, Ferenc, 94, 167

Teuchert, József, 71
Tildy, Zoltan, 4
Tito, Josip, 7, 11, 21, 154–155, 172, 180–181, 190
Tóth, Lázló, 106

Viczián, Lajos, 191
Voroshilov, Kliment, 5, 111

Wailes, Edwin, 79, 116–117
Wallach, Yehuda, 121, 137
Wisner, Frank, 83

Zedong, Mao, 127, 131
Zhukov, Georgy, 73, 75, 89, 118, 127, 134, 145, 166